ON BEING THE CHURCH

ON BEING THE CHURCH

Essays on the Christian Community

Edited by

Colin E. Gunton and Daniel W. Hardy

T. & T. CLARK

EDINBURGH

Copyright © T. & T. Clark Ltd, 1989

Typeset by Buccleuch Printers Ltd, Hawick
Printed and bound in Great Britain by Billing & Sons Ltd, Worcester

for

T. & T. CLARK LTD
59 George Street, Edinburgh EH2 2LQ

First printed 1989

British Library Cataloguing in Publication Data

Gunton, Colin E.
On being the church
1. Christian Life
I. Title   II. Hardy, Daniel W.
248.4

ISBN 0 567 09501 0 HB
0 567 29501 9 PB

CONTENTS

EDITORS' INTRODUCTION

1. *Unity and Diversity*

A book of essays written by six different authors is unlikely to have the unity of a dogmatic treatise from a single pen; nor do the authors wish to be regarded as members of a 'school' of theology, for they have not sought the kind of unity which would justify the label. The careful reader of this volume will find, below and sometimes upon the surface, differences of approach, emphasis and content. Yet, on the other hand, the collection is far more than a miscellaneous set of papers loosely centred on a general topic. The authors have worked closely together in deciding which particular topics should be treated, and in subjecting each other's work to careful and sustained criticism. They would wish to claim not the unity of a school, but that there is a mutuality and complementarity about the papers and, above all, shared central focuses and concerns.

The concern we all share derives from a conviction of the massive loss in recent years of a theological basis for a doctrine of the Church. Nor is it simply a matter of doctrine, for the evidence suggests that it is the Church itself which is in question. Moreover, the loss is not a problem for the Church alone, for the loss of a basis for its common life is a feature also of modern Western society in general. There is a crisis there, too, and it does not require great imagination to appreciate the importance of militant Islam's contempt for Western civilisation. The inadequacy of the two competing but in reality closely related philosophies of the West, individualist liberalism and state collectivism, to answer the true needs of human being in community marks a parallel crisis to the Church's failure to attend to the roots of her being.

In all this, the position of the English Church has its own unique features, as several of the papers will reveal. But we do not wish our deliberations to be limited to England. The group that has co-operated in the work contains members who derive from or teach in America, Ireland and mainland Europe. It contains both lay and ordained, as well as those with different ecclesiastical commitment—Catholic, Anglican and Reformed. Yet all share the concern for our life together which has been reflected in some recent writing about the West's loss of a common culture. It is in that general context that the overall unity of our direction should be understood.

The directional unity which we wish to claim for our co-operative enterprise is to be found in positive and constructive features of our thought as well as in the more negative and critical points which are their other side. Positively and above all we affirm a common commitment to the affirmation and restoration of what the first essay calls *sociality*. We do not apologise for the use of what to some readers may appear an unfamiliar technical term. It is employed because we want to bring to light a central and neglected feature of our human condition: that we are what we are by virtue of our membership of one another. We are social beings, and without sociality become less than human. Moreover, this sociality is a feature of our createdness, of the kind of beings that we are, not something that the Church attempts to tack on to an otherwise foreign reality. When, therefore, we speak of redemption, or of redeemed sociality, we do not wish to conceive it as a denial of created sociality, but as its restoration and fulfilment. A central focus of all the essays is the affirmation of the cruciality of sociality for life in the world and in the Church, although we do not wish to deny that here, as in other respects, the authors do not understand and express that centrality in quite the same way. What we do share is a belief at once in the importance of the feature of our life that is indicated by the concept and in the disastrous consequences of its neglect in so much life and thought.

The second direction we share is a commitment to the possibility of the Church. By 'possibility' we do not mean—quite definitely do not mean—the affirmation of some ideal community other than and apart from the concrete assembling of the actual people of God. It is a constant temptation for theologians and other élites to suppose that they can create their own sociality apart from the rest of humanity. In our view, as will be evident from a number of the papers, the arrogation of power and authority by élites is part of the problem. Our concern, rather, is to suggest possible approaches to the question of the Church as a vehicle of true sociality. As members of the body, we want the Church to be able to be itself. The essays we have written are diverse ways of coming to terms with the vacuum that we believe we, along with many others, have discerned. They are intermediate rather than claiming any definitive status. We wish to suggest possible directions rather than definitive answers. Inevitably, our work is rather theoretical; that is the nature of our calling. But good theology is theory that is not content to remain as theory, for it points us beyond ourselves to what can be true for all sociality.

The third common focus of our work will be evident from the fact that there is in the book little direct discussion of the question of the ordained ministry. Our views of the nature and ordering of that ministry differ; what we share is a concern to place the question within what we believe to be the more central matter of the Church's sociality. We are concerned that in so many discussions of ministry it is equated with the ordained ministry, in practice if not in theory, at the expense of engagement with the ministry of the whole people of God. We believe that ministry is a function of the ecclesial community as a whole, and that the structure of the ordained ministry in the existing Churches is often inimical to the development of that of the Church as a whole.

A fourth focus, closely related to the third, is the matter of authority, which is treated directly in Dr Jeanrond's paper, but is also the concern of us all. Again, our views are not precisely the same, and the weighting we would give to the various focuses of authority—traditional, biblical, rational, institutional—differ, in places markedly. Yet we share a common belief that the Church has tended to operate with a secularised conception of authority in which merely political considerations have overridden a theology grounded in the power of grace in the gospel; rooted, that is, in the way God meets us in Jesus' life, death and resurrection. To put it in the terms of the discussion of sociality, we would want to say that the neglect in both thought and action of the social basis of our existence leads us finally to dehumanise other human beings by treating them simply as objects for the exercise of power.

A fifth focus is related to the Church's failure to develop a theology of authority, and it is found in the fact that contemporary discussions of ecclesiology rarely engage with the matter of the constitution and being of the Church. Much modern discussion is devoted to the elaboration of images of the Church derived from the Bible, but that is inadequate because it tends to isolate ecclesiology from the wider theological task. The outcome is disastrous at every level. On one level, it prevents a critical engagement with the questions of human sociality and its rootedness in the divine creation and redemption. On another level, because it leaves in abeyance the question of the nature of the community, it encourages an approach to the practicalities of Church life which owes more to contingency management (or the exercise of power) than to a discerning of the way of the people of God in the world.

The five shared concerns which have been isolated provide the common framework for the questions which are asked in the different contributions. Some of them are more prominent in some papers than in others, but all appear and reappear like threads of different colours in a tapestry. And, to correct that simile, if the book does not have the unity of a single work of art, we hope that it will have the effect of six different floodlights illuminating different aspects of a single building.

This first part of the introduction has been designed to explain something of what the authors share. The book is itself offered as an instance of sociality in practice, in the hope that its strengths will be seen to derive from what the authors in all their differences have contributed to the overall richness of the whole. Theology, particularly in England, is often treated as a pursuit engaged in by talented and competing individuals. Our work together, which has included a number of meetings, three of them containing intensive and sustained discussion, has confirmed for us something of the truth we are seeking to express, and has given us delight in our shared discipline. In the second part of the introduction we turn to an outline of the particular contributions both in themselves and in the links that can be made between them.

2. Particular Contributions

The first paper, 'Created and Redeemed Sociality' is by

Daniel W. Hardy, who after about twenty years in the Department of Theology at a secular university, Birmingham, moved in 1986 to become Van Mildert Professor of Divinity in the University of Durham and at the same time Canon of Durham Cathedral. An American, he has for some years been involved in the development of theological education in the Church of England, and has long had interests in the interrelation of theology with modern culture, particularly scientific culture. His essay provides a preface to ecclesiology proper, and a spelling out of its essential context. It centres on the development and deployment of *sociality*, which we have already seen to be a central concern of the book, and begins from the fact that modern society appears to lack a rationale and a basis on which to cope with the increasing complexity of modern conditions, so much so that it may be in process of destroying itself. In response to such a need, the body of the essay is devoted for a quest for sociality as a transcendental, that is as one of the fundamental features of reality, 'forms through which being displays itself' (p. 25).

Without paying attention to sociality, it is argued, we fail to understand who we are, who is our neighbour and what our life on earth and in society is about. The opening sections of the paper demonstrate the failure of thought since Kant to encompass the social nature of our being, and the almost universal collapse into individualism or idealism. The outcome has been an inability to distinguish between the theory and pragmatics of sociality, so that ideologies like Apartheid become easier to justify. The quest for a more adequate sociality is rather like that for a doctrine of creation: it is a project of thought in the process of which it is hoped to lay bare basic features of our world in such a way that the theory may enable the pragmatics of society to be more adequately informed. Thus the project is not a matter of abstract theory, for it is concerned to establish a transcendental which is dynamic and helps to bring about both the affirmation of richer social forms and criticism of inadequate ones.

During the course of the argument examples of social thought in the theologians P. T. Forsyth and Dietrich Bonhoeffer are discussed, with a view to showing that theological accounts of merely churchly or redeemed sociality, unrelated to the sociality which is God's work in creation, run the danger of divorcing Christian faith from society and unduly restricting our conception of God's work in the world. Such a limitation is contrasted with what happened in Paul's missionary activity, which was not simply the result of a personal call but had to do equally with the discovery of Christ among the peoples of the world. The theological basis of sociality, always near to the surface of the paper, now becomes explicit. The Word of God active in all creation is the one who realises in time the eternal divine sociality which is the triune God.

The theme of the Trinity in relation to human society is taken up in the second paper, 'The Church on Earth: the Roots of Community', this time explicitly linked to the doctrine of the Church. Its author's activities also span the worlds of university and Church. Professor of Christian Doctrine at King's College, London, Colin Gunton is also associate minister of the United Reformed Church in Brentwood, Essex, and convener of the United Reformed Church's Doctrine and Worship Committee. His argument begins with a contention that, despite all the talk about the Church in the tradition, there has been little real theological engagement with the questions of what kind of community or institution the Church is. Theology too early slipped into an uncritical tendency to assimilate the Church to patterns of the political and legal institutions of the society in which it was set. In addition, the way in which the doctrine of the 'invisible Church' developed encouraged the emergence of a belief in a 'real' Church which was different from the actual worshipping community. The result was an almost unavoidable tendency to identify the Church with the hierarchy or the ordained ministry rather than with the community as a whole. (The virtual exclusion of the laity from a real part in the Church in one of the institutions of Christendom, the Church of England, is the burden of Richard Roberts' paper, the fifth in this collection.)

Professor Gunton argues that it is of the greatest significance that the theology of the Trinity—the sociality that God is—scarcely influenced the development of ecclesiology, and that when it did it was in a lop-sided way. Traditional ecclesiology makes much of the fact that the Church owes its institution to the divine Christ, but this has often led to the making of arrogant claims for the institution, leading, for example, to excessive self-confidence in its rightness and to the misuse of authority (a theme taken up by Werner Jeanrond in the following paper). To use the language of the fourth paper, by Christoph Schwoebel, the Church has been unable to delimit between what is of divine and what is of human agency, and so has been led into distortions of its gospel.

In this paper, it is argued that there is urgent need for the development of an ecclesiology of community. As a help to it, various witnesses from the Christian tradition are called in evidence, notable among them the English Puritan, John Owen, who uses both Aristotelian analysis and conceptuality drawn from early trinitarian theology to that end. In general, it is argued in the paper that two theological reorientations need to be made. The first is to a greater stress on the humanity of Jesus, especially with respect to his dependence on the guidance of the Holy Spirit, with a corresponding emphasis on the humanity of the Church. The second is to a more explicit basing of the being of the Church in the being of the triune God. God is what he is by virtue of the relations to each other of the three persons, Father, Son and Spirit. Should not the Church be understood by analogy with this, as the community called and enabled by God to echo in the world his eternal sociality? Again, as was the case with the discussion of sociality in the first paper, the author does not wish his argument to be seen as merely theoretical. Although it is theoretical, for it is concerned with the way we understand the being of the Church, its practical importance is illustrated by its implications for the ordained ministry and for the relations of men and women in the community.

The third paper, 'Community and Authority: the Nature and Implications of the Authority of Christian Community', is by Werner Jeanrond, a lay Roman Catholic from Germany, with a doctorate from the University of Chicago, who teaches theology at Trinity College, Dublin, originally a Protestant foundation but which now has an explicitly transdenominational constitution. In what is in some ways the most 'congregationalist' paper in the collection, he takes up a theme which is of central importance for all the churches, but has come to the fore with particular force in the Roman Church since the Second Vatican Council. Just as in the preceding essay it was argued that the Church has allowed herself to be secularised by attending to monarchical and military models in developing an understanding of her character, so here Dr Jeanrond claims that the Church has fallen victim to unchristian and authoritarian conceptions of authority. Another link with the preceding paper is to be found in its critical analysis of what it calls the mediaeval ontology in which clergy and laity were regarded as separate kinds of being, a conception still to be found in the documents of the Second Vatican Council.

Dr Jeanrond is highly critical of past and present ways of exercising authority in the Church. For example, he regards what he calls the practice of absolute ordination, deriving from the mediaeval ontological dualism, and the imposing of clergy upon communities, as depriving them 'of their basic dignity as Christian communities' (p. 99). Similarly, and in common with the other essayists, he regards the question of the ordained ministry as secondary to the question of how the faith should be embodied in institutions. He is not an idealist who denies the need for institutions and structures, but argues that in thinking about the Church we should beware of succumbing to the temptations of ideology, of justifying an indefensible practice by means which shield us from reality and endanger community.

The constructive side of his development looks forward to the questions asked by Christoph Schwoebel about where we are to locate divine and human action in relation to the Church. What is true 'theonomy', acting in response to divine calling, if it is not to be found in rule by a self-perpetuating hierarchy? There are, it is argued, three ways in which the Church is continually called back to obedience to God's authority: 'a communal organisation, an elected leadership, and the ongoing prophetic critique of both.' How these take shape is a matter of the needs of the time, but unless all have due place, there is danger of distortion. Moreover, the centre of their operation must be in the local Christian community, although the process must also involve 'universal and mutually critical co-operation among Christian communities.' (p. 103).

The fourth paper, 'The creature of the Word: Recovering the Ecclesiology of the Reformers,' may appear on the surface to introduce rather different matters from those so far considered, but its relevance is direct. It is by Christoph Schwoebel who, after a period teaching theology in Marburg, moved in 1986 to be Lecturer in Systematic Theology at King's College, London. Now a lay member of the United Reformed Church and of its Doctrine and Worship Committee, he brings to bear the advantages of one brought up outside the confused British ecclesiastical scene. The other members of the group are in general agreed that since the nineteenth century the Reformation has received a disgracefully pejorative treatment in English thought, with the effect that sheer propaganda and long-term denigration have blinded us not only to the part which the Reformation has played historically in the development of Anglican ecclesiology but, more important still, to the contemporary relevance of the thought of the Reformers.

Many of the problems which are the burden of the critical aspects of the other papers in the book derive from a failure to distinguish and delimit the spheres of the divine and the human in the Church. As was implied in the two previous essays, too much claiming of divine authority for the Church as it is leads to authoritarianism and a denial in practice of the Church's dependence on grace for its being and health. Similarly, lack of a theology of the relation between the gospel and the Church's being leads to a tendency, only too apparent in all branches of the Church, to make decisions on merely pragmatic—or power-political—grounds. Because the Reformers faced just such a problem, their careful attempts to delimit the spheres of divine and human action have much to teach us.

Much of the body of this paper is devoted to an

exposition of the ecclesiological thought of Luther and Calvin in its historical context. Luther's stress on the divine action as the sole source of the being of the real Church was designed as a counterweight to those that claimed too much for the authority of the actual institution. At the heart of his theology is a programme to delimit the spheres of the human and the divine, but not at the expense of seeing them out of relation to each other. In this respect, Calvin's thought is in essential continuity with Luther's, although in his different historical circumstances different needs came to the fore. In particular, Calvin had to pay more attention than Luther to the way in which the Church should be ordered.

Dr Schwoebel's conclusions are similar to Dr Jeanrond's proposal for a functional understanding of the ordained ministry, and he contends that there can be no identification of the Church that is God's action with any particular form of organisation. Two other chief points are made about the contemporary relevance of the thought of the Reformers. The first is that it raises fundamental questions about the relation between the Christian faith and the constitution of the Church. This, as we have seen is a part of the whole thrust of the book. The second is equally pertinent to our condition, and is one not made in the other papers. Much contemporary ecclesial practice takes place in the realm of what has already been called contingency management. Dr Schwoebel points out that if the Church is the creature of the divine word, it can be free from anxiety about self-preservation, and base its programmes on a response to grace rather than on a desperate concern to preserve existing institutions at all costs.

Dr Schwoebel's paper began with a discussion of the characteristically Anglican failure to engage with the heritage of the Reformers. It derived, he argued, first from the largely political nature of the English Reformation, and the resultant tendency to concern itself with the question of authority in the Church at the expense of the authority on which the Church is founded (p.112f); and second from the success of the Oxford Movement in 'catholicising' the Church. The fifth paper, 'Lord, Bondsman and Churchman: Power, Integrity and Identity in Anglicanism', engages with the theological vacuum which has resulted. It is written by Richard Roberts, a lay Anglican who lectures in systematic theology in the University of Durham. This paper has caused the group some controversy, because much space is devoted in it to a highly critical discussion of the ecclesiology of a colleague. About this, we wish to say that Dr Roberts' paper, which was seen in draft by the object of the critique, Professor S.W.Sykes, is to be understood not as an attack so much as a disscussion of the direction in which certain ideas can lead if taken to their logical conclusion. His paper is not intended to be an exhaustive or final critique so much as part of a process of conversation. It is, to use the jargon of literary criticism, a *reading* of the work of a leading Anglican theologian designed to bring to focus a central question of Anglican ecclesiology. In other writings, Dr Roberts has criticised the lack in Anglican ecclesiology of an adequate theology of the laity, whose place is obscured by an excessive stress on the bishops and other clergy. His contention is that with the breakdown in the modern period of the traditional basis of authority, there is a danger that the Church will reassert its central authority in a new and potentially arbitrary way. The hidden dangers can, he believes, be revealed in conversation with Professor Sykes' work.

His chief theses, accordingly, are two. The first is that the lack of an adequate theology of the whole Church may, in the crisis brought about by critical refutation of earlier bases for the Church, generate an authoritarianism of the centre, in which 'crisis management' replaces the authority of grace in the governance of the people of God. The second is parallel with Werner Jeanrond's characterisation of the crisis of authority in the Church of Rome. It is that the Church of England, in the absence of an adequate ecclesiology, is always tempted to behave as if the real Church is to be found in the clergy. The historical context for the development is seen in K. E. Kirk's collective work *The Apostolic Ministry* which in 1946 claimed for the Episcopate (rather than for the clergy) plenipotentiary powers. The development was in response to the weakening of the traditional christological base for ecclesiology. As criticism undermined christology, there developed a corresponding resting of weight upon the hierarchy. The outcome is demonstrated by reference to Hegel's parable of the Lord and Bondsman, which Dr Roberts believes to be in this respect highly illuminating. The laity are not really the Church, because they are regarded and treated as the suppressed bondsmen of the aristocratic bishops and their semi-dependent clergy.

Overall, the paper is a plea for a recognition of the situation and in particular of the need to find in ecclesiology an adequate account of the place of 'the spiritual proletariat, the laity.' This would require an ecclesiology centred in a quality of human relation rather than one preoccupied with the relations of orders, and would be a kind of theology of liberation, as Dr Roberts shows by references to the ecclesiology of Leonardo Boff. Along with the other papers, this one calls for a theology of the whole Church on the basis of which the intellectual and practical vacuum left by recent developments can be filled.

The final paper is by David Ford, a lay Anglican who is Lecturer in Theology in the University of Birmingham and has been for the last eleven years a member of a congregation in urban Birmingham. 'Faith in the Cities: Corinth and Urban England' has been placed at the end for a number of reasons. First, it explicitly draws together a number of threads from the preceding papers, and thus performs at the end of the book a similar function to that of this introduction, of making manifest some of the common themes and directions. Second, by its more direct use of the Bible it lays open something of what we hope is a central point of reference for all the contributions. Third, it is more directly and explicitly oriented to practical considerations than the other papers.

Such a point, however, must not be misunderstood. As has been made clear in this introductory essay, we regard all the papers as carrying considerable practical importance. They suggest ways of understanding human sociality in general and ecclesial existence in particular, and therefore have implications for how sociality shall take shape. But they are, for the most part, primarily theoretical because it is the theological basis of sociality that we regard as both important and neglected. Dr Ford's paper, by forging links between first-century Corinth and the modern city, brings the concerns of the book into direct practical focus.

The title makes reference to the recent Church of England report, *Faith in the City*, because David Ford believes the report to be both very important and seriously flawed in its most crucial dimension. On the one hand, it brings to bear concern for general sociality, and is not limited in its interests to a redemption found merely within church walls. Its informativeness and concern for the quality of life in England make it in that respect of great value. On the other hand, however, there is a danger that it will be read simply as law and not gospel, because it lacks the dimension of the hope that is the mark and the motivating power of the gospel. Moreover, 'it does not challenge deep patterns in the Church of England's ways of distributing power and authority, nor does it offer a vision of what authority centred on the Gospel might be like' (p. 253f). Overall, it lacks an explicit ecclesiology, and its implicit one is inadequate.

The Corinthian correspondence is here of great moment, because the situation it addresses—a traumatic transformation of the social structure—is both different from and similar to ours. Moreover, there is at Corinth a genuine sociality, despite all the problems, and by studying the interaction between Paul and the community we can observe how Paul essays, in the light of the gospel, 'a redescription of reality with (its) accompanying social embodiment' (p. 230). Dr Ford shows how in one area after another Paul related matters of ordinary church life to the gospel. In common with others of the papers, there is here much consideration of the nature of authority, and particularly its need to be embodied in and distributed throughout the Christian community.

In conclusion, it must be said that the six authors do not claim to speak as authoritative representatives of their churches. The work began as an attempt to bridge the gap between the academic study of theology—which is often supposed to sit light to, of not actually to subvert, the concerns of the churches—and the often narrowly focused and pragmatically oriented procedures of official church conversations and committees. We are representatives of the churches in the sense that we are committed to their lives under the gospel. We are also concerned that discussions of ecclesiology should take place in relation to the wider concerns of systematic theology to state the Christian faith in the context of today's thought and culture. We therefore offer the book in the hope that our suggestions and proposals will advance the process of engagement not only within the churches, but also between the churches and the world in which they are set.

CREATED AND REDEEMED SOCIALITY

by Daniel W. Hardy

1. Introduction

If we compare societies in the modern world with those in the ancient, we find modern societies much less cohesive. Furthermore, they do not expect to be cohesive. It seems that a reduction in expectation for society has taken place. And correspondingly, there is no sense of loss when societies do not in fact function well, as at present.

It does seem that the social institutions of the Western world are now in a state of disarray, despite the valiant efforts of many good people to make them otherwise. And, since many religious institutions have followed the patterns of secular society, directly mirroring them or depending on their stability in order to carry on an independent existence, the problems of society have affected religious groups very deeply as well. Even if one is much more optimistic, it still seems that society and its institutions lack a rationale by which to proceed on firm pathways; and lacking this they are prey to shifting policies or to the manoeuvres of the powerful.

The possibility of human society needs to be intelligently grasped and acted upon to achieve its highest potential, the more so with the growth in complexity which characterises human society through history. What we seem to see in our day is the effects of such a growth in complexity outstripping the intelligent grasp and action by which society may fulfil itself, with a corresponding instability—if not decay—in society and its institutions.

There is another dimension which must be added to such an explanation, for natural human society, as well as the means by which it is grasped and acted upon, manifests a pathological tendency whereby society becomes self-destructive, turning against itself and undermining the conditions which are necessary for its fulfilment. Society is not simply the unwilling victim of its own complexification: it is also active in its own self-destruction.

It is of great importance, therefore, that the foundations of the possibility of society be intelligently grasped, and the possibility thus revealed acted upon. Only thus may the direction of society be identified, and pathological deviations discovered and remedied. To address this task is to ask about the position of society in the Doctrines of Creation and Redemption, from which the issue of society has come to be disconnected. To ask about the basis of society in creation and redemption is also to ask about the nature and life of the Church, whose witness is to the possibility of a true society in the wider society around it.

2. Foundations and the Problems of Individualism and Idealism

What are the foundations of the possibility of society? One way of approaching the question is to recall one of Coleridge's most well-known, but not well understood, aphorisms:

> He who begins by loving Christianity, better than truth, will proceed by loving his own sect or church better than Christianity, and end in loving himself better than all.[1]

---

[1] S. T. Coleridge, *Aids to Reflection in the Formation of A Manly Character*, London: Taylor & Hessey, 1825, p. 101.

At first sight, this looks simply like practical advice about priorities. But closer examination shows that it is intimately tied to Coleridge's view of reason as the transcendent capability of man for truth. The view was dangerously similar to Kant's, as Coleridge knew, and might carry him along the trajectory which Kant had begun; the book *Aids to Reflection* was intended as a corrective to Kant's moral philosophy. The problem was that, though Kant had allowed a vestigial place for God, the implication of his view was that the human subject should replace the divine subject as the locus of the plenitude of being and truth. (And, for those who followed, this meant that the creator God must die and be resurrected as the creative human subject; he must die for the human subject to achieve his true place.) As God created the world through His word, so man creates—constructs—a world through his conscious activities and unconscious projections. In the last analysis, therefore, the 'other' was always found to be a dimension of the subject's relationship to himself. Since it is the solitary human subject which stands at the centre, this 'turn to the subject' always left the individual subject 'constructing' other subjects, or conceivably being deconstructed by them, finally perhaps achieving absolute knowledge when the other is fully reflected in the subject (Hegel). But, for Kant as well as Hegel and those who came after, the end was limited by the beginning, and since the beginning was individuality, the end was no true society, only intersubjectivity; and the way commended from the one to the other was no true way, but ultimately the exercise of power.

But Coleridge avoided the trap of displacing God by the human subject. He saw reason as the organ of the supersensuous in man, as the organ there of a truth beyond man. And this was not simply a philosophical view; it was

23

also a religious one, for human reason and will—when properly used—were seen to correspond to the divine reason and will which were themselves trinitarian in form. For man, therefore, loving truth was primary, as a co-ordination of will and reason, and this brought a correspondence of man's will and reason with those of God, the Trinity. It was unacceptable, therefore, to begin otherwise.

> He who begins by loving Christianity, better than truth, will proceed by loving his own sect or church better than Christianity, and end in loving himself better than all.

Since loving the truth brought participation in the Trinity, for man to love something else (in this case, Christianity) before truth was to undercut the proper use of will and reason, and in doing so to undercut their correspondence with God the Trinity, and replace them with something less. And once the rot had started, it would naturally lead to further debasements; when man no longer loved the truth, loving a lesser substitute would bring him to love still lesser substitutes. He would enter a downward spiral, whose end was in the least of all, self-love.

What is particularly interesting for our present purposes is that Coleridge's dynamic transcendentalism has a direct social implication. Loving the truth provides a universal sociality which is lost when preference is given to a particularised form of society; and preference for one particular society breeds more limited particularisms: love of Christianity stimulates sectarianism, and eventually the social disappears altogether; the only thing left is the individual self loving himself. Adhering to anything less than the universal sociality which arises in loving the truth is the entrance to a downward spiral to the least social.

What lies under the surface of Coleridge's remark is a concern with transcendentals—what have been called 'necessary notes of being', such as unity, truth, goodness, beauty. As traditionally conceived, these are the forms through which being displays itself, through which being is determinate; they constitute an answer to the search for the fundamental features of the cosmos. In the 'secularised' discussion of transcendentals which marked the 'turn to the subject' in Kant's philosophy, they were not 'necessary notes of being' but embedded in 'consciousness as such' in such a way as to provide the presuppositions for the possibility of science and morality; they needed to be uncovered by a process by which their use was analysed. In its endeavour to provide a proper basis for science and morality, Kant's philosophy concentrated on the 'consciousness as such', and was therefore universal in intent, but this was the universal in the individual consciousness; this philosophy began and ended with the individual consciousness. Not surprisingly, most of those who came after Kant concentrated on the transcendental ego, even where they developed notions of intersubjectivity, thereby confirming Kant's individualism.

But does Coleridge reach full sociality? It is true that in Coleridge's discussion, Kant's concern with 'consciousness as such' disappears, and is replaced by the dynamics of reason in relation to truth whose operation needed to be uncovered by reflection upon practice (try it! was the motto of *Aids to Reflection*). But if his view of the dynamics of reason is not focused on the consciousness, it is still the individual who is operative in the dynamics of reason in relation to the truth, and it is the mode of his individuality which changes from universal to solitary: 'He who begins . . . will end by loving himself better than all.' In the beginning, that is, the 'he' is a universal individual and at the end a solitary one. Ultimately, this remains a theory of universal individuality, rather than one of universal sociality.

It is this view, whether in the extreme form found in Kant (and those, like Kierkegaard, who follow him in this respect) or in the modified form found in Coleridge, which leads to Bonhoeffer's suspicions about transcendentalism as the foundation for a view of society. He found the conceptualities provided by the 'metaphysical scheme' of transcendental idealism unsuitable for application to the church as an empirically real community of believers:

> We must reject the derivation of the social from the epistemological category as a *metabasis eis allo genos*. From the purely transcendental category of the universal we can never reach the real existence of alien subjects. How then do we reach the alien subjects? By knowledge there is no way at all, just as there is no way by pure knowledge to God. All idealist ways of knowledge are contained within the sphere of the personal mind, and the way to the Transcendent is the way to the object of knowledge, to grasp which I bear within me the forms of the mind: thus the object remains an object, and never becomes a subject, an 'alien I'.[2]

These objections are well-founded if the transcendental category of the universal is individualist and idealist. For in such a case, the individual could reach neither the alien subject, nor his real existence. It is understandable why Bonhoeffer should therefore turn to the ethical sphere as a means of recovering responsibility to the alien subject in his empirical reality. As he saw it, it is only in the ethical sphere, where one acknowledges the thou of another person and God, that the other is truly acknowledged and genuine sociality is established.

But it is not necessarily the case that the transcendental universal is individualist and idealist. And we suggest that

[2] D. Bonhoeffer, *Sanctorum Communio*, London: Collins, 1963, p. 28.

it is neither. In the first place, both Kant and Coleridge, and also Bonhoeffer in his reaction to them, mistake the alienation of individuals in empirical reality for transcendental reality. The transcendental universal is sociality; and this, rather than individuality, must be the basis for understanding. In the second place, there is no necessary cleavage between the transcendental and the empirically real, of the sort often attributed to Kant and assumed by Bonhoeffer; rather, the transcendental should be understood as the basis of the real. By either of the two major traditional accounts of transcendentals, for example, they were understood as general features of the empirically real, not distanced from the real. On one account, as suggested earlier, transcendentals are 'necessary notes of being', the forms through which being displays itself, and through which being is determinate; as such they constitute fundamental features of the cosmos. On the other account, transcendentals comprise the presupposed basis for the establishment of knowledge through argument and agreement. They are:

> what is *ultimate and irreducible* for all who argue—no matter what their position. For by arguing—and this means even in the light of any doubt however radical, which, as doubt, should have a meaning—they have established for themselves and implicitly recognised both the transcendental presuppositions of epistemology and the theory of science in terms of the language game of an unlimited communication community.[3]

By either account of transcendentals, therefore, the transcendental universal should manifest itself in the empirically real.

---

[3] K.-O. Apel, *Towards a Transformation of Philosophy*, London: Routledge & Kegan Paul, 1980, p. 138.

3. Transcendental Sociality as Practical

Given the ideologies and events of modern times, one might readily doubt whether there could be a transcendental sociality manifest in the real which was either Godly or fully human. That is why, in their turn, Coleridge's concern for the consequences of a displaced love, the turn by Bonhoeffer to the ethical sphere and the concern for the pragmatics of human communication which has marked twentieth-century philosophy, are significant. With the exception of Coleridge, all alike abandon the discussion of transcendental sociality and instead concentrate on what is necessary for the practice of human community. They do so in many ways: Bonhoeffer's consideration of ethical responsibility in relation to one's fellow man and God, and Habermas's more rational attempt to achieve mutual understanding in communication that is free from coercion, might serve as two examples.

There is now strong pressure to concern oneself only with the practical or pragmatic, and to develop intermediate notions with which to do so, and to concentrate attention only on those. Hence the prominence given to the pragmatics of human communication or the ethics of human relationships. But this strategy is inadequate for several reasons. The conventions of pragmatics and ethics rest on the supposition of a transcendental sociality which is not only possible, but actually present in the practical or pragmatic. Secondly, pragmatics and ethics cannot necessarily provide insights into overall behaviour or the structure of sociality. Thirdly, what is found in pragmatics and ethics cannot readily be transferred to uncharted fields, where knowledge is scarce.

Rather than abandon the attempt to find a transcendental sociality manifest in the real, one which is Godly and fully human, we should treat the two as equally necessary aspects of sociality, and as importantly different levels which are not necessarily in conflict. Coleridge's concern with the transcendental basis of 'being-with' must, so to speak, meet the concern with that which occurs in practice as one is with another (or, in Bonhoeffer's words, answers the call of another).

How are we to conceive of the relation of the transcendental basis of sociality to practical sociality? The most fruitful way is to regard them as interconnected levels, the one testable only through the other. Thus, the social transcendental is like what is sometimes called a 'generic semi-interpreted theory' in science, such as general classical field theory, quantum field theory, game theory, information theory, network theory, etc. Like such a theory, it is comprised of notions which are assigned no factual interpretation, has a reference class consisting of a whole family of genera; and it is testable only conceptually unless it is given further specification (which makes it another kind of theory). In contrast to such a theory, what we have called practical sociality is like a 'generic interpreted theory' such as classical mechanics, general relativity, or the synthetic theory of evolution, etc. Like such a theory, it is comprised of notions which are assigned a factual interpretation, has a reference class with an indeterminate number of species; and it is only conceptually testable until there is added to it a concrete situation through which it can be empirically testable.[4] (Practical sociality is actually only practical when it is dealing with a concrete situation.)

Such a clear distinction between transcendental and pragmatic levels is important for the issue of sociality. This can be seen by considering one notorious example of the

[4] M. Bunge, *Method, Model and Matter*, Dordrecht: D. Reidel, 1973, pp. 38–43.

way in which the social transcendental (though not identified as such) has been 'fleshed out'. At various times, the accounts of creation and the formation of society in Genesis have been used to support the notion of 'orders of creation', which in turn was used to establish a hierarchy of races or preferred groups, thus justifying claims to superior races and providing support for the policies of Aryanisation in the Nazi era and Apartheid in South Africa, not to mention a myriad of other subjugations. In such cases, as one often finds in an improperly developed theology of creation, one finds a dualism selectively breached, a wrong view of human self-sufficiency and a confounding of God with aspects of the world and its history: God's presence in the world is recognised only through the medium of the history of a particular people (the 'superior race'), the people elevated by that history are allowed a wrong self-sufficiency (national autonomy) and God's will is wrongly confounded with a particular state of affairs (the existing racial divisions).

There are two strategies noticeable in the response to this use of the 'orders of creation' argument. (1) One mistakes an *interpretation* of a 'generic semi-interpreted theory' for the theory itself, and because that interpretation is falsified, abandons the theory itself. Thus Barth and others mistook a false use of the 'orders of creation' argument for the argument itself, and abandoned the very possibility of such an argument. (Barth abandoned it after his *Ethics*, and others did likewise; there has been confusion about the argument ever since.) In effect, that strategy involves the abandonment of the possibility of a social transcendental. (2) The other recognises that the particular interpretation of the theory (that which established a hierarchy of races) was falsified by its consequences, and then restates the argument in another form. (Bonhoeffer attempted to transform the argument into 'orders of preservation' which prepared for the coming of Christ, thereby nullifying the supposition that some were to be subjugated.) What is important here is to recognise that a failure at the pragmatic level does not falsify at the transcendental level; it only shows that the particular interpretation of the transcendental level has failed.

As can be seen from such a case, arguing that there is a social transcendental does not guarantee the quality of a particular content for it. That requires a further movement identifying the basis of the unity, truth, goodness and beauty of society. Such a movement, like the Doctrine of Creation itself, is a fundamental operation of human thought and life, and perfect results should not be expected.

4. Creation and the Social Transcendental

One way of pursuing this has been the doctrine of creation, and we may use that as an illustration of what is involved.

(i) In classical Christian theology, 'creation' is a summary indicative word for two things: (1) for all the formed or ordered cosmos, as distinct from that which is unformed or lacking in order on the one hand, and from God on the other hand; and (2) for the primary relation which this bears to God. In the first sense the word 'creation' designates that which has its own proper 'nature', through its inner constitution for example, whether by reason of its distinction from that which lacks such a nature or by reason of its constitution by God. In the second sense, the word designates the fundamental relation of this 'nature' to God: since, by reason of the primacy of God, there can be no other source for the ordered cosmos, the fundamental relation is seen as causative, e.g. derivation from God's action.

Theology of creation raises questions which are pertinent to these two senses of the word 'creation'. In their classical form, questions pertaining to the first sense have to do with the constitution of this cosmos as distinct from that which is not itself, and from God, and how this is to be explained. Those pertaining to the second sense have to do with the constitution of the cosmos by God, and how this is to be explained; hence they are concerned with the theology of nature, whether as understood from God's action or presence in nature ('natural theology'), or purely by reference to God's self-communication (as in 'revealed theology').

(ii) While 'classical' forms of thinking about creation take the cosmos in its relation to its source as their starting-point and emphasise the importance of explanation, the advent of modern understanding, which is traceable to humanistic, philosophical and theological influences, has brought a concentration on fields of inquiry within the cosmos. This concentration has in effect removed reference to God as the necessary source of the cosmos, and replaced it by reference to factors within the cosmos considered in their own right, each of which has become the province of specialists. The main areas of modern investigation— cosmology (including anthropology), history, epistemology, semiotics—have been steadily developed by reference to themselves, largely in contradistinction from each other, and it has been taken that each should be understood in terms of rational patterns which can be found within the area being investigated. Correspondingly, since interest has been transferred to factors operative in each area, pursued by the appropriate specialists, the possibility of a unified view of the cosmos has receded, and interest in God as the source has diminished sharply, almost to the vanishing point. Where interest in creation as a whole has remained, it has been transferred to specialists in a particular area, usually the physicists. Where interest in the Creator has remained outside the field of specialists (the theologians), attention has been concentrated on maintaining the 'fact' of the createdness of the world as such, and showing the 'necessity' of God as presupposition, whether for the cosmos, human life, history, truth, or authentic communication. These have proved so difficult, in the presence of powerful explanations developed within each area, that development of particular issues in the createdness of the world (such as sociality), and of their relation to the Creator, has been left to one side.

We see, then, that the notion of creation was used in two senses: (1) for all the formed or ordered cosmos, as distinct from that which is unformed or lacking in order on the one hand, and from God on the other hand; and (2) for the primary relation which this bears to God.

These senses of 'creation' designate the *results* of a fundamental operation of human thought, that of thinking the formed or ordered cosmos to its limits, to the frontier which distinguishes it from what is not itself, beyond which this ordering is lost. The process requires ascertaining the fundamental features of the formed cosmos, the division of the formed from the unformed, how this forming occurs, and by what agency it occurs. These are the typical movements involved in thinking of creation. It is not, of course, that such thinking does (or should) take place in a vacuum, or move according to its own trajectory. It begins from the formed cosmos, penetrates to its most basic conditions, ascertains the limits beyond which these conditions are not present, meets the elemental forces by which these conditions are constituted, and finds how they come to be present, determining by what means they come to be. Of course, such movements are not limited to rational operations such as those mentioned. They are also found in life itself, where one becomes aware of the elements which constitute life, and also the point at which they are absent, beyond which these elements of life are lost, in the process meeting fundamental life-giving forces by which the elements of life are constituted, discovering how this happens, and by what agency this occurs. Questions about the 'meaning of life' very often take this form.

Intimately associated with such operations are all kinds of 'sins' of omission and commission. Fundamental features of the ordered cosmos may be omitted or falsely placed; limits may go unrecognised or false limits may be established, wrongly placing the division of formed from unformed; the forming of the cosmos may be falsely identified; and the operative agency may be falsely understood.

As a fundamental operation of human thought and life, and with such difficult tasks, we should not expect the consideration of creation to produce perfect results; it must instead be a project of thought and life which should be capable of self-correction. This is not to suggest that it is simply a human construct; that would be to prejudge the issue of its correspondence with truth. The process is a dynamic order, and therefore always contingent, but in its contingency should correspond with truth.

In just such a fashion, the movement to a social transcendental is a project, which in its contingency should correspond with truth, but which should be capable of self-correction. The same is true for the social transcendental. The aim is to establish an element which will justify a true society, and thus inform the pragmatics of human society. But the danger of establishing an ideological substitute is very great; to paraphrase Lukacs, 'to say "we" is the beginning of ideology'. On the one hand, the supposition of universal human solidarity provides a fundamental consolation for human social life; on the other hand, the threat of a restricted or wrong basis for human solidarity is a constant accompaniment—the highest always seems to contain the lowest. As the discussion of the 'orders of creation' argument showed, universal human solidarity is too often based on the notion of assimilation to a particular social group, whether that is based on suppositions about national identity, economic and political practice, culture or religious belief.

5. The Dynamic of Social Truth

What kind of dynamic should therefore be employed in the project of establishing the social transcendental? Above all, it will need to be of such a kind as to allow the emergence of a social transcendental which corresponds with the truth of sociality. At the same time, it will have to take account of the manifest failure, through irrationality and wicked-ness, of human thought and life to appropriate a social transcendental which corresponds with this truth. This suggests a dynamic which is both affirmative and critical. As affirmative, it will be a projective realisation of society, and thus a raising of the most basic conditions for this by affirming them in thought and life. Furthermore, it will be capable of generating 'richer and more open-structured forms of order' in a social universe of constantly expanding complexity. As critical, it will identify and negate in-adequate conditions based on unsatisfactory categories or particular societies, whether subhuman (e.g. mechanical, organic or animal) or human (e.g. particular human groups, practices, cultures, beliefs). In different terms, the dynamic is a dialectic of hope and 'reality'. But it must be remembered that both affirmation and criticism are directed to the emergence of a social transcendental which corresponds with the truth of sociality.

Two further consequences follow from this brief statement of the dynamic which is necessary for the establishment of the social transcendental. On the one hand, the affirming, projective realisation of society will bring an aversion (a) to the confinements of what has been deemed to be 'natural' law or social order, and (b) to the moralistic following of patterns found in nature or history, of the sort advocated by Stoicism or such neo-Stoic movements as Capra's *Tao of Physics*.[5] Instead, it will respond to higher possibilities for society which are found through affirmation. On the other hand, the critical negation of inadequate categories for society will mean that society will not be 'natured' (understood through subhuman categories) nor will nature be 'socialised' (as providing 'a mute and purpose-less basis and pre-history for human society'),[6] with the concomitant possibilities for the exploitation of the natural world for the 'good' of society.

Nonetheless, the dynamic by which the social transcendental is established, whether relatively true or ideological, testifies to the search for a common meaning which is necessary for the formation of society. In formal terms, what is achieved *a posteriori* testifies to the presence of a social transcendental *a priori*. Another way of expressing this would be to speak of meaning as constituted through a determinate/indeterminate relation, in which anything meaningful is 'constituted only in relation to the general host of other possible determinations that are excluded in this particular case and are therefore indeterminate'.[7] If so,

[5] F. Capra, *The Tao of Physics*, New York: Bantam Books, 1977.

[6] G. Lukacs, *Hegel's False and His Genuine Ontology (The Ontology of Social Being, Vol. I)*, London: Merlin Press, 1978, p. 9.

[7] N. Luhmann, *Religious Dogmatics and the Evolution of Societies*, Lewiston: Edwin Mellen Press, 1984, p. xvii.

the establishment of societies testifies to a common determination involved in the meaningfulness of society as such, and this is the social transcendental. Such a common determination or meaning would include the 'necessity' of society and social order, whether as a universal feature (or 'fact') of the human condition, or as a feature of the evolution of humanity, or as that which justifies attempts to establish the pragmatics of human social behaviour.

It remains the case that this social transcendental or common meaning, though universal to the human condition, is contingent; it could conceivably be otherwise; and those who claim for it a particular content—the primacy of individuals or of the state, for example—suggest that it is otherwise. And the dynamic of establishing it, which has its own proper operations (the affirmation and critical negation mentioned above), is also contingent. How then are such operations formed and preserved?

One important answer is that they simply are. That is to say, though contingent, they are also necessary to the human condition. Human beings, to be such, are social and form societies; and they do so in the diverse ways which are appropriate to a world increasing in complexity. This is not to suggest that human beings are subject to some kind of mechanical or organic necessity; the necessity is a social freedom which arises from the presence of the social transcendental. Looking for another with whom to share life, for example, is not in the first instance a cultural or sexual necessity; it is founded in the social character of human being as such.

6. *The Formation of the Social Transcendental and Its Dynamic*

It is more difficult to say how the social character of the human being, the social transcendental, as the element

which justifies all society and thus informs social pragmatics, is formed and preserved, and the dynamic of
bringing it to its true form perpetuated.

Let us look briefly at two answers from modern
Christians. One is provided by Bonhoeffer in a programmatic (though largely unexplicated) statement:

> Social community is in essence given with community with God.
> The latter is not what leads to the former. Community with God
> is not without social community, nor is social community without
> community with God.[8]

Bonhoeffer derives sociality directly from relationship to
God; human sociality arises in (is given with) relationship
with God—as a necessary part of it, not as a *post facto*
addition to it. Therefore human sociality is inseparable
from community with God; human and human-divine
community are mutually necessary.

P. T. Forsyth supplied one of the few, and admirable,
parallels to Bonhoeffer's view:

> I desire to write of a holy Church as the moral guide of society.
> By a holy Church I mean a Church holy in its calling rather than
> in its attainment either in work or truth. I do not allude to the
> Church as an authority, but as the apostle and agent of the
> authority . . . The great problem before civilisation is the moral
> problem . . . the whole social problem. It is the issue on which
> civilisation depends for its permanence; and yet it is the problem
> which civilisation alone is least able to solve. But it is the problem
> on whose solution Christianity stands or falls . . . (1) The main
> work of the Church is determined by the nature of the Saviour's
> work in the cross, and not by human demands. (2) This work was
> the condensed action of His whole personality—His whole holy
> personality. (3) The Saviour's work being personal was therefore
> ethical, and not official. But by ethical I mean that its keynote was

[8] Quoted in E. Feil, *The Theology of Dietrich Bonhoeffer*, Philadelphia:
Fortress Press, 1985, p. 8.

holiness. The great need of the Church therefore is not work, but sanctity in the ethical evangelical sense. (4) The *essence* of Christ's work was the securing once for all of the Kingdom of God in the real world unseen, by an ethical and spiritual victory ... The historic scope of this work of the Saviour was the whole of society.[9]

As few others have done, Forsyth recognised the social problem as primary for civilisation and for Christianity; there is an inseparable connection between the two. And the Church is called as an apostle and witness to society as a whole on behalf of One whose work was for the whole of society, its witness being determined by Christ's achievement in securing the Kingdom of God through an ethical and spiritual victory.

Bonhoeffer and Forsyth alike recognise the centrality of the 'social problem', and that there is an inseparable connection between society and God. Furthermore, both recognise that the Church shows by what it does (as apostle and witness, not by the authority of its being) that God in Christ and the Cross has brought about ethical holiness, not for individual human beings so much as for all society. But there are two problems with their views. One is that they suppose the necessity of God's specific work in Christ as the solution of the social problem; the other is that they suppose that witness to the work of God is specific to the Church. In the first case, Bonhoeffer, for example, states the mutual necessity of social community with community with God as a matter of definition, without explication or defence. And both Bonhoeffer and Forsyth base the solution offered by God to the social problem on what can be called the ontology of 'gift': social community is the response to the gift of God, fulfilled in

[9] P. T. Forsyth, *The Church, the Gospel and Society*, London: Independent Press, 1962.

his achievement in Christ. In the second case, both Bonhoeffer and Forsyth suppose that the Church is the place where this response is made, not as cause for pride in the Church or for claims to its authority independent of Christ, but as apostle to society as a whole.

One effect of these views, therefore, is to eliminate what one could call 'general sociality' or created sociality present in the human condition; there can be no such thing as the social transcendental present in human society as an element of nature, because its place is always taken by the specific gift of God in Christ. The other effect is to eliminate the general dynamic whereby the social transcendent should be brought to correspondence with truth; its place is always taken by the specific apostleship and witness of the Church to something which occurred in Christ. Confronted with the need for sociality, both leap immediately to the specific gift of God and to the apostolicity of the Church on behalf of this gift.

There are two wider effects which result from their claims. First, in moving immediately to the specific gift of God in Christ proclaimed by the Church, they lose their commonality as created social beings with the society to which they speak. They put themselves outside the society to which they speak, and put Christian faith in the position of pronouncing God's work to society. Second, in proclaiming the specific gift of God in Christ as one of the grace which comes through God's victory, without relating this to God's work in creation, they narrow God's work unduly.

The consequences of these views are damaging. In the first place, despite the fact that Bonhoeffer and Forsyth identify the importance of Christian faith for sociality, and do so with such power and earnestness, they set Christian faith apart from common sociality, in effect privatising the

Christian contribution to sociality. In the second place, because they unduly restrict God's work to that of redemption, they lend substance to the views of those who underrate the importance of religious faith. In the presence of sharply increased contingencies in modern life, not only those which have to do with the disappearance of external natural resources but also those related to crises in institutions and personal freedom and meaning, it is widely claimed by social theorists that religions are obsolete because they are incapable of dealing with these contingencies. And where religion does deal with the contingencies which are common to modern life through 'contingency management praxis' (Luhmann), it is a 'bourgeois stabilisation of capitalistic action systems', and obsolete as a medium of identity formation.[10] The challenge thus presented to religion is powerful. It undercuts any unduly simple view of God's work in sociality, of the sort to be seen in one restricted to redemption and the Church.

But there is another danger to be seen amongst those who oppose the contribution of religon, that of what could be called social solipsism, or confinement within self-established parameters. In such a case, the theorist (or practitioner) overcomes social complexity by a constructed (or supposed) social theory which is basically incapable of being affected by anything that is other or different from itself. This is a self-closure within a particular social theory which ultimately disallows anything else, and is ultimately more sterile than the religions which are excluded. Ironically, this is the kind of crisis-management which was decried in religion. Unquestionably, if religion requires richness in meeting contingencies, social theory and practice do also.

[10] R. J. Siebert, *The Critical Theory of Religion*: The Frankfurt School, Berlin: Mouton, 1985, pp. 372–3.

Rather than trace the social transcendental, as the element which underlies all society and thus informs social pragmatics, to God's specific act of redemption in Christ, it should be traced to the Logos of God operative in creation. This divine ordering is what ultimately implants in the human condition the 'being-with' which is natural to it. And rather than trace the social dynamic (of bringing the use of the social transcendent to its true form) to the apostolicity of the Church, it should be traced to the truth of God present in creation. Hence it is to this dynamic that we trace the capacity of human beings to generate 'richer and more open-structured forms of order' in a social universe of constantly expanding complexity.[11] As stated earlier, the social transcendent—by virtue of its presence in finite human beings—is, though a necessary feature of human beings, contingent in form. But this contingency manifests the sociality of God present for humanity in created society. And the social transcendent is 'raised' to its true form in a social dynamic. We can now understand that for it to be raised to its true form is for this dynamic to generate richer possibilities of social order to meet the contingencies to which human beings are subject, particularly in the modern world, rather than simply to maintain the same range of possibilities for social order which were available in simpler situations.

This identifies the existence of social being in humanity (the social transcendental), and the movement of social being through the social dynamic, as due to the presence of divine sociality and hence the trinitarian presence of God. To carry the argument further, as we should properly do, would require an extensive discussion of the contingency

---

[11] cf. T. F. Torrance, *Divine and Contingent Order*, Oxford: Oxford University Press, 1982.

of God as social; but this is more than can be undertaken here.

7. The Social Transcendental and the Practice of Society

In conclusion, we must remark briefly on the ways in which the concept of the social transcendental requires further development. Strictly speaking, the social transcendent is what might be called a 'nest' of categories, and requires refraction through them all. Another way of speaking would suggest that the social transcendent, as a project of thought and life, requires specification through appropriate themata. A more technical designation of such categories or themata would be 'generic interpreted theories', those patterns of thought and life which are assigned a factual interpretation and have a reference class with an indeterminate number of species, as distinct from the higher level 'generic semi-interpreted theories' such as the social transcendental itself, which are not assigned such factual interpretations and have a reference class consisting of a whole family of genera, in this case societies. They are not, therefore, to be regarded as empirical descriptions, but as intermediates between the social transcendental itself and practical or empirical sociality. In a sense, they serve as a two-way street between the transcendental and the practical, enabling the social transcendental to guide the practical and also serving as a testing ground for a particular understanding of the social transcendental. They might be called 'intermediate' categories or themata.

In order to arrive at a conception of the social transcendental in its fullness and simplicity, it would be important to pursue the number and inter-relation of such categories; but we shall not attempt to do this now. Instead we shall give a first sketch of the areas in which they fall, and of the dynamics to be found in these areas.

In identifying the categories or themata, it is important to recognise those which are conditions for human society and those which are conditions in human society, and to recognise that such conditions are ramified through history —as, for example, conditions through which the social transcendental is realised are historical (though perhaps in different degrees) rather than timeless. The conditions for human society are, loosely speaking, situational: sociality is formed and constrained by ecological conditions, such as location on a delimited land area and the natural resources which are available there. The conditions in human society are: (1) those of social institutions, the presence of laws, customs and political organisation, with the constitution of leaders such as rulers, governors or a 'superior' class; (2) those of economic arrangement, including those of production and distribution; (3) those of personal relationship, including natural bonds (whether of blood affinity or loyalty) and those constructed bonds of a more 'spiritual' kind such as friendship or compassion; and (4) those of communication, such as language, symbols and culture.

All of these are also, in a sense, both the product and the producers of a history in which their effects have become, and become, more distributed and complex. And there is a sense in which the history which they produce is also the history of the world, and thus in turn provides the conditions for human society itself. For there can be little question that human society provides the organising activity by which the world itself emerges, a world which then provides the 'materials' for human society. More simply, that which causes finds itself caused by what it has caused. But that is too simple. The historical dimension is not so simple as many would have us believe: sharp distinctions are not only created but blurred through constant mobility and merging; there is great difficulty in maintaining clearly defined social differentiation except through blind adherence to the 'simple fact that they are different'.

Human social activity, occurring in these ways, is therefore capable of reconstituting its own ways. While, for example, laws, customs and political organisation appear to be an immutable 'social cosmology' by which people and things are assigned positions and powers, such a 'cosmology' can be transformed, even reinvented, to meet new demands. Hence the institutionality of society has its own historical dynamic. Indeed, it must have if it is to escape the premature stability of which modern social theorists complain, or the injustice of repressive societies to which those concerned with social liberation are opposed. For these are complaints about the fixation of society in inadequate forms which can be answered only by recovering the dynamics of institutionality.

The social transcendental of which we have been speaking, in its manifestation of the Divine Trinity, is found in such primary themata, as the witness of the Old Testament and the New makes clear—despite the tendencies of modern interpreters to personalise their message in individualist terms or to treat it as cultural history. In fact, one of the most important aspects of recognising the social transcendental is that it provides a corrective to widespread misinterpretations of the Bible, enabling us to grasp its meaning through a fuller set of themata than are normally in use.

In order to achieve a full picture of the social transcendental, it would be necessary to look at these themata one by one; but to do so would require a book. We must content ourselves with a sample, considering the issue of territoriality.

It is quite clear that the community of the Jews in ancient times was formed in part by their occupation of distinct territories, and the gradual coalescence of territorially identified groups through organisations serving some special purpose (e.g. the amphictyony). The availability of the conditions for a viable economic life was also important. Early Christianity presents an interesting transformation of this means of social formation. Places remain important, but the astonishing missionary journeys of St Paul seemed to be motivated, not simply as the result of a personal call, sustained by the companionship of Christ. They had more to do with his discovery of the presence of the risen Christ in the world itself. He found that the world itself was not empty but filled with the presence of Christ—a Christ-like place, so much so that travelling the world was for him a constant finding of Christ. And he found that the peoples of the world were themselves Christ-like; speaking to them was a constant rediscovering of Christ. If the social transcendental is found in the formation of societies by place, the determining element of places is here found to be Christ: they are Christomorphic. This is the basis for Paul's conviction that Christ is the head of all creation and salvation, without confinement to place. This has the effect of annulling social identities constructed by excluding others from an identifying place.

In order to understand the existence and quality of the social transcendental in such circumstances, we would need to consider all those conditions in human society which we mentioned before: (1) those of social institutions, the presence of laws, customs and political organisation, with the constitution of leaders such as rulers or governors; (2) those of economic arrangement, including those of production and distribution; (3) those of personal relationship, including natural bonds and those constructed bonds of a more 'spiritual' kind such as friendship or compassion; and (4) those of communication, such as language, symbols and culture. Each and all not only come into existence but also achieve a qualitative difference in the history of the Jews and the redemptive work of Christ. That is what forms from *created sociality* a truly *redeemed sociality*. And the one is necessary to understand the other.

2

THE CHURCH ON EARTH:
The Roots of Community

by Colin Gunton

1. The Drive towards Monism

'What on earth is the church for?' In Lent 1986 there took place an inter-Church study programme under that heading. The question, however, appears to carry a remarkable assumption: that we know what the Church *is*. At one level, of course, we do, and can answer fairly accurately the question of what it is in a number of ways, in the terms of sociological and historical analysis, for example. But at another level there is a case for saying that the question of the being of the Church is one of the most neglected topics of theology. We speak of the Church as 'one, holy, catholic and apostolic', but disagree on how the concepts should be understood because their meaning is determined by different assumptions and theologies. Similarly, while the choice of metaphors does make a difference—classically in the case of the Second Vatican Council's use of the notion of the people of God as a control on the metaphor of the body—there is little doubt that they too can be used in different ways and therefore with varying ontological content.

The case to be argued in this paper is that the manifest inadequacy of the theology of the Church derives from the fact that it has never seriously and consistently been rooted in a conception of the being of God as triune. Here, certainly in the British context, the deficiencies of ecclesiology are matched only by a failure to give due place as a matter of general practice to trinitarian theology. There is a widespread assumption that the doctrine of the Trinity is one of the *difficulties* of Christian belief: a kind of intellectual hurdle to be leaped before orthodoxy can be acknowledged. If that is the case, it results from a failure to realise both the interrelationship of the doctrine with other theological topics and its centrality for all areas of belief, worship and life. Because the Trinity has been divorced from other doctrines, it has fallen into disrepute, except as the recipient of lip service. But because it has been neglected, the Church has appropriated only a part of its rich store of possibilities for nourishing a genuine theology of community.

The first evidence for the thesis is that Harnack, who, unlike some others, devotes much space in his *History of Dogma* to the development of ecclesiology, can find little systematic reflection upon it in Eastern theology, and points out—accurately—that there is no dogmatic treatment of it in John of Damascus' *On the Orthodox Faith.*[1] In the West, attention centred, as it has ever since, on the clergy, and it is not much of an oversimplification to say that ecclesiological discussion in our time nearly always centres on, or degenerates into, disputes about clergy or bishops, the result being that the question of the nature or being of the Church is rarely allowed to come into sight. What then is missing? The answer can be approached by way of a contrast. The efforts of early work on christology were devoted to an examination of the question of the *being* of Christ: of who and what kind of being he is in relation to God the Father and the Holy Spirit, on the one hand, and, on the other, to the rest of the human race.

---

[1] Adolph Harnack, *History of Dogma*, E.T. by Neil Buchanan and others of third edition, London, 1897, Vol. III, p. 235.

Similarly, trinitarian reflection centred on the nature of God and of his relation to the world. Together, the two central strands in early Christian thinking have some claim to have generated an ontology that was distinctively different from those prevailing in the ancient world and, though in greater continuity, yet different also from the ontology (-ies?) implicit in the Old Testament writings.

Did anything similar take place in ecclesiology? There is some case for saying that, at the very least, a process of similar rigour was not carried through; and in some cases that here was a sphere where, far from developing a distinctive theology of community, the theologians mainly conformed their views to those of the world around, with baneful consequences. Here, if anywhere, the thesis assoc-iated with the name of Harnack, that the implications of the gospel came to be overlaid with an ideology foreign to them, is more than amply confirmed. Evidence in the East for the development of ecclesiology is not easy to find, chiefly for the reason that there appears to be none. Harnack, without giving references, asserts the East's acceptance of 'the fancy that the earthly hierarchy was the image of the heavenly'.[2] 'The idea of the Church that had the most vitality in the East was that of something which, regarded as active was "the lawful steward of the mysteries . . ." and conceived of as passive, was the image of the "heavenly hierarchy"'.[3] Too much should not be made of unsubstantiated allusions to hierarchy. But may it not at least be suggested that in a world where neo-platonism was influential, the urge to think in terms of degrees of reality, of a hierarchically structured world, was compelling in the absence of a drive to think otherwise? And is it not also true that a major achievement of ancient

[2] Harnack, op. cit., Vol. II, p. 85.
[3] Harnack, op. cit., Vol. IV, p. 279.

christological and trinitarian theology was that it did call in question that very way of thinking about reality?

The development in the West is both more explicit and more dismal, for the theology of the Church appears to have derived in large measure by analogy from the conception of an earthly empire.[4] A crucial phase in the development is to be observed in 'Cyprian's idea of the Church, an imitation of the conception of a political empire, viz. one great aristocratically governed state with an ideal head'.[5] There is, in the letters of Cyprian to which Harnack refers, little if any direct comparison of the Church with an empire. He prefers the analogy of the military camp.[6] But Harnack's comment is justified, in that the letters breathe a spirit of authoritarian commitment to the unity of the Church above all else. Appeals to scripture are allegorised or arbitrary (Cyprian likes texts which can be employed against heretics and schismatics—i.e. anyone outside the 'enclosed garden', 69:2), and so far as I can see, rarely to the texts which express the nature of the Church as a community. The theological basis is equally jejune, with Cyprian's God operating mainly as a principle of unity.[7] As von Campenhausen has shown, such remnants of the primitive ecclesiology as do survive are found in

---

[4] In explicit contradiction of dominical command and example, as in their anti-papal polemics Puritans like John Owen were not reluctant to point out. See his *Of Toleration*, in *Works*, edited by W. H. Goold, Edinburgh, 1862, Vol. VIII, pp. 163–206.

[5] Harnack, op. cit., Vol. II, p. 85, note 1. Harnack recognises, as should we, the constraints under which Cyprian was operating, but that is not the point here.

[6] Cyprian, *Letters* 46:2, 54:1.

[7] See especially the approving quotation in *Letters* 49:2 of the confession 'that there is one God and that there is one Christ the Lord . . . , one Holy Spirit, and that there ought to be one bishop in the Catholic Church'.

Cyprian's conception of the relationship of mutual love of the bishops, who accordingly become the 'real' Church.

When we come to Augustine, the picture is more complicated. A conception of the Church as the community of believers is undoubtedly important for him, but it is overlaid by developments deriving from the Church's change of status after Constantine. The official recognition of the Church meant that it was no longer certain whether it was a community of believers at all, so that it appeared rather to be a mixed community of the saved and the lost. This in turn led to two developments: the first a strong stress on the institutional nature of the Church, which fostered a tendency, with us to this day, to see the clergy as the *real* Church. The Church does not have its being from the congregating of the faithful—because not all of the faithful *are* faithful!—but from its relation to a hierarchical head. The mixed nature of the Church necessitates in turn an imposed, rather than freely accepted, discipline. The second is the platonising distinction between the visible and invisible Church. The real Church—represented by the clergy?—is the invisible Church, those known only to God, the elect. It is ironical, but not surprising, that such a conception, too, required increasing stress on the institutional and clerical organisation of the body.

The conclusion must be that the conception of God as a triune community made no substantive contribution to the doctrine of the Church. It is a semi-Harnackian conclusion in the sense that it shares Harnack's views that the original teaching of Christianity was overlaid with a philosophy that was foreign to it, but qualifies it in an important respect. Harnack's view, which is apparent throughout his great *History of Dogma*, was that the whole apparatus of early dogmatic theology was the imposition of a false metaphysic upon the gospel. I would hold rather, with

John Zizioulas,[8] that the development of the doctrine of the Trinity was the creation, true to the gospel, of a distinctively Christian ontology; but would add that its insights were for the most part not extended into ecclesiology. What happened was that the vacuum was readily filled by rival ontologies. There appear to have been two complementary influences. The first is the neoplatonic doctrine of reality as a graded hierarchy. From where, if not from such an influence, did the notion of hierarchy derive? There is scarcely biblical evidence worthy of the name. But Aquinas implies, without ever spelling the matter out, that the hierarchy of the Church—that there is in the Church an ontological grading of persons—is modelled on that of heaven.[9]

The second is the legal-political, which we have already met in Cyprian and will meet again. It is sometimes claimed that up to and including Aquinas in the West the conception of the Church was largely legal. The outcome can with little exaggeration be said to have been catastrophic, for the essence of a political institution, defined by its law, is that it employs constraint in order to maintain its unity. It can, therefore, be argued—with much support from the actual course of historical events—that the monistic drive with which this ideology has imbued the Church has, far from being the cement of Church unity, in fact been its solvent, because rebellion against its constraints has had its inspiration in Christian sources. It is then quite reasonable to speculate whether things might have been otherwise if the advice of Gamaliel in Acts (5:38f) and Paul to the Corinthians had been heeded. In his *Of Toleration* and in dispute with Bellarmine, John Owen

[8] John D. Zizioulas, *Being As Communion. Studies in Personhood and the Church*, London, 1985.
[9] Aquinas, *Summa Theologiae*, 1a:108:4, cf 108:2.

points out that according to 1 Cor. 11:19 'heresies' are 'for the manifesting of those that are approved, not the destroying of those that are not . . .' Quoting 2 Tim. 2:25, 'Waiting with all patience upon them that oppose themselves, if at any time God will give them repentance . . .', Owen comments: 'Imprisoning, banishing, slaying, is scarcely a patient waiting.'[10] The point of this citation of past controversy is not to raise old spectres, but to argue that bad ecclesiastical practice is at least in part the outcome of bad theology, and that awareness of this is a necessary step for modern ecclesiology.

2. The 'Heretical' Contribution

The reference to heresy and its treatment brings us to the next stage of the argument, and the claim that there is much wisdom to be found in the history of those who have been called heretics because their teaching and behaviour endangered not so much the creed as the seamless unity of the institution. If the effect of Constantine's settlement was a movement towards the clericalism of the invisible–visible polarity, the waning of that social order is calling attention again to the need to rethink the structures of the Church as a community. If we look at some representative figures, we shall see a pattern beginning to emerge. First among them is Tertullian, whose denial that the Church consists in the number of its bishops is often cited. But its context is also important. The polemic of the *De Pudicitia* concerns in large measure the abuses consequent upon the arrogation of the power of the keys to the clergy. Tertullian realises that the other side of the coin is the need to call attention to the fact that the Church is first of all a community:

[10] Owen, *Works*, VIII, p. 202.

> The church itself is, properly and principally, the Spirit himself, in whom is the trinity of the one divinity, Father, Son and Holy Spirit. (The Spirit) gathers (*congregat*) that church which the Lord has made to consist in 'three'. And so . . . every number which has combined together into this faith is accounted a church by its author and sanctifier.

The point is obscure, and the Latin almost untranslatable. But its point is clear in drawing links between three terms: the trinity, the community of faith and its free act of congregating.[11]

Harnack's remarks on Novatian are equally illuminating, because they make a comment about the institutionalising of the Church and the relation between Church and gospel. Novatian appears to be in a measure of continuity with the Tertullian of the *De Pudicitia* on the question of the forgiveness of sins. He has a different ecclesiology from his opponents because he has a different soteriology and eschatology. According to Harnack, he operates, on the one hand, with a theology that limits the power of the bishop to absolve because he believes that gross sin must be left to the eschatological judgement of God; and, on the other, with a view of the Church not so much as the place where people are prepared for salvation (the 'orthodox' conception) as the community where salvation is now being realised—in both cases, positions which arguably have greater biblical support than those of his opponents.

---

[11] Tertullian, of course, operated before the temptations of state support had come to wield their corrupting appeal. But his arguments for toleration maintain their validity: Nec religionis est cogere religionem, quae sponte suscipi debent, non vi. Quoted by Owen, op. cit., p. 184, to whom the argument that religion requires free adoption would naturally appeal. The use of Tertullian here should not be taken to imply adoption of that less attractive side of his thought chronicled by Hans von Campenhausen, *Ecclesiastical Authority and Spiritual Power in the Church of the First Three Centuries*, translated by J. A. Baker, Stanford, California, 1963, pp. 231ff.

'To the Novatians . . . membership of the Church is not the *sine qua non* of salvation, but it really secures it in some measure.' Harnack's comment reaches the heart of the matter:

> His proposition that none but God can forgive sins does not depotentiate the idea of the Church: but secures both her proper religious significance and the full sense of her dispensations of grace: it limits her powers and *extent* in favour of her *content*. Refusal of her forgiveness under certain circumstances—though this does not exclude the confident hope of God's mercy—can only mean that in Novatian's view this forgiveness is the foundation of salvation and does not merely avert the certainty of perdition.[12]

As Harnack represents it, therefore, Novatian's position is a denial of the Constantinian view of the Church that we have met in this connection: it is not a mixed community existing in some contingent relationship to the 'real' Church but 'As the assembly of the baptised, who have received God's forgiveness, the Church must be a real communion of salvation and of saints . . .' (ibid.). In that respect, we can see a real link between this early protester against the development of ecclesiology and the concern of, for example, the Puritans with Church discipline. It is surely not a historical accident that Western Christendon has thrown up a series of movements whose extremes have sometimes dabbled in millenialist violence, but whose more orthodox branches, labelled as heretical because of the extreme narrowness of the institutional definition of orthodoxy, have dedicated themselves to the same kind of

[12] Harnack, op. cit., Vol. II, p. 119. Harnack's diagnosis is confirmed by a similar report made by von Campenhausen of Cyprian's position, that 'the assurance of real here-and-now forgiveness was replaced by a mere likelihood and possibility of salvation', op. cit., p. 288.

community ecclesiology that seems to underlie the arguments of both Tertullian and Novatian.[13]

What is theologically at stake in this contradistinction of 'orthodox' and 'heretics'? The heart of the matter is pneumatological. Somewhere between the disputants is a major difference on the way in which the Spirit is conceived to constitute the Church. On the one side is a drive for unity, and a corresponding and growing emphasis on the structure of the institution; on the other a rebelliousness deriving from a different priority. To each corresponds a difference in the temporal framework, the conception of history, of the two sides. The one is increasingly dualistic: this life is a preparation for the next, a training ground for a future destiny. The other stresses more strongly the community as the place where the conditions of the life to come may be realised in the here and now. The reason for the divergence is the major deficiency in the development of pneumatology in the West, certainly in so far as it is measured against the New Testament. In the latter, there is considerable emphasis on the eschatological dimensions of the Spirit as the one by whose agency the life of the age to come is made real in the present. When that is lost, the Spirit tends to be institutionalised, so that in place of the free, dynamic, personal and *particular* agency of the Spirit, he is made into a substance which becomes the possession of the Church. It can be argued, then, that the criticism of the mainstream common to many of the 'heretical' movements of European Church history is that they see the institution as *claiming* too much of a realisation of eschatology,[14] while

[13] For numerous instances, see Norman Cohn, *The Pursuit of the Millenium*, London, 1957.

[14] The underlying theological problem is that historical churches make dogmatic claims on the basis of an appeal to a history whose actual course often appears to contradict the claims.

expecting too little of the community as a whole. It is significant that the extreme millenarian sects are like the official institution in claiming on their side too a realisation of the last things. Both alike deny the freedom of the Spirit and the contingency and fallibility of their embodiment of the Church. Corresponding to the imbalance in ecclesiology and pneumatology that this reveals there is, inevitably, an equally problematic christology. How that may be conceived to be is the subject of the next stage of the enquiry.

3. Christ, the Spirit and the Church

When we seek the christological dimensions of ecclesiology, the enquiry is complicated by the fact that there are two interlocking factors in operation. There is first the matter of what can be called the historical determination of the Church, the way in which we may suppose that in the economy of things the Church was instituted by Jesus, and that, of course, means a Jesus conceived to have been invested with divine power or authority. Most would hold to the fact of the instituting; disagreements arise over the manner and character of the action, and how it affects the present. Second, distinguishable but not separable from the first, is the way the Church is conceived to be patterned or moulded by the shape and direction of Jesus' life and its outcome: here the stress is as much on the dogmatic as on the historical significance of Jesus.

The effect of a belief in the christological determination of the Church according to the first, historical, category, is to be found in a number of places. Its force is determined by what it is believed that Jesus is doing in, for example, choosing twelve disciples. If, on the one hand, the twelve represent a reconstituted Israel,[15] the emphasis will be on the creation of a historical community—as, for example, it is understood in Schleiermacher; if, on the other hand, the disciples are the first of an order of clergy, to whom is transmitted authority over the community, a more strongly clerical ecclesiology will—and did—emerge. Even at this stage of historical enquiry we are presented with a dogmatic question, that of the end and direction of Jesus' exercise of instituting authority. Both of the interpretations we have noted can be employed to create or to attempt to create direct causal and therefore ontological and logical links between past historical events and present conditions. But both are questionable. There is considerable doubt whether direct links should be drawn between past historical happenings and consequent ecclesiologies. The attempts of denominations to trace their Church order to dominical institution are now discredited, though not in such a way as to prevent the continuation of the practice. Worse, such a procedure runs the danger of introducing a rent in the fabric of history, overstressing the newness of the Church and underplaying its continuity with Israel. It is worth noting here that in connection with his point that Jesus institutes the Church, John Zizioulas has remarked that even Jesus has to be freed from past history.[16]

Dogmatically—and now we move directly into the second of the factors which operate in this sphere—the point develops as follows. Christology's tendency is to

[15] R. Newton Flew, *Jesus and his Church*, London, 1960, p. 38.

[16] Zizioulas, op. cit., p. 130: 'Now if *becoming* history is the particularity of the Son in the economy, what is the contribution of the Spirit? Well, precisely the opposite: it is to liberate the Son and the economy from the bondage of history. If the Son dies on the cross, thus succumbing to the bondage of historical existence, it is the Spirit which raises him from the dead. The Spirit is the *beyond* history, and when he acts in history he does so in order to bring into history the last days, the *eschaton*.' Op. cit., p. 130.

universalise, and the way in which christology universalises ecclesiology determines the way in which we conceive of the createdness and, consequently, catholicity of the Church. Something of the force of the matter can be seen with the eyes given us by the doctrine of election. The logic of Barth's claim that 'God is none other than the One who in His Son or Word elects Himself, and in and with Himself elects His people'[17] has often been taken to imply a doctrine of universal salvation. The moment of truth in the contention is that if election is ordered christologically, and with greater emphasis on the divine Christ than on the human Jesus of Nazareth, the fate of us all appears to have been predetermined in eternity. A like ordering of ecclesiology to a monophysite or docetically tending christology has even more disastrous effects, and if I discern such monophysite tendencies in the christology underlying the *Dogmatic Constitution of the Church* in the documents of the Second Vatican Council, it is not to suggest that the error is only found in the Catholic tradition. 'As the assumed nature . . . serves the divine Word as a living organ of salvation, so, in a somewhat similar way, does the social structure of the Church serve the Spirit of Christ . . .'[18]

What kind of ecclesiology would derive from a greater stress on the fact that the ecclesiological significance of Jesus derives equally from the humanity of the incarnate? To hold, with Chalcedon and the Letter to the Hebrews, that Jesus is without sin does not imply that he is omniscient, or even infallible. 'But of that day . . . no one knows, not even the angels in heaven, nor the Son, but only the Father' (Mk.13:32). It is part of the being of a human

[17] Karl Barth, *Church Dogmatics*, translation edited by G. W. Bromiley and T. F. Torrance, Edinburgh, 1956–69, Vol. II/2, 1957, p. 76.
[18] Vatican Council II, *The Conciliar and Post Conciliar Documents*, edited by A. Flannery, Leominster, 1975, p. 357.

person to be contingent and fallible (though not, of course, to be sinful). If our christology take on board the full implications of the contingency and fallibility of Jesus, what of the Church? In view of the temptations and the trial in Gethsemane, may we claim even indefectibility of Jesus? He did, indeed, escape defection. But how? Not through some inbuilt divine programming, though that is the way it has often been made to appear, but by virtue of his free acceptance of the Spirit's guidance. How far then may the Church, consisting as it does of still sinful people, claim more than we claim for him?

A second area in which we may examine the effect of the christological determination of ecclesiology is in the area of authority. The modern Church must acknowledge with due penitence that it has rarely exercised authority after the manner of Jesus of Nazareth. To discover whether there is any theological reason for this—any reason, that is, other than attributing it to human sinfulness alone—we return to the question of the relation of christology and pneumatology. What is the relation between the Spirit and the Church? Sometimes it has appeared that because a *logical* link has been claimed between Spirit and institution, the institution has made too confident claims to be possessed of divine authority. The outcome, as we saw in the previous section, has been too 'realised' an eschatology of the institution, too near a claim for a coincidence of the Church's action with the action of God. Against such a tendency it must be emphasised that, as christology universalises, the direction of pneumatology is to particularise. The action of the Spirit is to anticipate, in the present and by means of the finite and contingent, the things of the age to come. This is true even christologically: it is only through the Spirit that the human actions of Jesus become ever and again the acts of God. Has the historical

Church made the mistake of claiming a premature universality for her works and words instead of praying for the Spirit and leaving the outcome to God?[19] Certainly, as James Whyte has argued, untenable and circular claims have been made for the operation of the Spirit in relation to the Church. He summarises the logic of the statement of the Anglican-Roman Catholic International Commission on authority.

> The decisions of councils or pope on fundamental matters of faith are not true because they are authoritative. They are authoritative because they are true. They are true because they are authentic interpretations of apostolic faith and witness. They are authentic interpretations of apostolic faith and witness because the Holy Spirit guards from error those who have been given the authority to make such pronouncements.

He points out that such arguments are not only circular and self-justifying, but are dogmatically flawed, in making too much of the divinity of the Church, too little of its humanity.[20]

What is required, therefore, is a reconsideration of the relation of pnuematology and christology, with a consequent reduction of stress on the Church's institution by Christ and a greater emphasis on its constitution by the Spirit. In such a way we may create fewer self-justifying and historicising links with the past and give more stress to the necessity for the present particularities of our churchly arrangements to be constituted by the Spirit. Such a reconsideration would begin by re-examining the relation of christology and pneumatology in general. The persistent vice of Western theology has been, because it is so

[19] See John Howard Yoder, *The Politics of Jesus*, Grand Rapids, 1972.
[20] James Whyte, 'The Problem of Authority', *King's Theological Review VII*, 1984, 39,38.

christologically oriented, a tendency to premature universalising, and in that respect the authors of *The Myth of God Incarnate* are at one with the tradition to which they take exception. The form that the universalising has taken has been docetic in direction, producing a tendency to conceive the motive force, so to speak, of Jesus' life as being the eternal Word. The outcome, as we know so well, is that his humanity becomes problematic: it appears to be almost conceptually inevitable that it is either loosely joined to the Word as in classic Nestorianism or overridden by it. Modern critics of the whole tradition, attempting to correct the balance by an appeal to the historical Jesus have made the mistake of generalising too soon from the supposed historical base, and have turned Jesus into an instance of some universal characteristic. What is needed is, rather, a greater emphasis in the action of the Holy Spirit towards Jesus as the source of the *particularity* and so historicity of his humanity.[21]

In view of the fact that the ecclesiology of John Owen will concern us later, it is not inappropriate to note here that his christology, in this respect anticipating by a century and a half that of Edward Irving, attempts precisely that reordering. In the first place, Owen *limits* the direct operation of the Word on the human reality of Jesus—in some contrast to Athanasius' incautious talk of the Word's 'wielding his body', using it as an 'instrument',[22] talk that was, of course, formalised by Apollinaris to rather different effect. In answer to those who would in effect make the Holy Spirit redundant in christology Owen holds

---

[21] It seems to me to be no accident that Schleiermacher, the father of modernist christology, was profoundly uncomfortable with the concrete Jewishness of Jesus. He was hurrying on to higher things. See *The Christian Faith*, translated by H. R. Mackintosh and J. S. Stewart, Edinburgh, 1928, p. 384.

[22] Athanasius, *De Incarnatione*, 17,42.

that 'The only singular immediate *act* of the person of the Son on the human nature was the *assumption* of it into subsistence with himself'. One implication of this is an assertion of the hypostatic union which does not entail 'a transfusion of the properties of one nature into the other, nor real physical communication of divine essential excellencies unto the humanity'. The humanity remains authentically human and is not subverted by the immanently operating Word. Wherein, then, consists its capacity to do the work of God? 'The Holy Ghost . . . is the *immediate, peculiar, efficient cause* of all external divine operations: for God worketh by his Spirit, or in him immediately applies the power and efficacy of the divine excellencies unto their operation . . .'[23]

Such a conception does much to create space for a conception of the humanity of Jesus which gives due emphasis to his freedom, particularly and contingency: they are *enabled* by the (transcendent) Spirit rather than *determined* by the (immanent) word. It also has important implications for the doctrine of the Church, which has, in most times and places been tempted—and, unlike Jesus, has usually succumbed—to behave as if she were immune from error. And if the Spirit which constitutes the Church is the one who was responsible for the shape of Jesus' life, we are still free to teach that he will give the Church a christomorphic direction. But it will be a different shape from the authoritarian one of the past, because it will be more oriented to the humanity of the saviour. It is some such concern which, despite its relative lack of pneumatological content, has informed the ecclesiology of John Howard Yoder. In *The Politics of Jesus* his concern was to argue that the Church's exercise of power should take its

[23] Owen, *Works*, op. cit., Vol. III, pp. 160–162. I owe these references to my student, Alan Spence.

direction from the way in which Jesus bore himself in face of the political forces of his day.[24] In more recent times he has turned his attention more explicitly to ecclesiology, arguing for a voluntary community which lives from the historical particularity of its origins.[25] All such enterprises enable us to reappropriate an ecclesiology of the humanity of Christ. That is the first and crying need if responses to the collapse of Christendom are not to take the form of new authoritarianisms, as they are indeed doing. Christology, then is the starting point. But of itself it does not take us far enough along the road, because we are seeking an ontology, some understanding of the nature of the Church, that is rooted in the being of God. Christology is only the starting point, because it is so closely related to the question of the status of the events from which the Church originated. If we wish to say something of what kind of sociality the Church is we must move from a discussion of the relation of christology to pneumatology to an enquiry into what it is that makes the Church what it is: and that first necessitates a move from the economic to the immanent Trinity; or from the ontic to the ontological.

4. Towards an Ontology of the Church

The argument stands as follows: that on 'economic' grounds one source of the weakness of the ecclesiological tradition has been identified. An overweighting of the christological as against the pneumatological determinants of ecclesiology together with an over-emphasis on the divine over against the human Christ has led to a 'docetic' doctrine of the Church. To recapitulate the argument of previous sections, it can also be said that much ecclesiology

---

[24] John Howard Yoder, op. cit.
[25] John Howard Yoder, *The Priestly Kingdom. Social Ethics as Gospel*, Notre Dame, 1984.

has been dominated by monistic or hierarchical conceptions of the Church, whose ontological basis is to be found in either neoplatonism or some other non-personal metaphysic. Where there is no explicitly Christian theological ontology, an implicit and foreign one will fill and has filled the vacuum. The contention is, accordingly, that a more satisfactory ontological basis will be found if we pay attention to the doctrine of the Trinity, which was, when first formulated, the means to an ontology alternative to those of the intellectual worlds in which Christianity once took shape, and must now reshape its form of life if it is to be adequate to the challenge of modern conditions. The doctrine of the Trinity, as it comes to us from the Cappadocian theologians, teaches us that the first thing to be said about the being of God is that it consists in personal communion. 'Communion is for Basil an ontological category. The *nature* of God is communion.'[26]

Suppose, then, that we begin with the hypothesis that the sole proper ontological basis for the Church is the being of God, who is what he is as the communion of Father, Son and Spirit. Where does it lead us? Great care must be taken in drawing out the implications of such a claim, and in particular the temptation must be resisted to draw conclusions of a logicising kind: appealing directly to the unity of the three as one God as a model for a unified Church; or, conversely (and, I believe, more creatively, though still inadequately) arguing from the distinctions of the persons for an ecclesiology of diversity, along the lines of the expression currently popular in ecumenical circles of 'reconciled diversity'. That would be to move too quickly, playing with abstract and mathematically determined concepts and exercising no theological control over their employment.

[26] John Zizioulas, op. cit., p. 134.

66

1. The crucial intermediate stage involves a trinitarian theology of creation. As many great thinkers, Coleridge prominent among them, have realised, a theology of the Trinity has important implications for the ontology of the creature. First, it forbids all monistic or pantheistic identification of the creation with the creator. More important, perhaps, in refusing to develop a logical link between creator and creation, it prevents back-door collapses into monism. The reason for this is to be found in the second, more positive, point, that the doctrine of the Trinity replaces a *logical* conception of the relation between God and the world with a *personal* one, and accordingly allows us to say two things of utmost importance: that God and the world are ontologically distinct realities; but that distinctness, far from being the denial of relations, is its ground. Such relation as there is is personal, not logical, the product of the free and personal action of the triune God. The world is therefore contingent, finite and what it is only by virtue of its continuing dynamic dependence upon its creator; or, to say the same thing in another way, by the free action of the Spirit on and towards it.

An inescapable characteristic of the Church in this context is that as part of the creation it, too, is finite and contingent. That is to repeat the point that was made in the previous section as an implication of conceiving the Church in the image of the humanity of Christ. The gospel is that the Father interrelates with his world by means of the frail humanity of his Son, and by his Spirit enables anticipations in the present of the promised perfection of the creation. What, then, is it for the Church to reflect, as part of the creation, the being of God? The answer, as John Zizioulas has shown, lies in the word *koinonia*, perhaps best translated as community (or perhaps sociality, compare the Russian *Sobornost*). One implication of the threefold community that is God is its dynamism: the being of God is a community of energies, of perichoretic interaction. As such, it is difficult to conceive its consistency with any static hierarchy. Such a hierarchy tends to generate or justify an ideology of permanent relations of subordination, as is instanced by Richard Roberts' telling use of the Hegelian phenomenology of the relation between lord and bondsman. Commenting on Kenneth Kirk's ecclesiology, he writes:

> The ministry has a final status in relation to the church; the Essential Ministry of the Episcopate creates and has contingent upon it a Dependent Ministry of the Presbyteriate and then, beyond that are the distant, dependent laity.[27]

We may glimpse behind such a conception further echoes of the imperial analogy, and there may also be traces of a misuse of trinitarian appropriations. But that takes us to a further stage in the argument.

2. We have seen that a central feature of the conception of the Church is the way in which its historical shape is formed by its (supposed) relation to the economic Trinity: to the Spirit-led Jesus in its past and to the Christ-shaped Spirit in its present. But caution has also been advised about arguing directly to the Church from the immanent Trinity. That is particularly important when appropriations are attempted from supposed patterns of relationship between persons of the Godhead. Moves of that kind can be used to justify theologically the dependent status of the

---

[27] Richard Roberts, 'Der Stellenwert des kirchlichen Amtes', *Zeitschrift für Theologie und Kirche* 83, 1986, 382f. Alan Sell similarly questions the Lima document's assertion that the ministry is constitutive of the Church's life and ministry. 'This would be to place the ministry above the gospel,' 'Ecclesiastical Integrity and Failure', Society for the Study of Theology, 1987, p. 15.

laity because it is supposed that the hierarchy is in some way more directly a reflection (ikon?) of the Father or Son.[28] The point can be illustrated by Derrick Sherwin Bailey's perceptive criticisms of Paul's argument in 1 Cor. 11:7 that 'a man ought not to cover his head, since he is the image and glory of God; but woman is the glory of man'.[29] Paul's exegesis and theology are both questionable. According to Genesis 1:26, it is man and woman together who are the image of God, a point which is itself of profound ecclesiological significance. Moreover, on a duly apophatic treatment of the trinitarian relations, it is illegitimate to attribute Fatherly, and so apparently super-ordinate, functions to man; but Son-like, and so sub-ordinate, functions to woman, as Barth continues to do.[30] Rather, we should not claim such detailed knowledge of the inner constitution of the Godhead that we can attempt direct and logical readings-off of that kind.

What kind of analogy between God and Church, Trinity and community, may there then be? If there is one, it should be of an indirect kind, in which the Church is seen as called to be a, so to speak, finite echo or bodying forth of the divine personal dynamics. How might this operate? Let me introduce the topic by developing a contrast between the Cappadocian and Augustinian conceptions of the Trinity. The latter is modalist in direction, if not actually modalist, in the sense that the three persons of the Trinity tend to be conceived as posterior to an underlying *deitas* or being of which they are, so to speak, outcrops. By contrast, the Cappadocian development, which Augustine so

---

[28] Henri de Lubac, *The Splendour of the Church*, London, 1956, p. 71, alludes to the possibility of deriving the hierarchy from the trinitarian processions.

[29] Derrick Sherwin Bailey, *The Man–Woman Relation in Christian Thought*, London, 1959, pp. 294ff.

[30] Karl Barth, *Church Dogmatics*, op. cit., Vol. III/4, 1961, pp. 188–202.

signally failed to appreciate, is that there is no being *anterior* to that of the persons. The being of God *is* the persons in relation to each other. The different Trinities generate correspondingly different ecclesiologies. Corresponding to the Augustinian conception there is an ecclesiology which conceives the being of the Church as in some sense anterior to the concrete historical relationships of the visible community. Such a conception is recognisable by two symptoms. The first is a platonising conception of the invisible Church which operates as ontologically prior—because it is the *real* Church—to the 'mixed' historical community. The second is the correlative teaching that an order of persons or ecclesiastical structure in some way undergirds or frames the personal relationships of the community: that the real being of the Church is to be found underlying the relations of the people rather than being a function of them. Such a conception is illustrated by a point made by de Lubac: 'no constituted assembly without a constitution, which includes a hierarchy . . . no realised community (*Gemeinschaft*) without a society (*Gesellschaft*) in which and through which it is realised'.[31] That gives the ontological game away. Why should there be no community without a society? May not the actual relations of concrete historical persons constitute the sole—or primary—being of the Church, just as the hypostases in relation constitute the being of God?

That things might conceivably be such is suggested by the ecclesiology of the seventeenth-century Puritan, John Owen. Owen is interesting because he is clearly seeking, as perhaps one of the first to do so, an ontology of the Church as a community. He is aware that he is breaking new ground, for he remarks that the Reformers, believing

[31] de Lubac, op. cit., p. 75.

that the reformation of doctrine was all that was needed, failed to develop a theology of the community.[32] That for Owen the being of the Church consists in its communion is clear from the use he makes of the terminology of Aristotelian causality. Speaking of what he calls the 'visible Church-state', he distinguishes between

(1) The *material cause* of this Church, or the matter whereof it is composed, which are *visible believers*. (2) The *formal cause* of it, which is their voluntary coalescency into such a society or congregation, according to the mind of Christ. (3) The *end of it* is, presential local communion, in all the ordinances and institutions of Christ . . .[33]

That is from an early essay, and in the later *True Nature of a Gospel Church*, he expands the idea slightly:

By the matter of the Church we understand the persons whereof the the Church doth consist, with their qualifications; and by its form, the reason, cause, and way of that kind of relation among them which gives them the being of a Church . . .[34]

What is intersting about the later formulation is the fact that the Aristotelian terminology now takes a back seat so that terms deriving from Cappadocian trinitarian theology —*person, cause, relation*—may come into the lead. The result is that Owen's definition of the Church is an echo of their theology of the Trinity. The being of the Church consists in the relations of the persons to each other.

A more speculative concern is whether we may develop an analogy between the free relations of the persons of the Godhead and the resulting conception of the Church as a

[32] John Owen, *The True Nature of a Gospel Church, Works*, op. cit., Vol. XVI, p. 20. Note the title's aspiration to ontology.
[33] John Owen, *Works*, op. cit., Vol. XV, p. 262.
[34] John Owen, *Works*, op. cit., Vol. XVI, p. 11.

voluntary society, if one whose voluntary coalescence is also and first conceived as the work of God the Spirit. The basis would again be the Cappadocian teaching that God is what he is in virtue of what the Father, Son and Spirit give to and receive from each other. There is, hardly surprisingly, in Owen a strong note of the voluntary exercise of membership in the visible Church. Is it possible to discern behind this the influence of the theology of the Trinity, for he is undoubtedly a deeply trinitarian thinker? At the very least, it is clear that ecclesiology is for him rooted in the freedom of obedience to the gospel. 'Wherefore *the formal cause of a church* consisteth in an obediential act of believers . . . jointly giving themselves up unto the Lord Jesus Christ, to do and observe . . .'[35] Nor is the resulting conception of the Church a static one. The Church is the work of the eschatological Spirit and so there is in Owen an emphasis, derived from the New Testament, on the *newness* of what is happening:

> If (the Church) constitute new relations between persons that neither naturally nor morally were before so related, as marriage doth between husband and wife; if it require new mutual duties and give new mutual rights among themselves . . . it is vain to imagine that this state can arise from or have any other formal cause but the joint consent and virtual confederation of those concerned unto those ends . . .[36]

For obvious historical reasons, Owen repeatedly emphasises the voluntary nature both of membership of the local church and of the federating of local churches with each other. All the most interesting developments in theology have come under the constraints of some historical pressure, and the fact that under the impact of his particular circumstances he moved so far towards a conception of the Church as a community of freely relating

[35] Ibid., p. 29.
[36] Ibid., p. 26.

persons must be accepted for what it is: an ecclesiology which echoes God's eternal being in relation. It is also to be observed that Owen uses what can be called the more subordinate of the Aristotelian causes to account for the voluntary combining of the people. It is clear that for him the 'efficient' and 'moving' causes of the Church—though he does not use such terminology—are the 'two hands' of God (Irenaeus), the Son who institutes and the Spirit who constitutes. We shall return to the point raised by that observation.

Another more recent essay in ecclesiology has produced some similar results. Edward Farley's *Ecclesial Man* is primarily an attempt to produce a phenomenological study of the Church as a community of redemption. On the face of the matter, phenomenology is the foe of ontology, in appearing to bracket ontological questions in order to describe appearances. But the way in which it is done in Farley's study appears to achieve not so much ontological agnosticism as a shedding of the weight of traditional ontological assumptions so that the structure of the visible community may be seen. The result is a description of the actual relations in which members of the community have their being, an ontology of the community which lives by its own descriptive strength rather than needing the support of—say—an ideal invisible background. A crucial passage is as follows:

> (Ecclesia) is not an exclusive form of social organisation such as a nation or tribe ... It does, however, involve a determinate intersubjectivity ... (I)n its concrete, everyday actualisation, ecclesia involves interpersonal relationships and reciprocities which occur in conjunction with its characteristic activities such as worship. These reciprocities presuppose an intersubjective structure in which participants constitute each other as believers.[37]

[37] Edward Farley, *Ecclesial Man. A Social Phenomenology of Faith and Reality*, Philadelphia, 1975, p. 152.

Once again, there are echoes of the Cappadocian Trinity. The participants constitute each other as believers, as the persons of the Trinity constitute each other as persons.

It is in the final clause of the extract from Farley that is to be found also the weakness of the phenomenological approach, and it corresponds to its strength. In saying that the participants constitute each other as believers, Farley appears to be ascribing to members of the Church the work that belongs to God the Spirit. By so doing he appears to have developed a rather idealising picture of the visible Church, and in two respects. First he has claimed too much for what is, as we are constantly reminded, a company of sinners, albeit of sinners forgiven and on the Christian way; and, second, he has read too directly from the being of God to that of the Church. He has, in sum, failed to distinguish satisfactorily between the divine and human determinants of the being of the Church.

Farley's phenomenology calls attention to the perils of attempting a theology of the Church, prominent among which is the danger of what could be called a printing of social reality in blithe disregard for the way things happen to be. Any ecclesiology must accordingly attempt to hold together two conflicting pulls. On the one hand if, with the New Testament, we are to speak of the Church of God, the being of the Church must be rooted in the being of God. On the other, however, a resulting ecclesiology must make due allowance for the fact that even as such the Church belongs to the created world, and that all finite organisms may fail to be nourished by their roots or may even be torn away from them. The Church remains this side of eternity a highly fallible community existing in a measure of contradiction of what it is called to be, and if as a matter of fact it has maintained a measure of integrity through the vicissitudes of its history, that may not be attributed to some inherent indefectibility. To be honest about our own history there is need to bear constantly in mind the temptations, by no means always resisted, to regression into a fallen past.

Too much is therefore not being claimed for the theology of the Church that is being attempted in this paper. The hope is to have created the framework by which a link may be drawn between the being of God and that which is from time to time realised by the Spirit. It is a kind of analogy of echo: the Church is what it is by virtue of being called to be a temporal echo of the eternal community that God is. What, then, is the point of such theoretical activity? 1. An attempt is being made to develop concepts with the aid of which the things we say about the Church may be understood. One simple example will suffice. Much has been made of the metaphor of the body of Christ, but, as the differences within Christendom reveal, it is by no means clear how it should be construed. It is an organic metaphor, and as such could be taken in a number of ways, totalitarian or pantheistic for example. There is much talk of organic unity of the churches, but the equally much used text from the Fourth Gospel (17:11), 'that they may be one, even as we are one' should give us pause, especially if we are aware of the trinitarian control. It is speaking not of an organic, so much as of an interpersonal unity: the personal unity of distinct but freely related persons. It is in some such light that we should approach the interpretation of the Pauline metaphor of the body, for we shall be aware that it is used in a number of senses: not only as a warning against disunity, but to stress the plurality of the Church's gifts and graces (1 Cor. 12:14ff, Rom. 12:4ff). The trinitarian ontology helps us to appropriate something of the richness and openness of that central ecclesial model.

2. Paul's misuse of trinitarian attributions has already been mentioned, and in fairness to him we should refer to another point made this time with his help by Sherwin Bailey, who in general refutes decisively the myth of Pauline misogyny.[38] Drawing on and correcting Barth's trinitarian anthropology, he concludes:

> Man . . . is in the image of God in its Manward aspect primarily by virtue of his essential structure as a bi-personal male–female unity in which (relationally . . . not numerically) the coinherence of Father, Son and Holy Spirit is reflected in terms of finite existence.[39]

Bailey's anthropology brings with it important ecclesiological implications, for if the image of God is primarily or even only largely realised in terms of the unity of the sexes, a major aspect of the Church's calling is to be a community of women and men:

> Against all one-sex institutions and orders . . . as against all vows of celibacy (compulsory, and even voluntary), there is set an insistent question mark; they are only justified if they do not hinder free and healthy partnership between the sexes . . . Nor are celibacy and monasticism alone in question; there are numerous Church societies, guilds and associations which are constituted on a single-sex basis, and are hardly calculated to uphold the obligation of partnership.

What that implies for the argument about the ordination of women should not be too difficult to realise. At the very least, it must be seen that the ecclesiology of community relativises, and not before time, the whole question of an ordained caste. More positively, as Bailey proceeds to argue, renewal in the image of God is essentially directed to 'harmonious creative relation between man and woman'.[40]

[38] D. S. Bailey, op. cit., ch. II.
[39] Ibid., p. 271.
[40] Ibid., pp. 284, 286 and 289.

That final point serves to introduce a more general consideration. Relations in the Church have so often been construed in terms of the permanent subordination of one group to another, even though the superordinate group has for the sake of appearances dignified its position with the rhetoric of 'service'. If, however, the attribution of particular positions to particular groups or orders is to be replaced by a pattern more reflective of the free personal relations which constitute the deity, should we not consciously move towards an eccesiology of perichoresis: in which there is no permanent structure of subordination, but in which there are overlapping patterns of relationships, so that the same person will be sometimes 'subordinate' and sometimes 'superordinate' according to the gifts and graces being exercised? And would that not more nearly echo the relationships of which Paul is speaking in 1 Cor. 12–14, from which the notion of a permanent order of leadership is completely absent? The concept may be thought to be hopelessly idealistic, but is that because we have so long been in thrall to the inherited stereotype? Whether that be so, the chief point of this section remains: that to base a theology of the Church in the Trinity is of great practical moment, because ancient questions tend to receive different answers if the primary control on ecclesiology is the tri-personal community of God. If it is true, as the opening sections of this paper held, that early ecclesiology failed to exercise appropriate control, and as a result produced authoritarian and monistic doctrines of the Church, it is important that the whole matter be reconsidered.

5. The Visible Community

In the previous section there has been attempted an ontology of the Church, in which it was suggested that a movement, carefully controlled by an apophatic doctrine of the immanent Trinity, can be made between a doctrine of God and a doctrine of the Church. The relation between the latter and the former has already been described as an 'echoing': the being of the Church should echo the interrelation between the three persons who together constitute the deity. The Church is called to be the kind of reality at a finite level that God is in eternity. Can further account be given of this analogy? Most obviously, it can be said that the doctrine of the Trinity is being used to suggest ways of allowing the eternal becoming of God—the eternally interanimating energies of the three—to provide the basis for the personal dynamics of the community.

Unless, however, everything is simply to hang in the air, there is need of some intermediate linkage, and this will be sought with the help of a return to some of the matters treated in the third section. What is the relation between the ontology of the Church—the so to speak theoretical framework with the help of which it is thought—and its actual being? That is to say: the source of our *ontology* of the Church is a doctrine of the Trinity; but how is God the three in one related to the actual historical and visible community? In what sense is our ecclesiology any more than a theory which is abstractly derived from an equally theoretical concept of God?

An essential intermediate step is that we ground the being of the Church in the source of the being of all things, the eternal energies of the three persons of the Trinity as they are in perichoretic interrelation. The primary echoes of that being are to be heard in the ways of God to the world in creation and the perfection of that creation in both Jesus and the Spirit. It is noteworthy that both of the supposedly deutero-Pauline letters to Colossae and Ephesus ground the being of the Church in the purpose of the Father to reconcile all things to himself through the Son and in the Spirit: that is to say, in the fulfilment of the destiny of creation. Scholars have sometimes argued that Col. 1:18a, 'He is the head of the body, the Church', is an interpolation into the logic of a hymn otherwise dedicated to a celebration of the cosmic Christ. But the text as it stands is precisely the point: the Church is the body called to be the community of the last times, that is to say, to realise in its life the promised and inaugurated reconciliation of all things. It therefore becomes an echo of the life of the Trinity when it is enabled by the Spirit to order its life to where that reconciliation takes place in time, that is to say, to the life, death and resurrection of Jesus.

The concrete means by which the Church becomes an echo of the life of the Godhead are all such as to direct the Church away from self-glorification to the source of its life in the creative and recreative presence of God to the world. The activity of proclamation and the celebration of the Gospel sacraments are temporal ways of orienting the community to the being of God. Proclamation turns the community to the Word whose echo it is called to be; baptism and eucharist, the sacraments of incorporation and *koinonia*, to the love of God the Father towards his world as it is mediated by the Son and Spirit. Thus there is no timeless Church: only a Church then and now and to be, as the Spirit ever and again incorporates people into Christ and in the same action brings them into and maintains them in community with each other.

To return whither we began, with an attack on the monism of the Church and its dominance by an ontology of the invisible, it must be said that there is no invisible Church—at least not in the sense in which it has usually been understood—not because the Church is perfect, but because to be in communion with those who are ordered to

3

COMMUNITY AND AUTHORITY:
The Nature and Implications of the
Authority of Christian Community

by Werner G. Jeanrond

1. Introduction

In this chapter I shall discuss the communal nature of Christian faith in God and the dimensions of authority for which this faith calls.

The question of who has authority in the Christian Church cannot be answered without analysing the question of wherein the authority of the Christian community as a whole is grounded. The problem of authority as a theological problem lies at the centre of the Church's beginning as a reform movement emerging from within Judaism. The traditional authorities in Pharisaic Judaism, such as law, temple, land and family, were reassessed and relativised by Jesus and his disciples as a result of their particular experience and understanding of God's presence in this world and of God's plan for this world. The recognition of God's presence does not require any special mediation by persons, procedures or rituals, rather every human being, Jew or non-Jew, is a potential 'friend' of God and therefore invited to participate in the 'Kingdom of God'.[1] The implications of this universalisation of God's

[1] Cf. Josef Blank, *Jesus von Nazareth: Geschichte und Relevanz* (Freiburg i.B.: Herder, 1983), 42ff., and Jürgen Moltman, *The Church in the Power of the Spirit: A Contribution to Messianic Ecclesiology*, transl. Margaret Kohl (London: SCM, 1977),114ff.

call to all human beings and the particular challenge to the salvific necessity of the religious and social institutions of Judaism led to the rejection of Jesus of Nazareth and of his theology by the religious establishment of his time. The religious leadership in Jerusalem condemned Jesus' theology as anarchical, inauthentic and dangerous; it felt obliged to protect the identity of religious orthodoxy and the authoritative order in society especially then, when it saw Judaism experiencing already considerable pressures and challenges to its identity from outside and from within. Yet in spite of the effort to suppress the Jesus movement, the spiritual energy of Jesus' disciples led to a new faith-praxis with, at least initially, a radically reformed understanding of relogous authority.

Any discussion of possible dimensions of Christian life today has to begin by developing criteria of authentic Christian discipleship. However, the search for such criteria leads immediately into the discussion of the authority attributed to historical sources which have been appreciated as 'normative' for Christian existence since the early times of the Church: Scripture and tradition and, as in the Roman Catholic Church, the authoritative interpretation of both by a particular teaching office (the Magisterium). Yet if the interpretation of such normative sources is to be critical it will require a critical theory, a *critical* hermeneutics, which is sufficiently suspicious of possible ideological distortions in all of these sources and in the interpretive process itself.[2] Only such a critical and self-critical hermeneutics will provide a basis both for a

---

[2] Cf. David Tracy, *Plurality and Ambiguity: Hermeneutics, Religion, Hope* (San Francisco: Harper & Row, 1987), and my own efforts of establishing such a critical hermeneutics in *Text and Interpretation as Categories of Theological Thinking*, transl. Thomas Wilson (Dublin: Gill and Macmillan, and New York: Crossroad, 1988).

more responsible interpretation of the sources of Christian faith and for a more responsible interpretation of human existence in the light of the renewed understanding of Christian faith. Although any individual and communal interpretation is always in danger of being distorted, the community of interpreters provides at least the possibility, although never a guarantee, of achieving more responsible interpretations and of developing more adequate criteria of Christian discipleship. While the history of the Christian movement is an essential source for the study of how previous generations developed criteria of discipleship, it does not represent a linear progression towards its ultimate consummation by God.[3] Such a view of an increasingly adequate discipleship would itself be an ideological distortion, an indefensible prejudgement of our own situation within the Christian movement. Thus, while we can never step out of the tradition of this movement, we may challenge the course and change the reality of it in terms of what we consider to be a more responsible response to God's call in our time. Thanks to our tradition which handed the Christian message on to us we can be critical of our tradition and reassess again and again the criteria of authentic discipleship.

2. *Christian Faith as Communal Response to God's Call*

Christian faith comes into being when people respond to Jesus Christ's life, death and resurrection by following him to God in their own lives. While the conscious decision to become Christ's disciple is always made by individuals, any such individual is always already related to other

---

[3] Michel Foucalt, *Von der Subversion des Wissens*, transl. and ed. Walter Seitter (Frankfurt/M.: Suhrkamp, 1982), 14, criticises the 'myth of evolution as the basic structure of history' (my translation).

disciples (from whom he or she has gained knowledge about the Christian faith) and to the world in which he or she lives. Following Jesus Christ to God means sharing the belief with other people—past and present—that in Jesus' story we see the ultimate disclosure of God's project with this universe (God's Kingdom).[4] The foundational experience of this belief is the recognition that God wants all forms of death ultimately to be overcome: physical death, spiritual death, the death of relationships between people, the death of the relationship between us and God (= the phenomenon of sin), and the self-perpetuation of all these threats to life (= the phenomenon usually referred to as 'original sin'). In Christian faith the resurrection of Jesus is seen as the ultimate victory of life over all these forms of death. Whoever follows the resurrected crucified one participates already in God's life.[5]

However, Christian existence faces the tension between this experience of new life and the continuing reality of all forms of death in this world. Throughout the history of Christianity many different efforts reacting to this tension can be observed. They comprise the organisation of military campaigns aiming at Christianising the world on the one side of a wide spectrum, as well as the various movements of withdrawal from this world as in certain hermetic and monastic traditions on the other side.

In our search for a more adequate relationship with our world we would need to consider the many different dimensions of Christian faith in more detail than is possible here. However, even a brief listing of major dimensions

[4] Cf. Paul M. Zulehner, 'Gemeinde' in Peter Eicher, ed., *Neues Handbuch theologischer Grundbegriffe II* (München: Kösel, 1984), 52–65, here esp. 52f. See also Glenn F. Chesnut, *Images of Christ: An Introduction to Christology* (Minneapolis: Seabury, 1984), xiii and 98f., where he translates the Greek concept 'hypostasis' with 'project'.

[5] Cf. Zulehner, 'Gemeinde', 53.

will help us to avoid unrealistic campaigns as well as irresponsible reductionisms in our efforts to participate already in God's life here and now.

Christian faith is *political*. While it always begins with a person's individual turn towards God's self-disclosure in human history and especially in the life, death and resurrection of Jesus of Nazareth, Christian faith points the individual believer immediately to other believers and ultimately to all human beings and our common human concern for the future of our universe. Thus, Christian faith is *social* and *public*. The organisation of Christian community, the Church, must reflect these dimensions and provide opportunities for every Christian to participate in the new praxis demanded by this faith. Christian faith is *historical* and *eschatological*: it is itself a phenomenon in human history and not outside it, and Christian praxis must be directed towards the transformation of this history according to God's will. That, however, means that Christians first of all take this universe seriously as willed by God and stop writing it off as the waste land of fights for another life. The 'eternal life' announced by Jesus Christ is not a temporal or geographical quantity, rather it is a spiritual category pointing to God's promise of renewing this world. Therefore, every individual Christian and every Christian community must be committed to becoming the 'salt of the earth', i.e. that force which prepares the way for God to become all in all in this universe. This principal commitment to the world must, however, always be *critical* of possible distortions in the specific acts transforming this world into God's place.

These and other dimensions of Christian faith show the complexity of the human response to the 'Spirit of Christ'. This spirit is kept alive by the Christian movement when it engages in a threefold praxis, namely in acts of proclaim-

ing, celebrating and sharing the new life.[6] (1) 'Proclamation' means the ongoing (critical and self-critical) retelling
of God's story with humankind from Abraham to Jesus to
us; (2) 'celebration' means the praise of God and of God's
gift of life;[7] and (3) 'sharing the new life' means active
solidarity with all human beings, especially with the needy,
the poor, the sick, the oppressed, i.e. with all those whose
existence is marked by some form of death. The term
which traditionally has referred to all three dimensions of
Christian faith-praxis is 'love': the recognition of God's
love calls for our love of God, of ourselves and of one
another. This is the spirit of the Christian community
which invites a continuous affirmation of God's creative
love of this universe.

The three dimensions of Christian faith-praxis can be
distinguished, but should never be separated. The entire
Christian community lives by proclaiming God's creative
activity in human history and especially in the story
of Jesus Christ, by celebrating God's presence in this
universe, especially though not only in the feast of the
eucharist, and by actively participating in the transformation of this world according to God's salvific plan. This
threefold identity of the Christian community is an
identity in process. That means the community can never
ultimately define its boundaries, because it confesses God's

[6] Cf. Zulehner, 'Gemeinde', 55–57, where 'Empfangen, Loben und Austeilen'
are defined as the fundamental Christian attitudes (*Grundgesten*). See also David
Tracy, *The Analogical Imagination: Christian Theology and the Culture of
Pluralism* (New York: Crossroad, 1981), 209, where he develops 'proclamation,
manifestation and historical action' as the three basic dimensions of the Christian
faith. Edward Farley, *Ecclesial Reflection: An Anatomy of Theological Method*
(Philadelphia: Fortress, 1982), 257: 'Proclamation, sacraments, and care are the
types of activities through which ecclesial existence occurs historically through
time.'

[7] Cf. Daniel W. Hardy and David Ford, *Jubilate: Theology in Praise* (London:
D L T, 1984), where 'praise' is developed as the fundamental Christian activity.

call as a universal call. Rather, the community must concentrate on its centre, that is God's presence in all the dimensions of the universe, and be willing to reassess again and again its faithfulness to its vocation as an instrument of God's reconciling love in this universe. This function of the community in the world has often been described as the community's 'sacramental' nature.[8]

This inclusive and dynamic identity of the Christian community finds powerful expression in the celebration of the eucharist. The eucharist can be experienced as the spiritual centre of the Christian community because it invites the individual person to participate in the threefold communal praxis of the Christian faith. The celebration of the eucharist includes the recollection and celebration of God's presence in human history, the recollection and celebration of Jesus Christ's sacrificial life and death and of God's affirmation of this person's way in the event of the resurrection; and here the community reflects its passionate concern for the need of our broken world to be reconciled with God. Thus, the eucharist can bring together all the different dimensions of the Christian community's identity: it can account for its egalitarian social fabric (though any exclusively male dominated organisation of the eucharistic feast does not). It can interpret the historical experiences and the local and universal manifestations of the community. It can spiritually prepare the community for concrete political action. And it can make the community painfully aware of its manifold failures while at the same time reminding it of God's love and forgiveness in order to enable the com-

---

[8] Cf. Wolfgang Beinert, 'Christsein ohne Kirche? Über die Notwendigkeit der Institution' in Johannes Hüttenbügel, *Gott-Mensch-Universum: Der Christ vor den Fragen der Zeit* (Graz: Styria, 1974), 677–703, esp. 693f.

munity to experience the freedom and the promise of a new beginning.[9]

This abstract description of the Christian community's identity has gathered only schematically the major characteristics of any local Christian gathering. Yet it has clarified already in principle the nature of authority of any Christian community. This community owes all of its authority to God and not to itself. God is the sole *auctor* of the community. God has called his people into a social, political, etc. existence by inviting men and women to respond together to his presence in this universe. Recognising God's ultimate and superior authority, the community is fundamentally suspicious of all *human* claims to ultimate authority and to superiority. Thus with regard to the forms of their organisation we can say that the members of a Christian community, by nature of their call should act in an 'anti-authoritarian' manner towards one another.

'Anti-authoritarian' refers to the need to question again and again the legitimacy of the forms of authority employed in the Church and does not mean that there should not be such forms at all. A Christian community like any other human community needs some structures and clearly designed social functions in order to minimise possible conflicts and tensions. However, Christian communities must be particularly mindful that no such function or structure develop into a system of oppression

[9] For the importance of the eucharist in the emerging Church see Josef Blank, *Vom Urchristentum zur Kirche: Kichenstrukturen im Rückblick auf den biblischen Ursprung* (München: Kösel, 1982), 236–244, and Peter Stuhlmacher, 'Das neutestamentliche Zeugnis vom Herrenmahl', *Zeitschrift für Theologie und Kirche* 84 (1987), 1–35: 'Indem die Tischgenossen in, mit und unter Brot und Wein Anteil an Jesu stellvertretendem Tod und neuem Leben erhalten, werden sie zur Gemeinde Jesu als Vorhut des neuen Gottesvolkes vereint. Das Herrenmahl ist schon in Jerusalem der entscheidende Kristallisationspunkt, der die Glaubenden immer aufs neue zur Gemeinde Christi zusammenschließt.'

where spiritually legitimised authority is replaced by spiritually unjustifiable exercise of power by one section of the community over the other.

3. What Authority is Necessary in a Christian Community?

(a) REFLECTIONS ON THE HISTORY OF THE PROBLEM

From a sociological perspective, 'the phenomenon of authority is basic to human behaviour'.[10] Authority can be defined as a property of a person or office, a relationship, a quality of communication or as a variation of one or more of these; it can be observed as parental authority (family), leadership in groups, as organised and bureaucratic authority (schools, churches, armies, industrial and governmental agencies, etc.), and generally as political authority.[11] With regard to 'authority' we have to analyse now whether or not the social reality of the Christian Church has been reflecting the theological identity of the Christian community as we have understood it here.

The history of the Christian Church illustrates the fact that different forms of authority have always existed in the Church and that there has always been a conflict about what constitutes 'authentic' authority in the community of Christians. For the early Church, Gerd Theissen's study of the sociology of the Jesus movement helps us to appreciate the important role of the homeless wandering charismatics who much more than any local group of Christians represented 'authoritatively' the new faith-praxis (cf. Paul

[10] Robert L. Peabody, 'Authority' in *International Encyclopedia of the Social Sciences I* (Collier and Macmillan, 1968), 473–477, here 473.
[11] Ibid. Cf. also Karl Rahner, 'Autorität' in *Christlicher Glaube in moderner Gesellschaft*, Vol. 14 (Freiburg i.B., Basel Wien: Herder, 1982), 5–36.

and Barnabas).[12] The authority of these wandering charismatics was recognised and affirmed by the local communities as superior to their own emerging leadership. However, the tension between the prophetic element and the more conservative forces within the local communities can be observed already very early in the Christian movement.[13] As the stabilisation of the local communities progressed, models for their organisation were taken at first from Jewish and other contemporary religious traditions (cultic offices and officers), and then, after the Constantinian changes, increasingly from the praxis of political and legal organisation in the Roman and subsequent secular empires. This latter source explains to some extent such organisational trends as the development of the territorial principle in parish structures, the growing distinction between clergy and laity, and the progressive centralisation within the church (cf. the primacy of Rome).

This way of organising Christian community was not accepted by all members of the community, as the development of monastic forms of Christian life documents. Various monastic communities tried to preserve some of the egalitarian and prophetic identity of the Christian community. Yet even these more adventurous forms of Christian community were in constant danger of being 'co-ordinated' by Roman or local bishops on the one hand and by local or imperial politicians on the other.[14]

[12] Gerd Theissen, *Soziologie der Jesusbewegung: Ein Beitrag zur Entstehungsgeschichte des Urchristentums.* Theologische Existenz heute 194, 3rd ed. (München: Kaiser, 1981), 14ff., esp. 16: 'Was wir an Nachrichten über die ersten urchristlichen Autoritäten haben, weist auf Wandercharismatiker.'

[13] Cf. Norbert Brox, *Kirchengeschichte des Altertums*, 2nd ed. (Düsseldorf: Patmos, 1986), 90ff.

[14] For a concise account of the monastic developments in the Middle Ages and of the relationship between monastries and the ecclesiastical and political world see Hans-Werner Goetz, *Leben im Mittelalter: vom 7. bis zum 13. Jahrhundert* (München: Beck, 1986), 65–114.

Structurally, the medieval Church consisted of two ('ontologically') different sections, the clergy and the laity.[15] The clergy had become the ruling class while the laity was the group to be looked after (not always only spiritually) by the clergy. This ecclesiastical organisation was questioned in the Protestant Reformation which retrieved the biblical image of the priesthood of all people.[16] But this retrieval was at first more of a programmatic nature, while the actual situation in the local church remained unchanged. The Protestant 'pastor' continued to take care of his flock, the Protestant potentate took over the role of the civil patron of the Reformed Church from his Roman Catholic predecessor. However, the ecclesial reorganisation in many (though not in all) Protestant movements led eventually to a much more substantial participation of the 'laity' in Church government, whereas in the Roman Catholic Church the principle of clerical authority was refined even further. Here the clerical absolutism has on the whole remained unchanged until today.

While the Protestant Churches consider the offices in the Church as 'functions' whose authority springs from the community, the Roman Catholic Church continues to defend the 'status' of its male clergy as willed by Christ. Thus, the organisation of authority in this Church is seen to come directly from God and to demand absolute

[15] Cf. my critique of the two-class system in the Roman Catholic Church in 'One Church: Two Classes? The Lesson of History' in Seán MacRéamoinn, ed., *Pobal: the laity in Ireland* (Dublin: Columba Press, 1986), 22–34.

[16] Cf. among other recent studies Horst Beintker, 'Aspekte zu Amt und Gemeinde in Bugenhagens und Luthers Kirchenordnungsprogramm', *Evangelische Theologie* 47 (1987), 120–137, and Paul-Werner Scheele, '"Eyn volck der gnaden": Ekklesiologische Implikationen der sakramentsbezogenen Sermones Martin Luthers aus dem Jahre 1519,' in Peter Manns and Harding Meyer, eds., *Ökumensiche Erschließung Martin Luthers* (Paderborn: Bonifatius, and Frankfurt/M.: Otto Lembeck, 1983), 154–168.

obedience from the members of the community. The model of vicarious representation of authority operative in the Roman Church has survived the changes of the Second Vatican Council. Although this Council's Constitution on the Church (*Lumen Gentium*) describes the Church as the people of God and emphasises the equal importance of all its members,[17] the equality of the faithful breaks down when in the same document 'we do not meet the view of one priestly character and diversity of function but two ontological qualities, resulting in two essentially different lines of functions, whereof the one is representative and the other is not'.[18] The tragedy of the Second Vatican Council lies in its failure to agree wholeheartedly on the redefinition of the Church as *communio* and to abandon the concept of the Church as *societas*.[19] As long as the final power over the community remains only in the hands of one section of the community, the essence of *communio* authorised by God is destroyed in favour of an ecclesial society authorised only by itself.

Nevertheless, the ambiguity of *Lumen Gentium* and the spirit of the Constitution *Gaudium et Spes* have been interpreted by some sections of the Roman Catholic Church as invitations to work for a more authentic communal faith-praxis with appropriate structures. The Latin American base-communities are an important example of this renewal in spite of the continuing authoritarian government of the Roman Catholic Church.[20]

[17] *Lumen Gentium* 7.

[18] Einar Sigurbjörnsson, *Ministry within the People of God: The Development of the Doctrines on the Church and on the Ministry in the Second Vatican Council's De Ecclesia.* Studia Theologica Lundensia 34 (Lund: Gleerup, 1974), 84.

[19] Cf. Severino Dianich, 'The Current State of Ecclesiology', *Concilium* 146 (1981), 92–97.

[20] Cf. Gotthold Hasenhüttl, *Freiheit in Fesseln: Die Chance der Befreiungstheologie* (Olten: Walter, 1985), 74–105.

Since the beginning of the modern period, particularly as a result of the Enlightenment, all the Christian Churches have been confronted with a radical critique of all forms of authority which cannot be accounted for by intelligible and persuasive arguments. As a result all the Churches are called to defend publicly all aspects of their organisational structure. Yet the leadership of the Roman Catholic Church in particular has failed to meet this critique from within and from outside the Church, and it continues to assert its status mainly by operating a sophisticated system of appointing and controlling bishops.[21]

Three responses to this situation can be observed in today's Roman Catholic Church: (1) An affirmative attitude towards this system found among 'obedient' lay-people who favour the shepherd-flock model of Church authority over against the organisation of a community in which every member shares the same rights and duties. (2) A twofold response among critical lay-people who would like to help build a local community with or without clerical leadership while at the same time trying to promote change in the system of Church government. (3) A radical departure from all Roman Catholic and similar forms of clerical absolutism in favour of alternative models of a Church of principally 'non-institutional' forms of Christian communities, so called 'house Churches', fellowships, etc.

In this situation of conflict and crisis, it must be the task of the theologian to reflect anew upon the theological foundation of Christian community and upon the dimensions of authority within the community, and to offer both a critique of existing forms of authority and proposals for a better organisation of Church.

[21] See Gabriel Daly, 'Catholicism and Modernity', *Journal of the American Academy of Religion* 53 (1985), 773–796.

(b) POSSIBLE ANSWERS

Any Christian ecclesiology will have to consider at least the following three aspects of the Church: (1) its institutional character, (2) its organisation of leadership and service and (3) its openness to critique and reform.

(1) The institutional character of the Church

The problem for Christians is not that they have organised themselves in ways which allow for stable and lasting communities and an uninterrupted tradition of response to God's call, but the question is which forms of institution are more equipped to promote the Christian faith-praxis and which are less, not at all, or no longer suitable. As we have seen, Christian communities have often adopted models for their own social organisation from the political context in which the communities developed. One of the reasons for this choice was the platonic understanding of Christian community as *societas perfecta*, i.e. the perfect earthly reflection of the divine essence of Church. As *societas*, the Church favoured institutional means by which it could rapidly accelerate its development all over the world, that is to achieve the highest possible realisation of its divine essence. This aim brought it into conflict with the secular powers interested in ruling the same world, so that the conflict between 'throne' and 'altar' arose. In this situation the Church leadership gave in to the temptation to understand the Church as a political power and often even as a military body in this world.

As a result of the radical cultural, political and theological changes in modern times, the image of the Church as perfect society has been widely discredited in favour of a more biblical image, namely the Church as community. This image describes a community which is no longer interested in conquering the globe in military terms, but which tries to witness as best it can to its foundational experiences of God's call in a more and more secularised world. This new self-understanding based on personal and communal experience rather than on metaphysical logic calls for a diversity of organisational models in order to fulfil its mission in a pluralistic world.

The experiential basis of Christian communities and their necessarily puralistic response demand forms of institution which are open to being adapted to the requirements of the local community rather than institutions which overrule the life of the community from outside. This 'inductive nature' (P. Berger) of the contemporary Christian communities in the West[22] implies then a rejection of all authoritarian forms of institution for theological and sociological reasons: the experiential consciousness of modern women and men and the belief that God alone has authority over the community unite in a forceful attack against all forms of *absolute* human authority.

In order to preserve the freedom of the individual in the Church on the one hand, and the theological dignity of the Christian community on the other, Gotthold Hassenhüttl suggested that the Church be organised as an 'institutional an-archy'.[23] Such an understanding of Christian community could promote the actual sharing of power and responsibility as well as the unmasking of all misuses of power in the Church. The need for a continuous transformation of the institutional elements in the Church arises for Leonardo Boff from the changing perception of what constitutes an adequate response to the Gospel in our time and its different contexts. 'No community can exist

---

[22] Cf. Peter L. Berger, *The Heretical Imperative: Contemporary Possibilities of religious Affirmation* (Garden City, New York: Anchor Press, 1979), 125–156.

[23] Gotthold Hasenhüttl, *Herrschaftsfreie Kirche: Sozio-theologische Grundlegung* (Düsseldorf: Patmos, 1974), 125.

without some institutionalisation that lends it unity, coherency, and identity. The institution does not exist for itself but is in service to the community of faith. As such, it evolves, following the same path as the historical transformation of the community itself that faces crises and discovers institutional responses to them. What we call ongoing conversion belongs to this historical process of fidelity and service to the community and the Lord.'[24] But it is important that the need for conversion is not limited to the individual believer. 'If conversion does not reach the institution of the Church, if it does not call into question the way in which power is exercised, if it does not reach the wider society, then we cannot speak of gospel conversion.'[25] The criterion for judging the adequacy of our religious institutions must remain the gospel.

Of course, the gospel must be interpreted anew in every generation. While such interpretation will always be pluralistic by nature of the different perspectives and contexts of the interpreters, this pluralism is not only no threat to the gospel; rather it alerts the community to realise its particular limitations and, thus, to look out to other Christian communities for critical correctives and encouragement.

Such an understanding of the need for and the limitations of institutional dimensions in the Church has direct consequences for our understanding of authentic leadership in the Church.

(2) Leadership and ministry in the Church

Leadership is a function of the Christian community and

---

[24] Leonardo Boff, Church: Charism and Power: Liberation Theology and the Institutional Church, transl. John W. Diercksmeier (London: SCM, 1985), 48.

[25] Op. cit., 55f.

not a status over against it.[26] The abolition of the 'laity' and the appreciation and integration of all the different gifts (*charismata*) in the community are preconditions for a Church trying to respond faithfully to the particular religious and social initiatives of Jesus Christ and his disciples. While the diversity of gifts in the community must be seen as a blessing, the organisation of these gifts for the benefit of the community's faith-praxis may give rise to conflict. However, the crucial point is not that there may be disagreement and diversity of opinions in the Christian community as to how to organise community, rather the essential question is how to handle such conflict and diversity in faithfulness to God's uniting and constructive spirit. Fortunately, the Christian tradition offers not only negative examples but also promising ways of handling conflict within the community for the benefit of the entire Church.[27]

The current discussion about equality between men and women in terms of access to the ordained ministry, as important as it is for a more adequate appreciation of the role of women in the Churches, has also a distorting effect on the general discussion of the nature of ministry. The particular focus on women has overshadowed the more general need for a radical reassessment of the nature of authentic Christian faith-praxis and its implications for appropriate organisation of the different ministries in the Christian community.

Edward Schillebeeckx has tried to revitalise this fundamental discussion on the nature of Church and ministry

[26] Cf. Edward Schillebeeckx, *The Church with a Human Face: A New and Expanded Theology of Ministry*, transl. John Bowden (London: SCM, 1985), 156ff.

[27] Cf. for instance the 'Antiochian Conflict' in Gal. 2. See Josef Blank, *Christliche Orientierungen* (Düsseldorf: Patmos, 1981), 243ff.

97

through his two recent books on the subject.[28] He has provided us with a rather detailed history of the development of ministry in the Church and reminded us of many often forgotten initiatives to reform the praxis of ministry. While these historical considerations are important, they do not spare us from the continuous task to reflect upon ways of organising Christian communities today. This task, however, can only be approached in the light of our answers to the preceding and more fundamental question of what constitutes authentic Christian faith.

Only in the framework of such a more fundamental theological debate can we reconsider the specific question of the ordained ministry. That a human community needs some form of leadership nobody doubts. That the Christian community needs an ordained ministry, however, cannot be taken for granted,[29] but needs to be dicussed with reference to both the theological demands of the Christian faith and the organisational demands of a contemporary human association. Given these requirements it seems rather odd that in some Churches the paricular understanding of the ordained ministry is still focused on the now obsolete metaphysical understanding of past times and on the organisational needs of medieval congregations.

Most urgently needed is a reassessment of the relationship between the ordained minister and the ordained community. The two-class system which developed particularly in the Roman Catholic Church with its practice of 'absolute' ordinations of priests and bishops, i.e. the ordination of men without any connection to a particular community, and the imposition of 'leaders' on communi-

---

[28] Edward Schillebeeckx, *Ministry: A Case for Change*, transl. John Bowden (London: SCM, 1981) and *The Church with a Human Face* (cf. note 26).

[29] Cf. A. T. & R. P. C. Hanson, *The Identity of the Church: A Guide to Recognising the Contemporary Church* (London: SCM, 1987), 144.

COMMUNITY AND AUTHORITY

ties or dioceses without their consent, cannot be justified either by reference to the New Testament nor by any other intelligible theological criteria. Of course, there may be emergencies where a community is unable or unwilling to ordain or appoint its own minister and is therefore in need of the support of other Christian communities, or where a community as a whole is engaged in a praxis which other communities regard as no longer Christian, that is, as no longer responding to God's call in Jesus Christ. In such situations it may well be necessary for fellow communities to become active and help out by making a more responsible leadership available for a particular period of time. But such emergencies must not be quoted in order to justify the current praxis of absolute ordination which deprives many Roman Catholic congregations and dioceses of their basic dignity as Christian communities.

The other argument often quoted in favour of the Roman Catholic organisation of a centrally managed leadership, i.e. the hierarchy of officers: pope, bishops, priests, is the need to preserve the apostolic tradition in the Christian Church. However, this tradition might be preserved equally well if not better through an organisation of Christian community where each member shares in the joy of witnessing to the presence of God's Spirit in their midst by being actively involved in the threefold praxis of the community as described above. Centralism as a principle of organisation does not guarantee the integrity of the gospel any better than a truly community based form of organisation; in fact it may well be that the latter will bring the Roman Catholic congregations to a new life, as can be witnessed already in South America and elsewhere, where Christian communities have successfully retrieved their own spiritual and organisational dignity.

(3) Prophetic critique in the Church

The recognition of God's authority in the Church and of the resulting theonomy of the Church is in itself a powerful corrective to all possible misuses of authority and power in the community. However, as the Roman Catholic interpretation of the vicarious foundation of ecclesiastical authority and power and its hierarchical results have demonstrated, 'theonomy' can be easily misunderstood and misused in a way which effectively splits a community into two or more classes instead of uniting it. Therefore Karl Rahner warns against all too quick references to God's authority in order to sanction or challenge human authority and power. He reminds us that our understanding of God's authority arises always already from human experience. Thus, we must always be critical of the distortions already present in our most basic sets of religious experiences. The authority of God is then the goal which we are to recognise better and better rather than the foundation of very concrete establishments of human power.[30] Moreover, as various developments of an uncritical self-righteousness in Christian Churches have shown, the faith-praxis of entire communities may in fact be distorted at a time. Thus, the recognition of the authority of the community and its theological foundation is not yet a guarantee against failure in the Church. The mere profession of faith in the guidance of the Holy Spirit does not yet protect us from more subtle forms of self-righteousness. Therefore, we have to acknowledge the critical dimension of that same Spirit and the tranformation it calls for.

The Spirit of God is the Spirit of truth. When we give up asking the question of truth we are in immediate danger of becoming self-righteous and distorted in our faith-praxis.

[30] Karl Rahner, 'Autorität', 8f.

Here lies a danger for all ecclesiological proposals which are developed on the basis of 'pure narrativity' while risking the neglect of the question of truth.[31] For when we no longer ask whether or not our particular Christian story is 'true', we have surrendered to our own story. Of course, we may not be able ultimately to answer the question whether a particular Christian story is true or not, but by at least asking the question we admit already in principle the fallibility of our response to God's call and may become open to critique. In the Jewish–Christian tradition it has always been the role of charismatic figures, such as the prophets, to interrupt the ongoing story by asking if it was 'true', i.e. if it corresponded to God's will. Individual Christians as well as entire local communities can become prophetic in this sense and serve the universal Church by calling it back to obedience to God's authority.

The Church needs these three elements of authority: a communal organisation, an elected leadership, and the ongoing prophetic critique of both. As soon as one of these elements is missing, the faith-praxis of the community is in danger of being distorted. The way in which a Christian community and its leadership treat criticism of their particular praxis will always be an indication of their inclination towards developing either a more loving community or a more powerful society. The Church needs the continuous reflection upon its theological identity and a continuous critique of all kinds of ideological distortions of this identity.[32]

---

[31] This seems to me to be a major problem with George A. Lindbeck's approach in his book *The Nature of Doctrine: Religion and Theology in a Postliberal Age* (London: SPCK, 1984), esp. 107ff.

[32] Wolfgang Beinert, 'Christsein ohne Kirche', 700: 'Reform der Kirche ist kein Geschäft für Beckmesser und Nörgler. Sie erfordert den Mut und die Heiligkeit des Propheten.'

4. *Local and Universal Church*

The existing plurality of Christian Churches and the ecumenical conversation in which most of them are involved have promoted an increasing awareness of the different possibilities of organising Christian communities. The exegetical retrieval of the plurality of ecclesial responses to the gospel already in New Testament times has further encouraged the appreciation of the fact that such a plurality in no way constitutes a threat to Christian faith. Rather it is a consequence of the many different contexts in which Christian faith lives. These insights have worked to highlight the need for a more detailed study of the relationship between faith and culture and of the status of the local Church within the Catholic Church.[33] 'Catholic Church' can have two meanings in this context: either it refers to the sum of all Christian communities or it refers to the Roman Catholic Church in particular. Whatever meaning is invoked, the principal question remains the same, namely what is the relationship between the local Christian community and the network of such communities?

In this regard the recent study by Robert Schreiter on *Constructing Local Theologies* is very helpful. Schreiter points out that the Christian Tradition is in fact nothing other than 'a series of local theologies, closely wedded to and responding to different cultural conditions'.[34] The consequence of this shift in perspective is that no particular local theology can claim any longer to represent the whole of the Christian tradition. Rather, the Christian tradition consists of all authentic Christian communities past and

[33] Cf. H. Richard Niebuhr, *Christ and Culture* (New York: Harper & Row, 1951).

[34] Robert J. Schreiter, *Constructing Local Theologies* (London: SCM, 1985), 93f.

present with their particular traditions. The crucial question arising from such a description of ecclesial reality then concerns the set of criteria by which to judge the authenticity of any particular local community, or in other words, the criteria for Christian identity.

However, even these criteria must be developed in a co-operative way by the various communities, rather than imposed by one community on another or by sections of the community on the whole of the community. All Christian communities are bound by the gospel to proclaim, to celebrate and to share the 'new life' in their particular situation. If they take this duty seriously they will have to become as aware as possible of the situation in which they live and of the particular cultural necessities for an adequate local appropriation of the gospel. This process of the inculturation of the gospel is never free of dangers. The local Church is by nature of its particularity in danger of losing sight of important dimensions of the Christian faith. It needs the co-operation and constructive critique of other Christian communities. While such a co-operation is in itself never an insurance against inauthenticity, it may at least contribute to keeping alive the consciousness of possible failures and distortions in any local appropriation of the Christian faith.[35] Since there is no blueprint for criteria of Christian authenticity the critical and self-critical participation of every Christian community in this universal and continuous reflection on the identity of Christian faith is essential.

This universal and mutually critical co-operation among Christian communities is the context in which we ought to consider the ecumenical movement in Christianity. Without disrespect for the progress achieved so far through

[35] Op. cit., 94.

ecumenical dialogue, the principles, aims and agenda of this dialogue also call for some critical observations.

First of all, the authority of the dialogue partners varies enormously. According to the particular constitution and self-understanding of networks of local communities, delegates are either appointed by a leadership body in the name and with the consent of the community or, as in the Roman Catholic Church, by a self-appointed body of bishops without proper consultation of the community. Similarly, proposals by ecumenical committees are either accepted by the Church communities or only by its leadership. That is one of the most severe drawbacks of the present ecumenical process, that committees are at work often without the full participation of the communities involved. The result of this situation is that the sophisticated formulas worked out by such ecumenical committees have no direct bearing on any of the local communities. Yet at the same time, the co-operation between Church traditions has progressed much more on the local level than the appropriate committees often realise and reflect.

The aim of the ecumenical movement has been to bring the different Christian Churches more closely together on the way towards a full Christian unity. However over the years the perception of 'unity' has changed.[36] In the light of the contemporary analysis of the complex relationship between faith and culture, Christian unity can certainly no longer mean a total doctrinal, liturgical and organisational uniformity or standardisation.

Standardisation and uniformity were the hallmarks of a

[36] Cf. Reiner Stahl, 'Grunddimensionen einer ökumensichen Ekklesiologie— Ein Versuch', *Theologische Literaturzeitung* 111 (1986), 81–90, and Miikka Ruokanen, *Hermeneutics as an Ecumenical Method in the Theology of Gerhard Ebeling*. Publications of Luther-Agricola Society B 13 (Helsinki: 1982), 9–19, where the recent developments of the concept of 'Christian Unity' are discussed.

eurocentric Church ever since the time of the Crusades. As long as Christian faith and European culture were exported as one single package, Christianity served more to destroy other cultures than to allow them to develop their own social, linguistic, philosophical and artistic forms of authentic response to God's calling in Jesus Christ.

Christian unity, therefore, must aim at fostering the mutually critical recognition of necessarily different, though not incompatible forms of Christian faith-praxis. The ecumenical movement could thus urge the different Christian communities within one tradition as well as the different traditions to declare such a unity, a true catholicity, rather than to limit its attention to theological and ecclesiological diplomacy.[37] In this context it is crucial to understand that Christian unity is not at the discretion of a (sometimes self-appointed) clerical leadership, rather it comes to life when local communities begin to respond in a co-operative, responsible and mutually critical way to God's universal call in Jesus Christ. Thus, Christian unity has an inductive-responsive and not a deductive-authoritarian character.

Primary expressions of the Catholicity of Christian faith-praxis could be among other activities 'inter-communion', that is the participation in another community's eucharistic celebration, and intercommunal solidarity and concern for the transformation of this world.[38]

5. Conclusion: Participating in God's Future

Our discussion of the authority if the Christian com-

---

[37] Cf. Ruokanen, op. cit., 18: 'A doctrinal consensus is not a presupposition but the gradually progressional result of a unity that has been proleptically declared.'

[38] Cf. Jürgen Moltmann, The Church in the Power of the Spirit, 284ff.

munity started with the recognition that the response called for by God's call in Jesus Christ is necessarily communal and contextual. In a particular situation, a particular time, and a particular culture we proclaim, celebrate and share God's new life as we see it disclosed in the story of Jesus Christ's life, death and resurrection. Faithfulness to this disclosure rules out any reduction of our response to an exclusively private and individualistic praxis on the one hand and any over-centralisation and over-standardisation of the various dimensions of our responses on the other hand. The first would limit the impact of Christian faith on the world, the second would hinder the appropriation of Christian faith in a given context and thus ultimately lead to the destruction of this faith's creativity in proclaiming the gospel in different contexts.

However, the theological and organisational insights into the communitarian character of the Christian faith-praxis do not yet free this praxis from possible distortions. Fear, the search for security, personal ambition, misguided efforts at conserving the ecclesial status quo of a particular age, the lack of self-criticism in terms of appreciating the particularity of any appropriation of faith, and the temptation to prescribe one appropriation as the only possible one for all times: the existence of these and other dangers will always need to be recognised and met with critical eyes and repenting hearts. No one Christian community lives outside the conditions of this universe, and thus, every community lives in the tension between the 'already' of God's call and promise and the 'not yet' of its response.

We understand God's call in Jesus Christ as a call to accept God's new life and thus to overcome the many manifestations of death in our world. However, if any Christian community wishes truly to respond to God's call it will have to detect and overcome first of all the manifestation of death in its own existence. To remain or to become *ecclesia semper reformanda* is not a pious wish but a costly programme for every Christian community. The community's institutional presence, its established leadership, and its commitment to prophetic critique and self-critique need to be examined continuously if possible distortions are to be detected. Hence, no claim to authority must be accepted unquestioned, rather any such claim must be assessed by the community in terms of its faithfulness to the gospel and its service to the community.

If the Christian communities wish to respond faithfully to God's call at the end of the twentieth century, then they must be free to meet the present world in which they live, and critically but co-operatively share the common concern of all people of good will for the future of this universe. With the dismantling of the eurocentric ideologies of 'true' Christianity, new and exciting possibilities of appropriating the gospel may appear and call for critical assessment. The fact that every new inculturation of the gospel entails the possible loss of the gospel's identity should not impel us to develop neurotic measures of 'saving' our identity by glorifying certain models of Church from the past, such as Tridentine and post-Reformation orthodoxies. 'Orthodoxy' and 'ortho-praxis' cannot be defined once and for all. Rather they have to be determined again and again by each one of the Christian communities and by all of them together.

The Church as the universal network of all Christian communities represents nothing other than the human and fallible response to God's creative and salvific activity in this universe. Hence, the Christian community's concern for the future of this world does not imply a loss of ecclesial identity, rather the Church finds its dynamic identity only in its critical relation to the world. In this sense, the Christian community must develop a spirituality of the world.[39]

The eschatological openness to God's ultimate transformation of this universe forces the Church to abandon all totalitarian explanations of and approaches to the world. Instead it is the task of the Church to proclaim to the world that God has invited every man and woman to join the process of transforming this universe according to God's plan. Because God has invited everyone, any lack of respect for the spiritual authority of any individual human being within the Christian community and of any particular community within the Church would mean failure to respect the full diversity of charismatic gifts present in the Church. Equally, any refusal to co-operate and the total or partial withdrawal from such participation in God's creative project by individual Christians and by Christian communities would limit the Church's response to God's call.

Even the often only too understandable frustration of individual Christians and of entire communities within the Church caused by the lack of 'progress' in the Church does not justify a withdrawal from God's project. Rather, it is important to remember that God did not call the perfect but the sinner to contribute to God's Kingdom. The experience of the resurrected crucified Jesus Christ has freed us from the pressures of judging the 'success' of our own or other people's contribution to God's creation. Rather, our experience of Jesus as the Christ is the foundation of our hope in God's ultimate fulfilment of his

[39] Cf. here the theological *opus* of Johann B. Metz. Especially *Zur Theologie der Welt* (Mainz: Grünewald, and München: Kaiser, 1968), and *Faith in History and Society: Towards a Practical Fundamental Theology*, transl. David Smith (London: Burns & Oates, 1980).

COMMUNITY AND AUTHORITY

creative project in spite of the limitations and failures of our responses. However, such a hope needs our active participation, otherwise it is only a pious projection.

4

THE CREATURE OF THE WORD:
Recovering the Ecclesiology of the Reformers

by Christoph Schwöbel

1. A Forgotten Heritage

When one considers the popular image of the Reformers, it seems that they are better remembered for their mistakes than for their achievements. The scandal of Luther's completely unjustifiable outburst of Antijudaism, the ambiguities of his stance in the Peasants' War, his misguided sanction of the bigamy of Philipp of Hesse and his linguistic creativity in peppering his assaults upon his theological opponents have created the picture of a powerful and thoroughly inconsistent personality given to cholerics that is difficult to reconcile with the claim to fundamental theological insights and profound piety attributed to him in Lutheran theology. One of the few things that seem to link him to the modern era is the famous and historically questionable 'Here I stand: I can do no other' at the Diet of Worms in 1521, which is celebrated as the moment where modern freedom of conscience entered the historical stage.

Calvin's popular image could hardly be said to be more sympathetic. Where Luther's personality appears to be riddled with inconsistencies, Calvin's seems almost too consistent. His attempts at establishing an authentic Christian community characterised by doctrinal soundness and moral integrity appears for many like the creation of an ecclesiastical police-state in which even the most innocent pleasure is sacrificed on the altar of a sour-faced moralism. His significance for the modern era is seen in the establishment of a firm link between personal salvation and worldly success which appears in the most secularised societies of the West as the hidden undercurrent driving capitalist economies to ever new extremes.

In view of these powerful popular images it does not seem surprising that the general impact of Reformation theology on the life and thought of the churches today is not very noticeable. Apart from programmatically confessional theologians from Lutheran and Calvinist traditions, and apart from historians specialising in the Reformation, the basic insights which motivated the Reformers seem to have the status of a forgotten heritage. Yet when one considers to what extent the Reformation shaped the theology and the institutional structures of the churches in the West, Protestant and non-Protestant alike, this forgetfulness seems to be far from unproblematical. The lack of awareness of the basic insights of the Reformers, which would appear as a characteristic of the life and thought of the churches today, is especially apparent with respect to the self-understanding of the churches which provides the basic orientation for their existence in contemporary society.

It is, therefore, not surprising that a notable characteristic of contemporary ecumenical dialogues and modern debates about the nature and mission of the Church is the relative absence of the basic ecclesiological insights of the Reformers. The fundamental ecclesiological *formulae* of Reformation theology are respectfully quoted, but they seem to provide not much more than historical references. Somehow it does not seem to be quite clear how this theological heritage could be related to the issues facing the churches today, and whether it could provide orientation in a situation where all parties can readily agree that fundamental orientation is needed, but disagree violently about its basic content. On the whole, it seems that the Reformers' reflection on the nature and mission of the Church belongs to that sphere of purely academic theologising which is better left to the professionals, because it seems to be quite irrelevant for the challenges encountered by the Church in a supposedly post-Christian era. What has been lost is an understanding of how the ecclesiological principles of the Reformation are connected to central aspects of Christian faith and how they relate theological doctrine and ecclesial practice. In the absence of this, the Reformers' conception of the Church seems to be either a historic monument of purely antiquarian interest or a doctrinal *shibboleth* which introduces an unpleasant note of divisiveness into the amiable atmosphere of ecumenical dialogue.

The reasons for this situation are complex and they differ from one denominational tradition to another. The unique character of the English Reformation as 'emphatically a political revolution'[1] in which the legal changes preceded the religious reformation has left its marks in the troubled relationship of Anglicanism to Reformation theology. The political character of the English Reformation did not only provide a problematical starting-point for the process of defining the theological identity of the Church of England, it also established a pattern in which ecclesiological issues were primarily treated as questions about polity and church-order and only then as questions about the nature and mission of the Church. Therefore the extensive discussion of ecclesiological matters from the time of

[1] Owen Chadwick, *The Reformation. The Pelican History of the Church*, 3 (Hardmondsworth, 1964, 1978), p. 97.

Elizabeth's accension to the Great Ejectment 1662 concentrated more on the problem of authority *in* the Church than on the primary question of the authority on which the Church is founded.[2]

It is against the background of the contentious history of debates about ecclesiastical polity and the theological principles implied in them that one has to understand the surprising success of the attempt at redefining the Anglican identity in the work of the more extreme representatives of the Oxford Movement.[3] How successful this attempt to 'unprotestantise' the Church of England was in the long run, even in those parts of the Church who would feel little sympathy for the theological presuppositions underlying the Tractarian programme, is nowhere more evident than in the recent discussion about the ordination of women. The theological helplessness documented in the constant confusion between theological questions and problems of practical reason is a strong indication of the absence of the main ecclesiological insights of the Reformers, because they concern primarily the relationship of the foundation of the Church and the practical problems of its organisation.

This situation is not confined to Anglicanism. Other denominational traditions show sometimes little more awareness of the ecclesiological principles of the Reformation. The peculiar pattern of the relationship of polity and theology established in the aftermath of the English Reformation did not only dictate the conditions of

[2] Cf. Robert S. Paul, '"A Way to Wyn Them": Ecclesiology and Religion in the English Reformation', in B. A. Gerrish, R. Benedetto (eds.), *Reformatio Perennis, Essays on Calvin and the Reformation. In Honor of Ford Lewis Battles*, Pittsburgh Theological Monograph Series 32 (Pittsburgh, 1981), pp. 91–103.

[3] Cf. W. J. Baker, 'Hurrell Froude and the Reformers', *Journal of Ecclesiastical History* 21 (1970), 243ff. and Paul Avis, 'The Tractarian Challenge to Consensus and the Identity of Anglicanism', *King's Theological Review* 9 (1986), 14–17.

ecclesiological reflection for the protagonists and representatives of the established church, but also for their nonconformist critics. The difficulty in seeing through the debate concerning questions of polity to the underlying theological principles is not only evident from historical examples like the tragically inconclusive careers of theologians like Thomas Cartwright and Robert Browne. It is also illustrated by the fact that it seems today much easier to argue for the procedures of decision making in nonconformist churches from the secular perspective of modern democracy than from theological principles underlying the idea of 'laocratic' government.

Even for the churches which emphatically stress their rootedness in the Reformation and which are characterised by a strong confessional tradition, the Reformers' thought about the Church does not seem to provide the basic orientation for confronting the questions which are encountered in the day-to-day existence of the Church. Very often the main aspects of the teaching of the Reformers about the Church seems to be buried under the complicated and contentious history of its interpretation. And often the institutional structures of the Church which were once established on the basis of the Reformers' ecclesiology seem to function quite apart from reflection on their foundation. But it cannot be denied that in the absence of a fundamental awareness of the foundation principles of church organisation in the historic churches of the Reformation the theological account they can give of their identity can only be deficient.

It would be interesting to speculate whether Roman Catholic theology could not also profit from an increased theological awareness concerning the basic insights of Reformation ecclesiology. This would not only enable the partners in ecumenical dialogue to assess how far the original conflict between the Reformers and the late medieval Roman church is still present, and to what extent the issues at stake have changed in subsequent time. It would also help to clarify perhaps more than it seemed up to now possible where precisely the crucial questions have to be located which would determine the possibilities for working towards a greater unity of the churches.[4] This might not be helpful for generating unqualified ecumenical enthusiasm, but it could help to increase the clarity of our theological perceptions and the realism of our ecumenical expectations.

The following remarks about the ecclesiology of the Reformers are intended as a reminder of this forgotten heritage. They are motivated by the conviction that the Reformers' view of the Church contains fundamental insights which are of crucial importance for the self-understanding of the Church, for the way in which the Church regards its institutional structures and for its ecclesial practice. These insights remain a challenge even in a situation where Reformation theology is widely disregarded and where the Reformers themselves seem to be presented in popular images which would hardly seem to invite anyone to try to recover their view of the Church. I do not attempt to present a historically and doctrinally complete exposition of Reformation ecclesiology.[5] Rather,

[4] It is one of the great merits of Eilert Herms' recent book on the unity of Christians in the community of Churches that it reintroduced basic elements of Reformation theology into the ecumenical discussion. It also contains one of the clearest and most condensed accounts of the theology of the Lutheran Reformation. Cf. E. Herms, *Einheit der Christen in der Gemeinschaft der Kirchen. Die Ökumenische Bewegung der römischen Kirche im Lichte der reformatorischen Theologie, Kirche und Konfession*, Veröffentlichungen des Konfessionskundlichen Instituts des Evangelischen Bundes 24 (Göttingen, 1984).

[5] A comprehensive historical and theological account of Reformation ecclesiology is Paul D. L. Avis, *The Church in the Theology of the Reformers*, Marshalls Theological Library (London, 1981).

I want to try uncover systematically the basic focus of the Reformers' understanding of the Church in order to recover its critical and constructive potential for the contemporary debate.

2. Luther's Basic Insight: The Relationship of Opus Dei and Opus Hominum

There is widespread agreement about the catholic intention of the Reformers.[6] They attempted to initiate change in the Church, but not with the aim of founding a new church or of propagating a new faith. Rather, they called for reform in order to preserve the Church's true identity, which they felt had been jeopardised by the late medieval Roman church. They were neither progressives who saw the real Church only in the future, so that it was the task of the present to effect the changes which would realise the future essence of the Church. Nor were they conservatives in the sense that they tried to return to a golden age of the Church in which it was still unambiguously itself, still unaffected by late distortions and ambiguities. Both elements can be found in their thought, but they are only aspects of a wider concern which is only partly represented in the term 'reform'.

The 'reformation' the Reformers intended to bring about was not simply a restructuring of the institutional order of the Church. And it was not merely the introduction of a new way of theological thinking about the Church. Both aspects, institutional reform and the reform of theological thought on the Church, are united in a wider perspective which is at the same time pragmatic and theoretical. It is, therefore, important not to treat the Reformers' ecclesi-

[6] Cf. Gustav Aulén, *Reformation and Catholicity* (Edinburgh and London, 1960), and Carl Heinz Ratschow, *Reformation heute* (Gütersloh, 1967), esp. pp. 10ff.

ology as a set of practical suggestions for the reorganisation of the Church or as a part of a new system of Christian dogmatics, although it contains both in itself. The Reformers' understanding of the Church is implied in their understanding of the nature of Christian faith and its practice, and of that which makes it possible: the action of God, Father, Son and Spirit in reconciling sinful humanity to himself by disclosing the truth about the relationship of the creator to his creation as the certainty of faith.

This essential interconnection between the practical questions of the life of the Church and the theoretical problems of the theological understanding of the Church, and their relation to the focal point of the nature of Christian faith and its constitution, is so important because we are today painfully aware of the gap between the factual existence of the Church in society and the theological formulae in which its nature is expressed. This leads to a situation in which the practical questions of day-to-day living in the Church are often decided on the basis of pragmatic and wholly untheological considerations, while the ecclesiology of academic theology, operating, as it seems, at one remove from the social reality of the Church, seems often unable to relate to the practical questions which face the Church in its struggle for survival in a society more and more shaped by a plurality of religious and quasi-religious world-views. The challenge of the ecclesiology of the Reformers is the challenge of a theological reflection on the Church which is closely related to the practical problems of Christian life in the Church, and which is at the same time theoretically rigorous.[7]

[7] Cf. Eilert Herms, 'Evangelische Katholiken? Zu einem aktuellen ökumenischen Problem', *Evangelische Kommentare* 18 (1985), 388–391, 389.

The interrelationship of theory and practice which characterises the ecclesiology of the Reformers is made possible by relating both aspects to the central point of their understanding of Christian faith: the distinction and relation of divine and human agency. It is this theological focus which explains why the conflict between Martin Luther and the Roman church could be triggered off by Luther's academic disputation theses on the theory of indulgences. Luther's theological reaction to the pastoral problems produced by popular indulgence preaching, which he experienced in the confessional, achieved a theological significance which shattered the religious legitimations of the power-structure of the late medieval Roman church when they were viewed from the perspective of the distinction and relation of divine and human work.[8] This focusing of all practical and theological matters in the question of the distinction and relation of *opus Dei* and *opus hominum* also explains why Luther's theology and his understanding of the Reformation developed step by step in confrontation with practical and pastoral problems which occurred in the daily life of the Church. It is in the practical situations of church life that it becomes apparent what kind of relationship between divine and human action is presupposed in the activity of the Church. The central question of the relation of *opus Dei* and *opus hominum* provides the framework in which Luther and the other Reformers interpreted the traditional

[8] On the theological significance of the 95 theses Heinrich Bornkamm's *Luther's World of Thought*, E. T. Martin H. Bertram (Saint Louis, 1958), pp. 36–54, is still helpful.

formulae for describing the nature and task of the Church and its ministry.[9]

According to the Reformers, God's action and human action have to be strictly distinguished in order to perceive their proper relationship. God's action in creation, revelation and inspiration establishes the relationship between the creator and his creatures, in which God is the creative ground for their existence and where he discloses the truth about his relationship to humanity and enables human beings to accept the truth of revelation as the certainty of faith. The action of God, Father, Son and Spirit makes human action possible and enables human beings to act in accordance with the will of the creator which is disclosed and authenticated through Christ by the Spirit. Because of this distinction divine and human agency can never compete or co-operate on the same level. God's work is always the condition of the possibility of all human action. But this distinction is not a separation. All human action remains forever dependent on God as its creative ground. Luther could summarise the unity of the action of God, Father, Son and Spirit in the metaphor of the creative Word of God, because God discloses the aim of his agency to his creatures in the promise of eternal life in the community of his Kingdom, and this disclosure of God's aim for his creation makes it possible for human beings to live in accordance with or in contradiction to God's creative will.

---

[9] The thesis that Luther's theology should be interpreted from the distinction and relationship of *opus Dei* and *opus hominum* as the basic insight of Reformation theology is not intended as another suggestion in the debate about the 'centre' of Luther's theology (e.g. his doctrine of justification, his concept of penitence, his theology of the Godness of God, his *theologia crucis*, etc.). Rather, it points to a common structural element presupposed in all these proposals.

To contest this fundamental asymmetry between God's action and human action is for Luther the primary characteristic of sin which for him is as much apparent in Adam's fall as in the preaching of the popular indulgence preachers and their claims for the authority of the bishop of Rome. In yielding to the Serpent's promise *eritis sicut Deus* human beings contradict their created destiny in their attempt to assume God's freedom, by interpreting their created and finite freedom as unconditional and self-created freedom. In trying to compete with God's agency human beings cannot experience God as the creative ground for their being and have to experience him as a threat to their existence and their chances of fulfilment.[10] Luther detected the same blurring of the distinction between God's agency and human agency in the popular indulgence preaching of his time and the claims for the status of the Pope and the Church of Rome implied in it. To say that the human action of the Church can co-operate with God in completing God's work of reconciliation in the distribution of his grace by the Church is to presume upon God.

The fundamental *asymmetry* of the relationship between the creator and his human creatures implies that human beings cannot restore their relationship to God once it has been disrupted by sin — a fact which is powerfully expressed in the doctrine of original sin.[11] Ascribing to human beings the ability to restore their broken relationship to God would entail ascribing the status of the creator to the creature. Only God the creator can restore the relationship with human beings by contradicting the

[10] Cf. Friedrich Beisser, Albrecht Peters, *Sünde und Sündenvergebung*, Fuldaer Hefte 26 (Hannover, 1983).
[11] Cf. Paul Althaus, *Die Theologie Martin Luthers* (Gütersloh 1980⁵), pp. 128ff.

120

human contradiction of sin. And the Christian Gospel claims that God *has* restored his relationship to humanity in Christ.[12] The Gospel of the restoration of righteousness by God's grace can only be passively accepted as the foundation for the human act of faith which is, according to Luther's interpretation of the First Commandment, the basic orientation for all human activity.[13] Luther could interpret the acceptance of God's grace as the restoration of the true feedom of a Christian, which is made possible by God and exercised in the service of our neighbours.[14] The reason why the doctrine of justification could be interpreted by Lutheran theologians as the *articulus stantis et cadentis ecclesiae* and as the centre for the presentation of Christian doctrine, is that it accurately depicts this interrelationship of divine and human action.[15]

[12] Luther describes the Gospel in his introduction to his exegesis of 1 Peter as a sermon and a cry of God's grace and mercy: 'Evangelion aber heisset nichts anderes, denn ein Predigt und Geschrei von der Gnad und Barmherzigkeit Gottes, durch den Herren Christum mit seinem Tod verdienet und erworben; und ist nicht eigentlich das, das in Buechern stehet, und in Buchstaben verfasset wird, sondern mehr eine muendliche Predigt und lebendig Wort und eine Stimme, die da in die ganze Welt erschallet und oeffentlich wird ausgeschrien, dass man's ueberall hoeret.' Epistle St. Petri gepredigt und ausgelegt (1523), WA 12, 259.

[13] Cf. *Luther's Primary Works together with his Shorter and Larger Catechism*, E. T., ed. with theological and historical essays by H. Wace and C. A. Buchheim (London, 1896), pp. 34ff.

[14] This is developed in unsurpassed form in Luther's *The Freedom of a Christian* (1520), in *Luther's Works* 31, pp. 329–377.

[15] Luther himself described the crucial role of the doctrine of justification in the following way (WA 3,335): 'Ille unicus locus conservat Ecclesiam Christi; hoc amisso amittitur Christi et Ecclesia nec relinquitur ulla cognitio doctrinarum et spiritus. Ipse sol, dies, lux Ecclesiae et omnis fiduciae ille articulus.'

3. Created by the Word: The Constitution of the Church

Luther's conception of the Church is decisively shaped by this understanding of the relationship of *opus Dei* and *opus hominum*. The Church is *creatura verbi divini*: the creature of the divine Word. The Church is constituted by God's action and not by any human action. It is not an association of people who have a shared taste for religion or the creation of some kind of human community spirit. It is not a community devoted to a common cause or to the realisation of a common aim, and in this the Church differs from other organisations. As the creature of the divine Word the Church is constituted by divine action.[16] And the way in which the Church is constituted by divine action determines the character and scope of human action in the Church.

The Church is created by the divine Word insofar as it evokes the human response of faith. 'The Word begets faith. Faith is our response to God's Word.'[17] The Word of God creates the certainty that makes the human act of faith possible. In Luther's view this only happens when the Spirit authenticates the Gospel of Christ as the truth about the relationship of God the creator to his creation. The revelation of God in Jesus Christ overcomes the self-deception of sin and discloses the truth about God's relationship to his creation as his faithfulness and grace by which he contradicts the human contradiction of sin. The

[16] This focus of Luther's ecclesiology is expressed in the slogan: 'Die Kirche macht nicht das Wortt, sondern sie wird von dem Wortt.' (WA 8, 491) This emphasis is systematically developed in *Concerning the Ministry* (1523) which culminates in the statement: 'For since the Church owes its birth to the Word, is nourished, aided and strengthened by it, it is obvious that it cannot be without the Word. If it is without the Word it ceases to be a Church.' *Luther's Works* 40, p. 37.

[17] Bornkamm, op. cit., p. 136.

content of this revelation is that God remains faithful to his aim of gathering his human creatures in the community of his Kingdom.

Luther explained the way in which God creates his Church with reference to the *external* and *internal clarity* of Scripture.[18] The external clarity of Scripture is the unambiguous meaning of Scripture as the Gospel of Christ, as the proclamation of the disclosure of God's grace in Jesus Christ which is his faithfulness to his fallen human creation. Scripture is (externally) clear insofar as it unambiguously witnesses God's revelation in Christ as the revelation of God's true relationship to his creation. The internal clarity of Scripture refers to the 'teaching of the Spirit in the heart' whereby God authenticates the truth of his revelation in Christ witnessed by the external clarity of Scripture as the personal certainty for the believer. Where the external word of Scripture is authenticated by the internal testimony of the Spirit it becomes God's Word, *viva vox Dei.* This certainty created by the authentification of the word of Scripture makes faith, the unconditional trust in God the creator, redeemer and saviour possible. And this faith is the only adequate response to the Word of God which constitutes the Church by making this response possible.

Within this framework of the doctrine of the internal and external clarity of Scripture, the human act of faith is made possible by God's agency as the agency of Father, Son and Spirit. God creates the world *ex nihilo*, and he establishes a relationship to his human creatures in which they can act in accordance with or in contradiction to

---

[18] Cf. H. Bornkamm, 'Das Wort Gottes bei Luther' (1933) in *Luther. Gestalt und Wirkung* (Gütersloh, 1975), pp. 147–186; and R. Hermann, 'Von der Klarheit der Heiligen Schrift' (1958) in *Studien zur Theologie Luthers und des Luthertums* (Göttingen, 1982), pp. 170–255.

God's creative will. In Christ, God discloses the truth about his relationship to his human creation against the contradiction of sin as his faithfulness and justifying grace. And by the Spirit God authenticates this revelation as the truth about his relationship to humankind and the world and thereby creates the certainty which makes faith possible.

For the believer this threefold condition for the possibility of the Church is passively constituted by God's agency and can only be actively acknowledged by the human act of faith as the basic orientation of all human activity. The Protestant Reformers emphasised no less than their Roman opponents that the act of faith has the character of obedience. But they differed in their understanding of the authority which can demand our obedience. In Luther's understanding only the Word of God, God in his revelation, can demand our obedience as unconditional trust in God, our creator, redeemer and saviour. This authority of the Word of God cannot be effectively represented by any human authority, however elevated in the ecclesiastical hierarchy it may be.[19] Just as no finite entity deserves our unconditional trust, no finite entity can demand our absolute obedience. The reason for this radical distinction between the authority of the Word of God and any human form of authority is that the revelation of God cannot be efficaciously transmitted by a human person, it cannot be administered by a human institution, and it cannot become part of a human tradition. Since only God can create the certainty that makes faith possible in authenticating the truth of the revelation of the creator in Christ, it cannot be effectively communicated by human action. It cannot be incorporated by any human

[19] Cf. E. Herms, *Einheit der Christen*, pp. 100ff.

work and it cannot be embodied in any human institution. Creating faith is something the Church or any of its representatives cannot *do*, the Church must leave it to God and must *let it happen—ubi et quando visum est Deo*.

Does that mean that God creates faith quite independently of the proclamation of the Gospel of Christ in the Church? Again the doctrine of the external word of Scripture and Christian proclamation can provide an important clue for Luther's understanding of the function of human preaching in the constitution of the Church. We have already seen that the Word of God cannot be incorporated in any human word. But God incorporates the human witness to the Gospel in his Word, insofar as he grants us certainty in authenticating the external word of Scripture and human proclamation by the internal testimony of the Spirit. God freely uses the human witness to the Gospel of Christ to create the certainty which makes faith possible in authenticating the external word of Christian proclamation.[20] But this relationship between God's creative action in constituting the Church and the human action of proclaiming the truth of the Gospel of Christ excludes precisely that human action could ever take the place of God's action in creating the Church, that the proclamation of the truth of revelation could ever effectively replace or represent the revelation itself.

In English theology this view of the constitution of the Church has been expressed with admirable clarity by P. T. Forsyth:

> The Church rests on the grace of God, the judging, atoning, regenerating grace of God which is his holy love in the form it must take with human sin. Wherever that is heartily confessed and goes on to rule we have the true Church. Insofar as the Church is

[20] Cf. P. Althaus, op. cit., pp. 42ff.

a creature, it is the creature of the preached gospel of God's grace, forgiving, redeeming and creating us anew by Christ's cross. The Church was created by the preaching of that solitary gospel and fortified by the sacraments of it which are, indeed, but other ways of receiving, confessing and preaching it. The Church is the social and practical response to that grace.[21]

4. The Essential Attributes of the Church

What follows from this understanding of the constitution of the Church for the nature of the Church and its ministry? Luther's various descriptions of the nature of the Church reflect very strongly the distinction and relation between divine and human action in its constitution as *creatura verbi divini*.

> Thank God, a child seven years old knows what the Church is, namely, the holy believers and the lambs that hear their Shepherd's voice. For the children pray thus: I believe in a holy Christian Church. This holiness does not consist in surplices, tonsures, long clerical gowns, and other ceremonies of theirs, fabricated by them without the warrant of Holy Writ, but in God's Word and in true faith.[22]

This description of the Church from the Smalcald Articles, Luther's only formal attempt at expressing the confessional basis of the Church, is justly famous—not only for Luther's apparently boundless confidence in the theological acuteness of seven-year-olds. It is in its extreme simplicity clear with respect to what it rejects, all holy institutions or objects for which it is claimed that they represent God in the Church, and it is equally clear with regard to what it affirms: That the true character of the Church consists in the Word of God and in true faith. Both

[21] P. T. Forsyth, *The Church and the Sacraments* (London, 1917), p. 31.
[22] Smalcald Articles, Pt.III, 12 cited in Bornkamm, *Luther's World of Thought*, p. 134.

constitute the *communio sanctorum* as the relationship of divine and human action in the Church.[23] According to this view, the Church can be viewed from two perspectives. In trying to determine the nature of the Church one has to talk about what makes the Church possible, i.e. the Word of God, and what is made possible in the Church, i.e. true faith. Both aspects together form the *communio sanctorum*, and of *this* Church the attributes of the Church expressed in the Creeds of the ancient church can be predicated.

The Church as *creatura verbi divini* which is made possible by the Word of God and in which true faith is made possible is *one*. This unity is grounded in the fact that in creating faith God authenticates his revelation in Jesus Christ as his grace and truth. The identity of the content of the revelation of God in Christ which is authenticated by the Spirit for many people in many different historical situations and cultural contexts constitutes the unity of the Church. In this way the unity of the Church has its foundation in the unity of God's action in creation, revelation and inspiration which—and that is the hope of faith—will find its perfect expression in the Kingdom of God.

This Church, the *communio sanctorum* as the *creatura verbi divini*, is the *catholic* Church. Its universality is grounded in the universality of the truth of revelation, because the revelation in Christ is the revelation of the true relationship of the creator to his creation. This universality of the Church is inextricably bound up with the truth of revelation. The revelation of God in Christ as it is authenticated by the Spirit does not concern a particular aspect of reality, but the very constitution of reality, the

[23] Cf. Gordon Rupp, *The Righteousness of God, Luther Studies* (London, 1968³), pp. 312–322.

destiny of human beings and of the whole of creation. The universality of the revelation is an implication of its ontological character. And the *communio sanctorum* that is made possible by the authentification of the revelation of the Father through the Son by the Spirit is universal, insofar as it owes its existence to the universality of the truth of revelation. The catholicity of the Church does not guarantee the universality of the truth of revelation. The universality of the truth of revelation is the foundation for the catholicity of the Church.[24]

The *communio sanctorum* is the *apostolic* Church, not because it is part of a chain of human tradition, but because it witnesses the identity and universality of God's revelation in Christ. The apostle is not defined by his or her position in a process of human tradition, but by the One who sends the apostle.[25] The apostolic succession is the *successio fidelium* which is constituted by the fact that God authenticated and authenticates the truth of the human proclamation of the Gospel of Christ.[26] To confine it to one tier of a human hierarchy, or even to the hierarchy itself, is to limit the activity of the Spirit to the power-structures of human institutions, and this is inconceivable, if the Church itself is the creature of the Word of God.

This Church which is as *creatura verbi divini* the one, catholic and apostolic Church is holy, not because it could

---

[24] This view of the catholicity of the Church was forcefully expressed by Michael Ramsay in his *The Gospel and the Catholic Church* (London, 1936): 'Catholicism, created by the gospel, finds its power in terms of the gospel alone. Neither the massive polity of the Church, nor its tradition in order and worship can in themselves seem to define Catholicism; for all these things have their meaning in the gospel, wherein the true doctrine of Catholicism can be found.' (pp. 179f.).

[25] Cf. Daniel T. Jenkins, *The Nature of Catholicity* (London, 1953²), pp. 18–94. Cf. also P. Avis, op. cit., p. 127ff.

[26] Cf. Bornkamm, op. cit., p. 143.

claim holiness as one of its very own, intrinsic attributes, but because it owes its holiness to the holy and sanctifying action of the Holy Spirit. To talk about the holy Church can only refer, according to the interpretation of the Lutheran Reformation, to the fact that it is constituted as the creature of the Word of God and not to any characteristic which the Church possesses independently of its divine constitution. And since the revelation to which the Church owes its existence always remains God's revelation and cannot be transferred to any human institution, the Church is holy only insofar as it is sanctified by the Holy Spirit—*ubi et quando visum est Deo*. Wherever and whenever the human witness to the Gospel of Christ is authenticated by the Holy Spirit the community of faith which is in this way made possible is a communion of saints.

5. The Visible Community of Witness

If we follow this interpretation of the traditional attributes of the Church which seems to be required by the ecclesiological principles of the Lutheran Reformation, we have to say that those attributes can, strictly speaking, only refer to God's action in creating the Church, and they can be predicated of the Church only with respect to its constitution as *creatura verbi divini*. Does this not imply an untenable spiritualism which neglects the factual existence of churches, of more or less organised groups of believers? Does this view not demonstrate the much debated weakness of the Lutheran conception of the Church, i.e. that it seems to concentrate almost exclusively of the 'invisible' Church? And is this not a patent falsification of the view offered above that Luther's conception of the Church was from the beginning directed towards the solution of practical problems in the life of the Church?[27]

One can only accuse Luther's ecclesiology of one-sided spiritualism if one interprets the distinction between *opus Dei* and *opus hominum* as a rigid separation and overlooks the essential relation of divine and human action in the Church. The 'invisible' Church and the 'visible' churches are not to be interpreted as separate realms, the one a spiritual Platonic society and the other a tangible body of believers.[28] Nor is the Church we experience as congregations and institutions only a fragmentary fore-shadowing of what will be made visible as the true essence of the Church in the future. What constitutes something cannot be separated from what is constituted, what is made possible cannot be divorced from what makes it possible. The 'invisibility' of the Church refers to God's act in constituting the Church which, as the power to create a visibile *community of witness*, is itself invisible.[29] The distinction between the 'invisible' and 'visible' Church can

[27] It cannot be denied that there is a certain development in Luther's thought from the emphasis on the ethical and social dimension of the visible community of witness to a more pronounced spiritualism in his understanding of the Church. This proved to be highly problematical in a situation where the legal establishment of the Church had already been achieved by the regional princes for political reasons. The historical consequences of this situation motivated Lutheran theologians at the end of the 19th and at the beginning of the 20th century to reflect on the possibility of an ethical conception of the Church which mediates between the theological and legal conception of the Church. Martin Rade's essay 'Der Sprung in Luther's Kirchenbegriff' (1914) is still a very valuable analysis of this issue. Cf. Christoph Schwöbel (ed.), *Martin Rade, Ausgewählte Schriften III, Recht und Glaube* (Gütersloh, 1988), pp. 151–166.

[28] Cf. the brief and precise discussion in P. Avis, op. cit., pp. 4ff.

[29] For Luther's view of the 'Invisible' cf. Ingolf U. Dalferth's important study 'The Visible and the Invisible: Luther's Legacy of a Theological Theology' in S. W. Sykes (ed.), *England and Germany. Studies in Theological Diplomacy*, Studies in the Intercultural History of Christianity 25 (Frankfurt/Berne, 1982), pp. 15–44.

be more adequately interpreted if we relate it to the question how the Church can be an object of faith which is confessed in the Creed and how it can be field of human action. Only as *creatura verbi divini* is the Church an object of faith, because only God's action in establishing and disclosing the true relationship between the creator and his creation that makes faith possible can be confessed as the content of faith. As the community of witness which proclaims the truth of God's revelation it is a human field of action.

The human actions made possible by God's invisible constitution of the Church are very much visible and — according to Luther — even more audible. They have to be defined as bearing witness to the creation of the Church by proclaiming the Gospel of Christ. The human community of witness is made possible by God's action in Christ through the Spirit, when God himself creates the certainty which makes faith possible by authenticating the Gospel of Christ as the truth about God's relationship to his creation. This certainty has to be understood as *personal* certainty, because it is created by the authentification of the Gospel of Christ for the individual believer. As certainty with respect to the reconciliation of God and humanity it confronts us where everyone of us is specifically herself or himself, because its content is the forgiveness of our personal sin. Our sin is always the most individual fact about ourselves, the extent of which is only known to us and to God, the judge and comforter of consciences. Although sin binds the sinners together in a collective which is referred to with a characteristically impersonal term as the *massa perditionis*, it is the destruction of any communion. In the forgiveness of sin God reconstitutes the relationship of the human creatures to their creator and this is—according to Luther—not only the reconstitution of human personhood, but it is also the reconstitution of our created sociality as redeemed sociality. Created sociality is reconstituted in the community of the Church by the personally authenticated recognition that in Jesus Christ God has overcome the contradiction of sin and that he has disclosed his eternal will of grace for the whole of his creation. Because the will of God as it is disclosed in Jesus Christ is the eternal will of the creator for all his creatures, the community of those who confess Christ as their Lord is the witnessing community which proclaims the truth of the Gospel of Christ as a truth which is valid for the whole creation. The missionary character of this community is grounded in the universality of the will of the creator which determines the fundamental solidarity of the Church with the whole of humankind.

6. The Ministry in the Community of Witness

The human action in the Church which bears witness to the divine action in constituting the Church is the *ministerium verbi divini*.[30] In being a community of witness the empirical community of the Church lives and acts in accordance with the constitution of the Church as *creatura verbi divini*. This ministry of the Church is demanded by the obedience of faith for *all* Christians and therefore all christians exercise the royal priesthood of the community of witness.[31] This ministry comprises the whole life of the Christian insofar as faith is not just one human act among others, but the basic orientation for all the activity of believers. Just as sin is the basic orientation,

[30] Cf. Avis, op. cit., pp. 81–130.

[31] One of the most distinctive attempts to spell out the implications of Luther's view of the universal priesthood is M. Rade's 'Das königliche Priestertum der Gläubigen und seine Forderung an die evangelische Kirche unserer Zeit' (1918), reprinted in C. Schwöbel (ed.), *Martin Rade, Ausgewählte Schriften* III, pp. 167–196.

or better: disorientation, of the activity of sinful humanity, faith is the basic orientation for all actions of redeemed humanity. In his interpretation of the Ten Commandments Luther introduced a number of distinctions which are crucial for his understanding of the relationship of faith, the ministry of the word and the witness to God's will which determines the whole life of a Christian community.[32] Obeying the first commandment is the fundamental act of faith in the relationship of unconditional trust to God which provides the framework for all other human activities. The second and the third commandments are concerned with those particular human actions in which the revelation of God is explicitly proclaimed as the determinative foundation for the life of faith in the Christian community. And this is the foundation for the ministry of the Word. Doing what the other commandments of the so-called second table demand is the fulfilment of the will of the creator in relation to the whole of creation.

The basic form of the ministry of the Word in the Church is witnessing the truth of the revelation of God in Christ which is authenticated by the Spirit. It is the proclamation of the grace of God as the truth about God's relationship to his creatures. This proclamation can never create faith or effectively administer the grace of God—this can only be done by God himself. The proclamation as a human act is the witness to the action of God, Father, Son and Spirit. It can only be a work of faith, if this distinction is constantly observed and safeguarded. And this applies to the Christian proclamation in preaching as well as to the administration of the visible words of the sacraments. They refer to the Word of God as the condition for their

---

[32] Cf. Herms, op. cit., pp. 108ff.

possibility, which they can never produce or reproduce.

The emphasis on the distinction between God's revelation and the human witness to that revelation does not mean that God does his work in creating his Church in total separation from the human community of witness. The relationship between the external word and the internal teaching of the Spirit implies that God freely makes use of the human activity of witness in authenticating the human word of witness as the truth about the revelation of God in Jesus Christ. The Augsburg Confession has cast this in the famous phrase that God acts through the word of preaching and the visible word of the sacraments *tamquam per instrumenta* in creating the certainty of faith that makes the Church possible. By the free grace of God the community of witness becomes a necessary condition for the creation of the Church as the creature of the Word. The human word of the ministry of the Word becomes instrumental for the divine work of constituting the Church. But this instrumentality is only granted by God's free grace, and any attempt at identifying the human word and the divine Word is to presume upon God's freedom, it denies the condition for the possibility of the ministry of the Word.

7. The Marks of the Church

The criteria by which the community of witness and its ministry have to be assessed derive from God's action in constituting the Church. The human act of witness must be in accordance with the disclosure of the truth of God's revelation through Christ by the Spirit which demands and makes the human witness possible.

The *Augsburg Confession* (VII) counts the pure preaching of the Gospel and the correct administration of the sacraments as the two necessary *notae ecclesiae* by which a community of witness can be identified. Luther himself presented a much longer list in his *On the Councils and the Church* (1539) where he summarises the characteristics of the true community of witness:

> There God's word is preached and believed purely and ardently; the children are accepted into the kingdom of God through Baptism; there hearts assailed by sin and temptation find solace and strength in Holy Communion; there sinners unburden their conscience in confession; there ministers are commissioned in orderly fashion for preaching the Word, for administering the sacraments, and for other pastoral ministrations; there a prayerful Christian people offers God praise and thanks in public worship; there people are opposed and persecuted for the sake of Christ and there they must bear the cross of their master.[33]

This description of the true marks of the community of witness is not only important because it demonstrates that the preaching of the Gospel and the administration of the sacraments are necessary characteristics, but not a complete list, of what characterises this community. It also hints at Luther's view of the specific offices in the universal priesthood of all believers. The correct practice of human witness which conforms to the creation of the Church by God's action requires rules which try to ensure this conformity. The question of church order must be raised in order to safeguard that the practice of witness is conducted in a manner most adequate to its objective and content. Therefore the congregation in which every baptised Christian is called up to witness to the Gospel has to make sure that no one presumes upon the right that

---

[33] This is Bornkamm's summary of the detailed exposition of the *notae ecclesiae* (op. cit., p. 145) in *On the Councils and the Church*, Luther's Works 41, pp. 147–167. Cf. also the discussion of the *notae* in *Against Hanswurst* (1541), *loc. cit*, pp. 194ff. and the corresponding criticism of the Roman Church, pp. 199ff.

belongs to all.[34] And therefore it is necessary that the congregation commissions specific persons with the public proclamation of the Gospel of Christ and with the administration of the sacraments. This ordination is the basic element in an institutional order which is strictly subordinate to its task: to safeguard the authentic and competent human witness to God's creative, redemptive and saving action. The commissioning of properly educated men and women for the task of preaching and administering the sacraments in the congregation of the royal priesthood has correctly been called a question of 'practical reason'.[35] But the principle of this practical reason is the faithfulness to the Word of God of what is witnessed and how it is witnessed.

This view of the office in the Church as a special commission on the basis of the universal ministry of all believers emphasises that the empirical community of witness is a field of human action and not, like the Church as *creatura verbi divini*, an object of faith. While the *notae ecclesiae* can be predicted of any given empirical church if it is a true community of witness, the essential attributes of the Church cannot be predicated of any empirical church or of the empirical churches in their totality. Nevertheless, in confessing the one, holy, catholic and apostolic Church as an object of faith, the community of witness proclaims its belief that God will use the faithful proclamation of the empirical churches in gathering his Church and building his Kingdom. In its proclamation the community of

---

[34] This is the central argument in Luther's *That a Christian Assembly or Congregation Has the Right and Power to Judge All Teaching and to Call, Appoint and Dismiss Teachers* (1523), in Luther's Works 39, pp. 305–314. Cf. on this point W. Härle, Gründzüge einer Theologie der Synode', *Anstösse* 33 (1986), 70–77.

[35] Rade, op. cit., p. 192.

witness affirms the unity of the Church as the creature of the Word by asserting the identity of God's revelation which is grounded in the unity of God's action. It witnesses to the catholicity of the Church by proclaiming the universality of the truth of revelation. And it practises its belief in the Apostolic Church in the confidence that God will use its ministry in continuity with the *successio fidelium* for the realisation of his purpose. This confidence implies trusting in the sanctifying activity of the Holy Spirit in enabling the community to live in accordance with its calling.

8. *Building on the Foundations: Calvin*

In Luther's conception of the Church the distinction of God's action in constituting the Church and of the human action in bearing witness to the Word of God is sometimes more strongly emphasised than their relation which is the basis for the description of the community of witness. In Luther's historical situation of conflict with the late medieval Roman church this is quite understandable. In this context it was required to turn the distinction between *opus Dei* and *opus hominum* against all claims that God's revelation could be effectively transmitted by means of the Church or that God's grace could be distributed by the priesthood. Against this misguided — and for Luther blasphemous — identification of God's action and a specific form of human action, this distinction had to be stressed as much as possible. For the understanding of the Church this implied that the *creatura verbi divini* as the object of faith had to be proclaimed against any claim of an empirical church to be this Church and therefore to be able to demand faith. This polemical situation accounts for the alleged 'spiritualism' of Luther's understanding of the Church, which is, however, misinterpreted if it turns the distinction between the *creatura verbi* and every empirical church into a rigid separation.

Calvin's conception of the Church is the outcome of a different historical situation. As Owen Chadwick remarks: 'Luther married an ex-nun, Calvin the widow of an Anabaptist; and the difference is symbolic.'[36] In Calvin's ecclesiology the original conflict with the Roman church is still a dominant influence, but side by side with it a new problem demands attention: the consolidation of the Reformed community over against the radical wing of the Reformation.[37] The shifting of the emphasis can also be observed in the development of Calvin's doctrine of the Church. Whereas the first edition of the *Institutes* of 1536 presents a doctrine of the Church centred around the 'invisibility' of the Church in radical criticism of the Roman Church's claims to incorporate God's action in the Roman Church, the last edition of 1559 develops the ecclesiology from the perspective of the 'visible' Church as a response to the practical problems facing the new Reformed community. But the concept of the 'invisible' Church is still retained and defines the framework for the discussion of the practical questions concerning the organisation of the visible community. It can be argued that in this Calvin preserved the fundamental insight of Luther's ecclesiology better than Melanchthon, Luther's successor in the second generation of the Reformers, who in his *loci communes* of

[36] Owen Chadwick, op. cit., p. 83.

[37] For a summary of Calvin's ecclesiology cf. Wilhelm Niesel, *Die Theologie Calvins*, Einführung in die evangelische Theologie 6 (Munich, 1938), pp. 174–200. A concise exposition of Calvin's doctrine of the Church in the 1559 edition of the *Institutes* can be found in Ulrich Kühn, *Kirche*, Handbuch Systematischer Theologie, ed. Carl Heinz Ratschow, 10 (Gütersloh, 1980), pp. 58–75. The most comprehensive recent presentation of the systematic structure of Calvin's ecclesiology is B. C. Milner, *Calvin's Doctrine of the Church*, Studies in the History of Christian Thought 5 (Leiden, 1970).

1559 restricts his discussion of the Church to the *coetus visibilis*, the empirical community of the Church.[38]

The difference of perspective between Luther's and Calvin's understanding of the Church should be seen as caused by the requirements of different circumstances which necessitated different emphases concerning the basic insight about the constitution and nature of the Church. From the view point of later history we have grown so accustomed to viewing 'Lutheranism' and 'Calvinism' as different denominational groups and theological orientations that we are prone to see Luther and Calvin as opposite expressions of Protestantism. This conceals the underlying continuity in their thought and the fact that at least some of their differences were occasioned by different historical circumstances and not by diametrically opposed doctrinal emphases. One could even argue that in certain respects Luther and Calvin are more closely linked in their theology than certain representatives of 'Lutheranism' and 'Calvinism' to the respective founder of their school.

Calvin's understanding of the Church has in common with Luther's conception that the Church as an object of faith is sharply distinguished from the Church as a field of human action, of church reforms and of the institution of church order. Therefore the Church which is professed in the creed is for Calvin not identical with the 'visible' Church, since it is the whole Church of God including the elect who have already died. God's action alone is the foundation of the Church, and since the scope of his action is identical with the range of his knowledge, he alone knows the members of his Church: '. . . To God alone must be left the knowledge of his Church, of which his

---

[38] Cf. Küehn, op. cit., pp. 39ff.

secret election forms the foundation.'[39] This Church which is grounded in God's election is the one of whom the essential attributes of the Church have to be predicated. Therefore the unity and catholicity of the Church cannot be predicated of any of the empirical churches, it can only be predicated of the Church of the eternal election. The principle of its unity is Christ as its head.

> All the elect of God are so joined together in Christ that as they depend on one head, so they are as it were compacted into one body, being knit together like its different members; made truly one by living together under the same Spirit of God in one faith, hope and charity, called not only to the same inheritance of eternal life, but to participation in one God and one Christ.[40]

Calvin's doctrine of election which is in many respects highly problematic serves here to distinguish between the Church that is created by divine action from the human congregations. Similarly to his soteriology, it is the function of this doctrine in Calvin's ecclesiology to safeguard the sole agency of God in redemption and in gathering together his Church. And this is the foundation for the certainty of faith. If it were in any way dependent on human action it would, according to Calvin, be a matter of considerable doubt for the believers whether they are in fact saved and members of the Church. By interpreting the fact of salvation and the existence of the Church as grounded in God's election, the believers are given confidence in the foundation of their faith. The foundation of the Church in God's action, which is the ground for belief in the Church (or believing the Church, as Calvin prefers), is twofold:

[39] Inst. IV, 1,2=John Calvin, *Institutes of the Christian Religion*, E. T. Henry Beveridge III, Edinburgh, 1846, p. 11.
[40] Ibid.

First, it stands with the election of God, and cannot change or fail, any more than eternal providence. Next, it is in a manner united with the stability of Christ, who will no more allow his faithful followers to be dissevered from him, than he would allow his own members to be torn to pieces.[41]

If we interpret God's action as the foundation for the unity of the Church we do not need the visible evidence of a united empirical church: '. . . in order to embrace the unity of the Church in this manner, it is not necessary, as I have observed, to see it with our eyes or feel it with our hands.'[42] The reason why Calvin nevertheless incorporates the *sanctorum communio* as an aspect of the external Church in the Church that is believed, is that the *communio* itself is part of God's gift in creating his Church. Therefore, Calvin can write about the true believers:

> . . . if they are truly persuaded that God is the common Father of them all, and Christ their common head, they cannot but be united together in brotherly love, and mutually impart their blessings to each other.[43]

The emphasis on the 'visibility' of the Church is evident when Calvin ascribes the title 'Mother' to the visible Church. The reason for this is that God freely uses the Church in bringing about his kingdom: 'We see that God, who might perfect his people in a moment, chooses not to bring them into manhood in any other way than by the education of the Church.'[44] God makes use of the instrumentality of the human proclamation of the Gospel to create faith, and the title 'Mother' can express the significance of the human proclamation of the Gospel as an

[41] Inst. IV, 1,3=Beveridge III, p. 12.
[42] Inst. IV, 1,3=Beveridge III, p. 13.
[43] Inst. IV, 1,3=Beveridge III, p. 12.
[44] Inst. IV, 1,5=Beveridge III, p. 14.

instrumental condition for the creation of the Church. It also emphasises the importance of the process of education that is in Calvin's view part of this constitution. God permits the instrumentality of witness in order 'that he may thus allure us to himself, instead of driving us away by his thunder'.[45] Calvin was acutely aware of the problem implied in the blurring of the distinction between the instrumentality of human preaching and the constitution of certainty which remains the work of the Spirit,

> as at this time there is a great dispute as to the efficacy of the ministry, some extravagantly overrating its dignity, and others erroneously maintaining, that what is peculiar to the Spirit of God is transferred to mortal men, when we suppose that ministers and teachers penetrate to the mind and heart, so as to correct the blindness of the one and the hardness of the other . . .[46]

Calvin maintains on the basis of key passages of Pauline theology that the efficacy of the ministry can in no way be regarded as a human work, but is always the work of the Spirit.

> And it is indeed necessary to keep these sentences in view, since God, in ascribing to himself the illumination of the spirit and the renewal of the heart, reminds us that it is sacrilege for man to claim any part of either to himself.[47]

On the basis of these considerations which demonstrate the necessity of the distinction between God's work and human work, Calvin can present his definitive exposition of both related modes of being of the Church. And as everything in Calvin's theology this distinction is presented as a result of scriptural exegesis:

[45] Inst. IV, 1,5=Beveridge III, p. 15.
[46] Inst. IV, 1,6=Beveridge III, p. 18.
[47] Inst. IV, 1,6=Beveridge III, p. 19.

I have observed that the Scriptures speak of the Church in two ways. Sometimes when they speak of the Church they mean the Church as it really is before God—the Church into which none are admitted but those who by the gift of adoption are sons of God, and by the sanctification of the Spirit true members of Christ. In this case it not only comprehends the saints who dwell on the earth, but all the elect who have existed from the beginning of the world. Often, too, by the name of the Church is designated the whole body of mankind scattered throughout the world, who profess to worship one God and Christ, who by baptism are initiated into faith; by partaking of the Lord's Supper profess unity in true doctrine and charity, agree in holding the word of the Lord, and observe the ministry which Christ has appointed to the preaching of it. In this Church there is a very large mixture of hypocrites; who have nothing of Christ but the name and the outward appearance: of ambitious, avaricious, envious, evil-speaking men, some also of impurer lives, who are tolerated for a time, either because their guilt cannot be legally established, or because due strictness of discipline is not always observed. Hence, as it is necessary to believe the invisible Church, so we are also enjoined to regard this Church which is so called with reference to man, and to cultivate its communion.[48]

The visible Church can be identified by the marks or symbols of the true Church:

Wherever we see the word of God sincerely preached and heard, wherever we see the sacraments administered according to the institution of Christ, there we cannot have any doubt that the Church of God has some existence.[49]

Everything else is excluded from the marks which distinguish the true Church. Even church discipline which the later Reformed confessions of faith count among the *notae ecclesiae* is missing from Calvin's list.[50] Calvin is not

[48] Inst. IV, 1,7=Beveridge III, p. 19f.
[49] Inst. IV, 1,9=Beveridge III, p. 21f.
[50] Cf. the discussion of this question which is one of the origins for dissensus among the Reformers of the second generation in Avis, op. cit., pp. 43ff.

prepared to withhold the name of a church from any society in which the ministry of the word and the ministry of the sacraments is properly conducted, however fragmentary and fallible it may appear. Wherever the Gospel of Christ is witnessed in a proper way, there is the Church as the community of witness.

9. Rules for Conducting the Ministry

These fundamental aspects of Calvin's ecclesiology give ample evidence for the common foundations of the understanding of the Church in the theology of the Reformers. Where Calvin differs from Luther is not in his view of the divine constitution of the Church as creature of the Word and not in his conception of the Church as a community of witness which can be identified by the preaching of the Gospel of Christ and by the correct administration of the sacraments. What Calvin offers in addition to Luther's conception is a sustained reflection on how the ministry of the word should be conducted and which rules regulate the procedure for appointing those who are commissioned to exercise it. These rules concern the competent fulfilment of the task of the Church in witnessing to God's revelation as the condition of its possibility. It is their function to safeguard the conditions under which true witness to the Gospel of Christ is possible. And insofar as God uses the human witness to his revelation in building his Church, the ministry belongs to 'the order in which the Lord has been pleased that his Church should be governed'.[51] The authority of the ministers is strictly derivative: it is the authority of their ministry, and this derives its authority from what it witnesses:

[51] Inst. IV, 3,1 = Beveridge III, p. 57.

Therefore, it is here necessary to remember, that whatever authority and dignity the Holy Spirit in Scripture confers on priests, or prophets, or successors of the Apostles, it wholly gives not to men themselves, but to the ministry to which they are appointed; or, to speak more plainly, to the word, to the ministry of which they are appointed.[52]

This derivative authority which is an authority that is witnessed and not an authority which is effectively represented makes it necessary to regard the ministers as 'instruments' and 'vessels'. In some places Calvin could develop this into a 'sacramental view'[53] of the ministry:

[Paul] is accustomed to speak in two different ways of ministers, as well as of sacraments. For in some cases he considers a minister as one who has been ordained by the Lord for . . . regenerating souls, . . . for remitting sins . . . Viewed in that respect, he . . . endows him . . . with the power of the Spirit . . . In other cases, he considers a minister one who is a servant, not a master, an instrument, not the hand; and, in short, as man, not God.[54]

This twofold perspective is to be interpreted from the relationship of divine and human action by which God the Spirit uses the human witness to the Gospel of Christ as the instrument for creating his Church. The human community of witness can only propose rules for the competent human witness, it can only suggest procedures for the election and ordination of ministers. The internal call of the minister remains outside the scope of human procedures. It is the personal gift of the certainty of faith which can only be given by the Spirit of God.

The four offices of the pastor, the teacher, the presbyter and the deacon which Calvin, following Martin Bucer,

[52] Inst. IV, 8,2=Beveridge III, p. 159f.
[53] Milner, op. cit., p. 137.
[54] Comm. 1 Cor. 3:7, Ioannis Calvini Opera Quae Supersunt Omnia (ed. G. Baum, et al.), XLIX, p. 350, cited in Milner, op. cit., p. 137f.

suggested for the practice of the ministry in the community of witness, are designed to guarantee the highest possible responsibility in the practice of the ministry.[55] And in arguing for this fourfold structure Calvin constantly mixes arguments from biblical key passages about the offices in the Church (e.g. Eph. 4:11) with arguments from the Fathers and pragmatic arguments with regard to the task of maintaining and conducting the ministry in a most comprehensive and effective manner. Calvin was quite conscious that this rearrangement of offices in the Church cannot claim to be literally scriptural or totally in accord with the tradition. But that is not the criterion by which the offices in the Church should be judged. Their only criterion is whether they enable the Church as the community of witness to perform its ministry in the most competent manner.

A characteristic feature of Calvin's ecclesiology is that large parts of his reflections are concerned with the power of the Church (Inst IV, 8–13), which is defined as 'the spiritual power which is proper to the Church and which consists either in doctrine, or jurisdiction, or in enacting laws'.[56] These sections of Calvin's ecclesiology have been subject to heated debate, especially since the Reformed confessions of faith gave the discipline in the Church the quality of a third mark of the true Church—a step which Calvin never took. It is easy to ridicule the extremes to which Church discipline concerning public and private morality was taken in Calvin's Geneva—which seem hard

[55] Cf. Otto Weber, 'Calvins Lehre von der Kirchen', in *Die Treue Gottes in der Geschichte der Kirche* (Neukirchen, 1968, p. 32. The fourfold ministry is developed in Inst. IV, 3,4=Beveridge III, p. 6of. There is a certain tension with Inst. IV, 4,1=Beveridge III, p. 74, where Calvin speaks of three orders of the ministry. Cf. the discussion in Kühn, op. cit., pp. 65ff.

[56] Inst. IV, 8,1=Beveridge III, p. 159.

to justify, even if it was like Savonarola's Florence.[57] It must, however, be observed that Calvin carefully limits these rules and regulations to the human community of witness as a human field of action. The Church cannot bind the conscience and it cannot presume upon God's judgement. The basic motivation which is often given for Calvin's conception of the enforcement of morality, i.e. that it has the function of aiding the ministry of the word and the sanctification which is effected where the human word is used by God's grace, is certainly one aspect of Calvin's conception. More important is perhaps that these reflections are concerned with those human actions which do not *explicitly* witness to God's revelation in Christ as it is authenticated by the Spirit in the ministry of the word, but which are performed as obedience to the will of the creator in relation to the whole of creation. As much as it is under the obligation to exercise the ministry of the word, the community of witness is also called to perform the works that are required by the second table of the Ten Commandments. The revelation of God in Christ which is authenticated by the Spirit concerns the relationship of the creator to the whole of creation. Faith as the active response to the truth of revelation is not only the restoration of our relationship to God, but since this relationship is restored, it implies the restoration of the relationship to ourselves, to other persons and to the cultural and natural world. Justification implies the sanctification of the believer, the reconstitution of the human person as a moral agent, i.e. as an agent who is enabled to act in accordance with the will of the creator. The community of witness does not only witness explicitly in the ministry of the word to the truth of the revelation, it

[57] Cf. Willem Nijenhuis, art. 'Calvin' in *Theologische Realenzyklopäedie* VII, p. 573.

also witnesses implicitly to this truth by doing the will of the creator. Only if this connection is grasped, can faith be the basic orientation for all human actions. And this is the continuing challenge of Calvin's reflections on church discipline.

Since the actions which are performed in response to God's revelation do not occur in a special field of action, the Church cannot avoid clarifying its relations to the institutions in which society is organised. Therefore the reflections on the relationship between the Church and the state with which Calvin concludes the presentation of his ecclesiology in the *Institutes* are inevitable.[58] But again it has to be observed that none of these relations belongs to the divine constitution of the Church, but to the Church as a human field of action. Therefore they are subject to revision and constant supervision whether they allow the Church to exercise its ministry to which it is called in the obedience of faith: of witnessing to the truth of God's revelation in the public proclamation of the word and sacraments and by doing the will of the creator in his creation.

10. What the Church Cannot Do

Confronted with the challenge of the ecclesiology of the Reformers which could only be sketched here in its basic outlines, we can still feel the clash of this understanding of the Church with the power-structures of the later medieval Roman church. But the challenge is not restricted to its original historical setting and to the opposing parties in this historical confrontation. It also concerns the churches in the tradition of the Reformation which cannot claim to have remained true to the fundamental insights of their

[58] Cf. Inst. IV, 20: Of Civil Government=Beveridge III, pp. 518–554.

theological Fathers in all periods of their history. One reason for the continuing challenge of the ecclesiology of the Reformers is that it relates the understanding of the Church to the fundamental character of Christian faith and its constitution. In the context of ecclesiological questions it raises the fundamental questions about the relationship of God's work and human work, of revelation and faith, which cannot be evaded by any church or theology.

The fundamental lesson to be learnt from the ecclesiology of the Reformers is the art of distinguishing and relating *opus Dei* and *opus hominum*. This art has to be practised both critically and constructively. The critical insight of the Reformers' understanding of the Church is that God's action in constituting the Church as the *creatura verbi divini* which is the one, holy, catholic and apostolic Church of faith cannot be identified with any human action in the Church or any human form of church organisation. Wherever divine authority is claimed for any form of human action or institution in the Church the *proton pseudos* of turning God's action into an instrument of human action has already been committed and the Word of God is taken captive. This applies to all attempts at incorporating God's action in human action. If we see the fundamental distinction between God's work and human work as a 'heresy-detector' we can note two basic forms of 'heresy' which blur this distinction.

The first could paradoxically be dubbed 'the heresy of orthodoxy' where a particular doctrine or set of doctrines (including, perhaps, a doctrine of the Church) is identified with the truth of revelation. Since the truth of the revelation of God can only be disclosed and authenticated through the Son by the Spirit, it cannot become part of a human tradition of teaching. All we can hope for is, according to the Reformers, that the Spirit authenticates our witness to the truth of the Gospel of Christ.

The second heresy which similarly blurs the distinction between the divine work and the human work could be labelled 'the heresy of orthopraxis'. This heresy occurs where the work of God is identified with a specific form of human action, whether it is an institution or office in the Church or a movement denying all institutional organisation. God's work cannot be embodied in any human act. According to the Reformers God's action cannot be represented by any human agent or institution. We cannot do God's work. Here the critical distinction of the Reformers does not only apply to those who identify a specific historical form of church organisation with the work of God, but also to those who identify God's action with the liberation from the historical institutions of the Church. According to the Reformers we can only hope that God will use our human actions and institutions which can do nothing but witness to God's work for achieving his work in creating his Church.

To recognise and to acknowledge what it cannot do could have a radically liberating effect for the Church. In a situation which seems to be almost universally characterised by a loss of nerve on the part of the churches, and where self-preservation seems to be the chief point on the hidden agenda of ecclesiastical existence, it could only be a liberation to see that the church cannot preserve its existence because it has not constituted itself. That there will always be a Church is an article of faith, but the continued existence of the Church cannot be guaranteed by our programme of Church reform or our programmatic appeals to resist any such attempt. We can only witness to God's faithfulness who will complete the work he has begun by creating the Church as the creature of the divine Word.

11. *What the Church Can Do and Must Do*

The critical side of the distinction of the Reformers between *opus Dei* and *opus hominum* concentrates on what the community of believers cannot do, but what it must let happen—*ubi et quando visum est Deo*. But the ecclesiology of the Reformers is not only a radical critique of all claims which identify divine and human agency, it also illustrates constructively what the Church as the community of witness must do and what it can do. What it must do is to witness the revelation of God in Christ which is authenticated by the Spirit by the proclamation of the Gospel of Christ in preaching and in administering the visible words of the sacraments. This witness to the revelation of God in Christ is the faithful presentation and interpretation of the truth of the Gospel as the truth about the relationship of the creator to his creation. In witnessing to the Gospel of Christ the individual believers are gathered in the community of witness. The community of witness only exists in particular communities which bear witness to the universal *communio sanctorum* as the *creatura verbi divini*. Witness is the character of all human acts in which God's action in creation, revelation and inspiration is confessed as the condition for the possibility of the human act of faith.

Since faith as unconditional trust in God is made possible by the certainty which, as the gift of the Spirit authenticates the truth of the revelation in the Son, is the basic orientation for all human actions, the community of faith is not only called to witness the constitution of faith in God's revelation by the ministry of the word, it has also to do the will of God the creator in relation to the whole of creation. The community of witness is an ethical community, a community of virtue and character whose actions have to conform to the will of the creator.

The human action of witness is made possible by the

divine action of creating the certainty of faith. The criterion which governs this human activity is that the witness conforms to what made it possible: the certainty of faith concerning the truth of revelation. This criterion implies that the human activity of witness must distinguish itself clearly from the divine action that made it possible.[59] If it does not maintain this distinction—and this was the basic accusation of the Reformers against the medieval Roman church—it implicitly denies the condition of its possibility.

What the community of witness *can* do is to organise its ministry and life in such a way that it can fulfil its fundamental obligation of the ministry of the Word in forms that are credible and convincing. The community of witness which is called to be absolutely obedient in its ministry of the Word is free in organising the conditions under which it can perform its task. This does not mean that the Church, when it rediscovers the promise of freedom that is implied in the acknowledgement of the Word of God as the only authority which commands absolute obedience, could somehow step out of history and start all over again from scratch. But it can recognise the traditions and institutional structures in which it exists for what they are: human traditions and institutions which cannot claim divine dignity. Insofar as they have their justification not in themselves but in the truth of the Word of God to which the community of witness owes its existence, all ecclesial traditions and institutions are open to criticism and change. The witnessing community that

[59] Herms, op. cit., p. 114 formulates this as the fundamental rule for the practice of the ministry: 'Das ministerium verbi ist in allen seinen Gestalten und Spielarten . . . *so zu vollziehen, dass es sich in allen seinen Tätigkeiten explizit gegen das Verwechseltwerden mit dem göttlichen Offenbarungshandeln selber schützt. Das aber kann nur so geschehen, daß es selber seine eigenen Vollzüge unmissverständlich von dem Offenbarungshandeln des göttlichen Geistes unterscheidet.*'

respects the freedom of God in using the human witness is free to organise the human forms which enable it to exercise its task in the institutions which prove to be most adequate for the practice of witness. Here all competence, imagination and constructive ideas available should be used in order to present an authentic, credible and attractive practice of witness to those outside the community of witness. With regard to this task the Church is free to be self-critical, which in the case of the community of witness means exposing itself to the criticism of the Gospel, and to revise and reform those rules and institutions which seem to impede a credible practice of witness.

This human freedom in organising the practice of witness which is possible in a community of witness that remains faithful to its task has important ecumenical implications. Whereas the community of witness has to insist on the distinction between the *creatura verbi divini* and every empirical church, no human institution or church office or set of rules for the practice of the ministry of the word can as such be a theologically necessary condition for community with other churches. Historically different practices of worship and different forms of Church organisation do not have to stand in the way of a communion of communities of witness which proclaim, but can never identify with, the universal Church which is created by God. An ecumenical practice which respects the distinction between the work of the divine economy and the work of ecumenical understanding in the different communities of witness can exercise freedom in finding shared rules and practices for the ministry of the word in the audible words of preaching and the visible words of the sacraments. Only where this distinction is blurred and the human work of ecumenical understanding claims to bring about the unity of the Church which can only be the work of the divine economy, the community of witness must, according to the ecclesiology of the Reformers, abstain from such forms of ecumenical practice.

What would the recovery of the forgotten heritage of Reformation ecclesiology mean for the churches today? Rediscovering the basic insight into the distinction between God's work and the human work of witnessing to the truth of the revelation would mean that the Church could be freed from the preoccupation with preserving its identity. The true identity of the Church as the creature of the divine Word can only be witnessed by the community of witness. This community of witness which confesses its faith in the one, holy, catholic and apostolic Church is identifiable by its ministry of the word. It is identifiable by the fact that it does *not* identify with the Church as the object of faith, but that it restricts itself to witnessing this Church in its ministry. Since the *creatura verba divini* cannot be identified with any empirical form of institutional order or church organisation or any programme of church reform, none of the human forms of organising the ministry of the community of witness has divine dignity. Therefore, the Church as an organised human community of witness can be an *ecclesia semper reformanda* which is open to change as long as these changes help the church to fulfil its fundamental task of witnessing to the truth of the Gospel of Christ in the specific historical, cultural and social circumstances in which it exists. What can never be changed is the truth of the revelation by which God discloses his unchanging faithfulness to his creation. Recovering the basic insight of the Reformers' view of the Church would mean that the Church is freed from fulfilling impossible tasks and free to turn to those possible tasks which are demanded by its ministry as a community of witness. Such a Church could find orientation and consolation in the promise that it will remain a true community of witness as long as it remains a community of true witness.

5

LORD, BONDSMAN AND CHURCHMAN:
Identity, Integrity and Power in Anglicanism

by Richard H. Roberts

Introduction

The pungent and abrasive title of this paper indicates the main aspects of an investigation we propose into some of the contemporary dilemmas of English Anglicanism as represented prominently today by a leading apologist for this tradition, Professor Stephen W. Sykes, Regius Professor of Divinity in the University of Cambridge. In two important and related, but perhaps not fully appreciated works, *The Integrity of Anglicanism* and *The Identity of Christianity*,[1] Professor Sykes has sought first to rework Anglican theological method and self-understanding, and then, second, to formulate and apply in the context of the Church universal, and its task of defining the identity of Christianity, the contribution he believes it is the distinct vocation of the Anglican Communion to make. These are the positive proposals to be found in Sykes' project, but underlying them is a yet more fundamental theme, that of power, and it is the latter, we believe, which is of the greater theological significance in the long term. Indeed we shall argue that the 'sub-plot' or 'sub-text' of the position developed in Sykes' two major works comprises the elaboration of a theory of theological power which is in effect the linking thread upon which hang glistening beads of historical and theological illustration.

[1] *The Integrity of Anglicanism* (London, 1978); *The Identity of Christianity* (London, 1984). Henceforth referred to as *Integrity* and *Identity* respectively.

This interpretation may appear to run counter to certain aspects of explicit authorial intention but what we develop below is a 'reading' of these texts that gives priority to the hermeneutic of power and accords relative status to the issue of 'identity'. We thus isolate a proposal with definite but questionable implications for the theory and practice of future Anglicanism.

In his two books Sykes has advanced a complex and sophisticated set of arguments which reflect his long-term engagement with German and North American theology, as well as with the intricacies of the English tradition. These arguments are promulgated at a time of almost unparalleled theological stress in which the positive formulation of the substance of the Christian faith (rather than its merely negative criticism) is a pressing necessity. Not only this but the social and cultural aspects of the contemporary crisis, in particular secularisation in all its complexity, press in upon an ancestral English Anglican tradition burdened with multiple ambiguities. What Sykes in reality offers is in the first instance an internal reform, a re-organisation of the relationship in theology between the pursuit of truth as such and the responsible management of power on the part of the theologian, whose task it is, within certain limits, to define what Christianity should be for his or her tradition and generation. This dual task is initially articulated in relation to the policy of a particular tradition, but the impact of Sykes' proposals applies in the context of Christianity as a whole and is conceived through arguments which make frequent if not systematic allusion to materials lying outside strictly theological confines. It is our contention that whilst Sykes' proposals are of fundamental importance, engagement with substantial discussions of the relation of truth and power both within and outside Christian theology indicates that without revision his hypothesis would lead to the inhibition, even the prohibition of that emancipation that ought in our view to accompany the grace and truth of the Gospel.

In order to justify these assertions we shall argue as follows: first, the historical context will be outlined in schematic terms indicating how theological developments are related to structural factors; second, a theoretical dimension will be opened up through reference to Hegel's ontological parable of the Lord and Bondsman which provides important parallels with attempts to restate a theological position; third, the *Integrity* will be analysed; and then, fourth, the *Identity* will likewise be 'read' from the standpoint of the emergence of the sub-text which contains the key 'structure' that, we believe, informs and unites Sykes' endeavours;[2] fifth, the theory of power present in the sub-text is then expounded at length in relation to the theoretical insights provided by the Hegelian parallel; sixth, in conclusion, it is argued that our reading and interpretation of this renewal of Anglican theology in terms of an identity of authority with power

---

[2] The term 'structure' merits explanation. The way in which Sykes' books are here 'read' is 'structuralist' in the sense that we seek to present his texts as 'unified *structures*, through an examination of the interrelation of the different levels of each work'. Thus David Robey comments on Tzvetan Todorov's study of Henry James in the introduction to *Structuralism: an Introduction* (Oxford, 1973) p. 3. The close affinity between the approach taken up here and applied to contemporary theological texts and Todorov's treatment of the stories of James became obvious to me after the composition of the first draft of this paper. Todorov's essay, 'The Structural Analysis of Literature: the Tales of Henry James' contains the following comment, analogously applicable in the present theological context: 'The secret of James' tales is, therefore, precisely the existence of an essential secret, of something which is not named, of an absent, overwhelming force which puts the whole present machinery of the narrative into motion . . .: on the one hand he deploys all his strength to reach the hidden essence, to unveil the secret object; on the other, he constantly moves it further and further away', p. 75.

contains possibilities which unchecked will lead to un-desirable consequences.

Our argument is, it must be emphasised, a *reading* of the texts of a contemporary theologian seen in their context. As such the approach taken to the work in question is *dialectical*; the latencies and potentialities present in the 'structure' of the texts are pressed to the limits and deliberately not resolved in a premature manner into compromise or *via media*. Thus the Hegelian model that overshadows much of modern critical epistemology like-wise serves to draw out the implicit possibilities of an argument which might otherwise remain relatively un-explored. On this basis we reach conclusions which will have demanded the direction of 'resistance' against a number of features in traditional Anglican theological method and its attendant ethos. This, I believe, is justified by the importance of the issues involved.

1. The historical context of the contemporary Anglican problem of self-definition

There has as yet appeared no full-scale study of English theology in the nineteenth and twentieth centuries which respects both the historical and the sociological factors evident in an era of progressive secularisation. In the absence of such an adequate contextualisation the follow-ing outline takes the form of an hypothesis generated on the basis of an appraisal of the broadest features of the developments of last century. Put in the most succinct way two fundamental tendencies are evident in Anglican theology and these underlie the detailed discussion of any particular facets of the whole situation. First, since the magisterial defence of classical Chalcedonian orthodoxy by H. P. Liddon in his Bampton Lectures[3] of 1867 there has

[3] *The Divinity of Our Lord and Saviour Jesus Christ* (London, 1867).

been a slow but inexorable decline of Christology 'from above' and a corresponding increase in interest in the themes of the humanity of Christ and in *kenosis*. Over the same period there has been a parallel and highly intransigent defence of a high doctrine of the ministry focused increasingly in the episcopate which extended from Charles Gore's attack[4] upon Edwin Hatch's Bampton Lectures *The Organisation of the Early Christian Churches*[5] through to K. E. Kirk's collective work *The Apostolic Ministry* of 1946. The latter contains within it what may be justly termed a triumphalist *plerosis* of the episcopate which was conceived as embodying the *shaliach* or divine plenipotentiary of God.[6] The historical conjunction of two such tendencies in the context of secularisation, that is the enforced retreat of the apparent reality of the sacred in society and the growth of pluralism, cannot but arouse the interest and ideological suspicion of anyone concerned for the integrity of the tradition. A struggle for and assertion of theological identity on the part of the ordained ministry would appear to have been contemporaneous with a loss of distinctive identity in the area of incarnational doctrine and the doctrine of the Church. In contrasting these impulses: a progressive *kenosis* in the doctrine of the Incarnation and a

[4] *The Ministry of the Christian Church* (London, 1881), new ed. 1919 by C. H. Turner.

[5] (London, 1881).

[6] (London, 1946). Kirk commented on the ultimate significance of the episcopate thus: 'But embedded in the system as we know it, is its foundation and justification, its only principle of continuity with apostolic times – the commission of the apostle or shaliach to act in our Lord's own Person. If it is this which we are offering to our separated brethren, and this which they desire to accept from us, all is well', p. 52. Acute controversy followed the publication of this work; my point is not based upon criticism of the historical basis of such a vision, but upon the ideological impulse implicit in its emergence and the essential – dependent – passive structure of theological priorities it embodies, to the acute detriment of a proper ecclesiology of the whole people of God.

corresponding *plerosis* in the doctrine of the ordained ministry, is it not plausible to assume some form of correlation if, as will become apparent, 'identity' is understood in the context of a competitive economy of meaning as one assertion made against others? Thus understood, the search for self-understanding on the part of the ordained ministry, the professional class within the Church, could not merely be the assumption of an identity given through ancestral tradition; it had, by contrast, to be sustained through assertion and struggle. In the often intellectually isolated world of theological reflection the disjunction between explicit self-understanding and the actual social function of ideas is often extreme. It is crucial to understand that the assertion required to focus and establish an identity is not an act perpetrated in a vacuum. On the contrary it is an act perpetrated against another. In re-establishing its threatened identity in the face of secularisation the Anglican (and here is meant the most theologically self-assertive catholic wing of Anglicanism) ordained hierarchy came to conceive itself by means of an identity which, in asserting itself, correspondingly denied theological identity to the other, that is the laity. This process of definition through appropriation to the self and negation of the other is, we shall later argue, intrinsic to the human condition as understood in that most illuminating of traditions that extends in its modern form from Hegel, through to, for example, the work of the French critic and historian Michel Foucault.

The more commonly raised issues concerning Anglican identity, in particular that of 'comprehensiveness', assume a conflict between alternatives within a framework originating in the Elizabethan Settlement and its initial rationalisation in Richard Hooker's *Laws of Ecclesiastical Polity*. It is one of the strengths of Professor Sykes' critique of contemporary Anglicanism that in it conflict is seen as inevitable. It is, however, our conviction that the notion of 'conflict' as conceived by Sykes is insufficiently developed and unnaturally restricted even when used in relation to the extended argument about 'power' within the Church and Christian theology. It is, furthermore, our contention that theology understood as a field of competitive forces, a *struggle for power*, involves the definition of the very nature of power itself. The history of English Anglicanism in the past century would indicate *prima facie*, that a largely silent struggle has taken place within the inter-related spheres of Christology and ecclesiology accompanied by the virtual absence of a theology of the laity, that is of the people of God as a whole. This is starkly apparent when the twentieth-century Anglican tradition is contrasted with the ecclesiology (albeit problematic) of Vatican II. Full engagement with these issues on the historical, theological and sociological level lies outside the scope of this paper. Less ambitiously, but no less pertinently, we confine ourselves to a critique of one significant attempt to confront these issues of integrity and power within Anglican theology and polity. Through a critical reading and analysis of the basic structure of Sykes' two important texts it will be apparent that the substantial and methodological issues and the putative answers afforded by Sykes are less than wholly satisfactory and indicate the need for a rather more ambitious conception of the role and nature of systematic theology itself as the primary tool to be used in the clarification of the task of the Church in its contemporary context. Before turning to the exposition of a reading of these texts in context it is necessary to generate theoretical insight into the dynamics of power as provided in Hegel's mighty parable of the Lord and Bondsman. The ecclesiological struggle for identity, a conflict of polarities, of essential and dependent ministry within the Church, parallels the ontological and epistemological 'moments' in Hegel's text. It is thus in the 'intertextuality' generated between the integrity and identity texts of Professor Sykes and the text of Hegel that some of the wider parameters of engagement will emerge. Above all, the question of social structure and hierarchy in relation to struggle *even within the Church* cannot be ignored without the possibility of ideological bewitchment and illusion.

2. Lordship and Bondage: Hegel's prefigurement of the sociology of knowledge and critical theory

The hermeneutics of power within Christian theology is underdeveloped although pioneering work in this area is present in liberation theology.[7] Behind the development of Marxism, the sociology of knowledge and critical theory there lies the seminal text, Hegel's *Phenomenology of Mind* of 1807 which is of no lesser importance for contemporary Christian theology. This work, and in particular so far as this paper is concerned, its second main section concerned with 'self-consciousness' (*Selbstbewusstsein*), is an account of the emergence of consciousness from simple sense-certainty to absolute knowledge, which, whilst it reflects the basic division of Kant's first *Critique*, is dialectical in the sense that it recounts the contrasting 'moments' in a processual development rather than as the merely static conditions underlying and implied in the enactment of knowledge. In the second section of the *Phenomenology* Hegel presents the construction of consciousness out of relation and division both within the subject and between

[7] Two obvious examples are J. L. Segundo's *The Liberation of Theology* (Dublin, 1977) and L. Boff's *Church, Charism and Power* (London, 1985).

subjects. The dynamic, conflictual pattern that emerges is represented in the parable of the Lord and Bondsman (*Herr und Knecht*), which is composed of resonant and suggestive images capable of multiple and complex interpretations.[8] At root, however, the imagery is expressive of relation of independence and dependence and the concomitant forms of consciousness. Implicit in the parable and its resolution into the confrontation of stoicism and scepticism in the 'unhappy consciousness' (*Unglückliches Bewusstsein*) is Hegel's final confrontation of the ancestral Christian, that is medieval, embodiment of a religious consciousness in the social antithesis of lordship and bondage with its dissolution in enlightened modernity. The juxtaposition of independent and essential and of dependent and inessential consciousness articulated by Hegel provides an exact formal parallel with the polarisation of pre-critical consciousness to be found in such anachronistic entities as the Anglican repristination of the theology of the episcopate (as essential ministry) and the presbyterate (the inessential ministry) that was implied in the previous section of this paper. The question that arises is this, can we move beyond the crude, unreflective polarity of the ancestral juxtaposition of *ordo* and *plebs* – albeit decked out with the full panoply of biblical and patristic adornment in its mid-twentieth century Anglican restatement – and, if so, how?

An answer to this question is not easy to determine but one plausible response is to set over against each other the dialectic of power as Hegel expounds it in the *Phenomenology* and as we see it in traditional Anglican ecclesiology and the renewed theory of theological power that is revealed in the crucial sub-text of the *Integrity* and the

---

[8] J. Baillie (tr.) *The Phenomenology of Mind* (London, 1949).

Identity. This, as we have already maintained, involves a 'reading' of both texts and a leap of intellectual imagination facilitated by the assumption that there is structure in both and that each writer is engaged with analogous confrontations of antiquity and modernity. For Hegel there are, in the simplest preliminary terms, three 'moments' in the emergence and completion of self-consciousness, a process analogous with the eruption of life itself:

> (a) pure undifferentiated ego is its first immediate object. (b) This immediacy is itself, however, thoroughgoing mediation; it has its being only by cancelling the independent object, in other words it is Desire. The satisfaction of desire is indeed the reflexion of self-consciousness into itself, in the certainty which has passed into objective truth. But (c) the truth of this certainty is really twofold reflexion, the reduplication of self-consciousness.[9]

Whilst Hegel could write out of a riven personal experience: 'I am not one of the fighters locked in battle, but both, and I am the struggle itself. I am fire and water . . .',[10] his concession to the reader comes in the imaged presentation of this conflict. Thus in the passage 'Independence and dependence of self-consciousness', self-consciousness is seen to exist 'in itself and for itself, in that, and by the fact that it exists for another self-consciousness; that is to say, it *is* only by being acknowledged or "recognised"'.[11] This first moment in the dialectic, the passage from unreflective unity into consciousness of existence 'for itself' can be put in parallel with the emergence of an epistemological and ontological elite in the Church by reference to whom those

[9] J. Baillie, op. cit., p. 226.
[10] *Vorlesungen über die Philosophie der Religion*, Glockner, XV, p. 80, as cited by G. A. Kelly, 'Notes on Hegel's "Lordship and Bondage"', in A. MacIntyre (ed.), *Hegel: A Collection of Critical Essays*, Notre Dame, 1976, p. 217.
[11] J. Baillie, op. cit., p. 229.

not so privileged define themselves. Thus, by analogy, an *ordo* invested with divine plenitude and existing for itself becomes the sociological reference point in which is located the Pneuma-Christ. An essential ministry serves as a source that must deny the other in order to affirm itself: knowledge of it comes only through acknowledgement of its ultimate distinction. Identification of the 'authority' of such a focused reality does not depend, as Sykes is to assert, upon 'self-assertiveness' but upon the assumption of plenitude, that is the totality of a prior, given essence – in theological terms the power of God. 'Self-assertiveness' belongs, as becomes apparent, not to the essential being, Hegel's 'Lord', but to the 'slave' or 'bondsman' who has to struggle *ab ovo*.

> The one is independent, and its essential nature is to be for itself; the other is dependent, and its essence is life or existence for another. The former is the Master, or Lord, the latter the Bondsman.[12]

This characterisation of the foundation of human existence in assertion and negation has entered the structure of modern thought in many forms, not least through Marx, Freud, Sartre and Michel Foucault (not to mention into feminist theory through Simone de Beauvoir). In Christian theology it is also present, be it in the epistemology of Protestantism (for example in Karl Barth) or the onto-logical hierarchy of Catholicism, and the pattern persists in the genteel ambivalence of Anglican polity. What comes next in the Hegelian conflict is less well understood and acknowledged. The Master exists for itself and mediates itself through the Other which becomes what it is through designation as a subordinate thing. The proof of essence, of

[12] J. Baillie, op. cit., p. 234.

being *through* the Other by the Master, strikes fear into the Slave, who is, despite the Master, a consciousness experiencing the threat of negation, of reduction to mere thinghood (*Dingheit*). In this 'trial by death' the Master in triumphing passes into the ultimate irony: at the moment of effectively achieved Lordship he finds that he is not fully independent but dependent; it is only *through* negation and isolation, the extinction of the Other as a *means* to self-fulfilment that the Master attains to his exaltation. Correspondingly, the Slave enters a life-and-death struggle in the face of negation, the death embodied in the Master who comes to swallow him into mediate thinghood. He must in effect fight back, he must labour to assert himself or face subsumption into the mediation, the self-projection of the Master. The theological affinities are obvious.

Hegel, unlike Sykes, is of course engaged in an analysis of the transcendental presupposition of reason and in this he is the successor of Kant. The parallel to be drawn here is limited: we are in the first instance concerned to juxtapose the archaisms of both Anglican hierarchy and the Lordship and Bondage passage with the critical 'modernisations' afforded by Hegel and by Sykes. The Hegelian polarity is not explicitly presented as a socio-historial entity or process but in terms of the mutual reality of the consciousness which 'finds that it is and is not another consciousness, as also that this other is for itself only when it cancels itself as existing for itself, and has self-existence only in the self-existence of the other.'[13] The correlate of this in theological terms is, as we have argued, the situation of the unchallenged *ordo*, a priesthood that mediates, unchallenged, on behalf of others and in terms of which a laity must understand itself, that is as negated. We find a

[13] J. Baillie, op. cit., p. 231.

potent example of this in the dubious repristination of the doctrine of the essential priesthood embodied in the episcopate in *The Apostolic Ministry* of 1946 where it is conceived as the theological presupposition without which the dependent presbyterate and the even more remote lay non-entity (or *Unding*) do not respectively exist.

In this section we have seen how the parable of the Lord and Bondsman provides an informative parallel with the structure of traditional Anglican (and indeed Catholic)[14] ecclesiology; both represent anachronistic archaisms in the modern world. Hegel provides a subversive account of this polarity in which Lord and Bondsman, Master and Slave co-exist in deadly conflict, and, with remarkable fluidity exchange attributes as the 'moments' of the *coincidentia oppositorum* engage in what amounts to a secularised *perichoresis*. Hegel's ontology and epistemology understand identity as the protest against a given, unreflective domination. Indeed the theologically trained genius of Hegel was to understand the essence of enlightened modernity in terms of the necessity of recognising the inevitability of assertion in the context of the void and even, in the final account, the identity of being and nothingness (*Nichtigkeit*). As we shall see there are further similarities between this position and modern Anglican attempts at self-definition. In the context of an abrogation of the historical transmission of identity through tradition, and the nihilistic and analytical reduction of metaphysical claims what can be done to re-assert identity? Not surprisingly tackling the analogous context involves a re-

---

[14] Yves M. J. Congar's assessment of the position of the laity in the opening sections of *Lay People in the Church. A Study for a Theology of Laity* (London: 1957) informs the approach taken in this paper, especially the juxtaposition of laity as religious proletariat in the Church and of a theology of laity as a theology of the *whole Church*.

engagement with the question of power. Integrity (the question of method) and identity (the assertion of a definition or the postulation of the conditions of achieving definition) issue in the consideration of power: it is only it would seem through the latter that the vacuum can be filled and meaning imposed upon the tradition. Thus we now see that a full the reading of the *Integrity* and *Identity* texts may now represent the contemporary dilemma of Anglicanism. On this basis we may later return to the question of power, informed by the parallel we have developed.

3. *Integrity: the quest for method*

The Integrity of Anglicanism begins with a definition of systematic theology: 'By "systematic theology"', Sykes maintains, 'I mean that constructive discipline which presents the substance of the Christian faith with a claim on the minds of men.'[15] This is but one of several definitions of the nature of 'systematic theology' which have an important bearing on the course of the exposition. It is fundamental to Sykes' whole argument that the demand for *substantive* definition has, however, to be translated into a *functional* quest; thus the term 'the substance of the Christian faith' has to be understood throughout as the struggle for definition which becomes the definition itself. There is, it need hardly be emphasised, no reference made here to those contextual, structural and conflictual factors which are in reality presupposed by the terms 'constructive discipline' and 'substance of the Christian faith'.

The 'integrity' towards which Sykes strives has two meanings: it is first 'the capacity to recognise the whole identity of the aspect or institution', and 'to inquire into

[15] *Integrity*, p. ix.

ON BEING THE CHURCH

the identity of Anglicanism is to ask whether there is any internal rationale binding Anglicans together as a "Church" ';[16] and, second, it is to recognise that 'stage of moral soundness' characteristic of an institution that knows what it believes in when it accepts and moulds Christian allegiance. That 'integrity' in both senses is at the very least endangered within Anglicanism is of central importance. Whilst it is important to recognise that Sykes is consistent in his commitment to Anglican theology as the informed reflection of a world-wide communion, that is a body 'in communion with, and recognising the leadership of the see of Canterbury',[17] it is also notable that his argument is focused upon a specific articulation of the distinctiveness of Anglicanism by the English theologian, the late Bishop A. M. Ramsey. Writing in *The Gospel and the Catholic Church* Ramsey saw in the Anglican Church a balanced witness to 'Gospel and Church and sound learning', but beyond this

> . . . its greater indication lies in its pointing through its own history to something of which it is a fragment. Its credentials are its incompleteness, with the tension and turmoil at its soul. It is clumsy and untidy, it baffles neatness and logic. For it is sent not to command itself as the 'best type of Christianity', but by its very brokenness to point to the universal Church wherein all have died.[18]

This apologetic invites the riposte that mere turmoil is elevated to the level of theory; Sykes' postulation of conflict as a defining characteristic of Christianity is, however, the translation of tension and turmoil into a rationalisation of conflict manageable through a theory of power. Thus what we find in the *Integrity* text is a

[16] *Integrity*, p. 1.
[17] *Integrity*, p. 2.
[18] (London, 1936), p. 220.

sophisticated, up-dated repristination of Ramsey's position, qualified by the careful distinction that 'incompleteness is something other than incoherence',[19] and complemented with insights drawn eclectically from a variety of sources. This is then worked out in its wider application to the complex quest for the 'essence' and 'identity' of Christianity. Reformulating the earlier and pointed questions of A. E. J. Rawlinson and Hensley Henson, Sykes asks:

> Is there an Anglican theology, a proposal many have denied? Is there an Anglican method in theology, which some have affirmed while denying that there is an Anglican theology? And what in any case is the present state of the Anglican study of the doctrine of the church, and why is there so little deliberate cultivation of doctrinal or systematic theology?[20]

The answer to these questions constitute the main body of the *Integrity* but they are all ultimately underlaid, so Sykes argues, by a single issue that emerges in the final chapter where he attempts 'to face directly the question which lies behind the whole Anglican hesitancy about its self-understanding, namely the question of authority in Anglicanism'.[21] It is the transmutation of the concept of 'authority' and its eventual identification with 'power' that unites the *Integrity* and the *Identity*. It is our purpose to map out critically this structure that unifies and informs the texts in the belief that there is an insufficiently explicit consistency in a position that merits further exploration in terms of the hermeneutic of power. The focus of conflict in Anglicanism is not understood by Sykes as structural but located in the diversity of theological positions that subsist

---

[19] *Integrity*, p. 3.
[20] *Integrity*, p. 5.
[21] *Integrity*, ibid.

in the Church. The *Integrity of Anglicanism* is therefore presented as an exercise in the 'ethics of belief' which takes as axiomatic the Anglican mode of ecclesial subsistence with its institutionally sustained cohabitation of theologically incommensurable traditions. Sykes' response to this is a demand for an adequate, formal justification for this state of affairs:

> A Christian Church, which is aware of a wide variety of diverse theological positions and which deliberately decides not to adopt one or other of them, but rather to tolerate diversity, has still to offer a definite reason for doing so and to justify that reason in the face of objection. If a Church both enforces the use of a liturgy which is thoroughly stamped by a particular doctrinal inheritance, and also permits wide latitude in the professed belief of its officers, then, again, there ought to be a thorough analysis and explanation of that dual position. And my complaint against the Church of England, in particular, is that its attempts to do so hitherto have been muddled and inadequate, partly by reason of the continued use of an apologetic which patently no longer meets the situation (if it ever did) and partly because of deeply rooted failures in its programme of theological education.[22]

In this passage the basic strands of Sykes' apologetic emerge: a diversity of theological positions coexists with the enforced use of a liturgy which is itself the vehicle of the doctrinal inheritance. It is in effect necessary to redefine and clarify the relationship between freedom and authority so embodied in the Anglican Church. It is not only that 'Toleration of diversity itself need(s) to be justified theologically if it is to be able to claim any kind of integrity',[23] but that this toleration has to be conditioned by its relation to the redefined 'authority' invested in the control of, and participation in, the ongoing liturgy of the Church.

[22] *Integrity*, p. 6.
[23] *Integrity*, pp. 6–7.

Sykes begins his argument with an account in chapter 1 of the origins of the idea of 'comprehensiveness', which in the context of Anglicanism 'means simply that the Church contains in itself many elements regarded as mutually exclusive in other communions'.[24] Seen in relation to the discussion of fundamental articles and the articulation of *via media* Sykes launches what are for him ferocious attacks upon F. D. Maurice (and to a lesser extent Bishop Gore). Maurice's romantic commitment to the union of opposites and to the exclusion of systematic reflection appears, so Sykes argues, to have done little more than sanction lazy and inadequate thought and what amounts to self-deception. Most questionable was Maurice's use of the 'principle of the complementarity of apparently opposed truths'[25] and at this juncture Sykes erects theoretical criteria in the form of a realist challenge supposedly superior to that operating in the sub-rational Maurician tradition:

> Lots of contradictory things may be said by those with a vested interest in refusing to think straight. What complementarity requires, if it is so to be used in a *rational* manner, is the demonstration that both of the alleged truths are true and necessary to the proper depiction of the reality being studied.[26]

Maurice's attempted containment of the liberal impulse by its confinement to a third church party in a supposed reconciliation of conflicting viewpoints only takes place in virtue of a 'suitable process of emasculation of controversial content'.[27] This in turn has led, so Sykes fears, to the propagation of 'a tame and Anglicised *tertium quid*' alien

[24] *Integrity*, p. 8.
[25] *Integrity*, p. 19.
[26] *Integrity*, ibid.
[27] *Integrity*, ibid.

to each of the consistent traditions it purports to represent.

In chapter 2 of the *Integrity* Sykes reviews the significance of liberalism as expressed in Anglican modernism and concludes that its radicality was more appearance than reality. Thus Sanday and his associates produced what amounted to a mediating theology between 'hard line orthodoxy and wild radicalism'.[28] This notwithstanding, Sykes endorses T. S. Eliot's view that 'liberalism is a negative phenomenon, a finding of the courage and the grounds *not* to hold views frequently held in the past and invested, it may be, with the venerable authority of tradition'.[29] Anglican 'comprehensiveness' is an abuse of the principle of complementarity when it is used to permit the cohabitation of views that may be really opposed and, moreover, the effort and courage required to be positive is greater than that invested in mere negative criticism. Realism has its own higher demands and Sykes finds evidence of these in the doctrine Report of 1976 *Christian Believing*, where it was argued that:

> The issues here—on the one hand loyalty to the formulae of the Church and obedience to received truth, on the other adventurous exploration and the Church's engagement with the contemporary world—appear to point in very different directions and to reflect different conceptions of the nature of religious truth. It is, to say the least, very difficult to explain away divergences of this fundamental kind merely as complementary aspects of the many-sided wisdom of God.'[30]

The polarity emerging here between obedience to truth and adventurous exploration lends support to Sykes' contention that liberalism is not a 'party' subsumable within a

---

[28] *Integrity*, p. 27.
[29] *Integrity*, p. 32.
[30] *Christian Believing* (London, 1976), p. 38.

structure containing 'catholic' and 'protestant' groupings but a phenomenon that presents, as becomes apparent, an alternative mode of management undertaken on the assumption that, 'tolerant though the Anglican Communion has become, it has a standpoint on matters of doctrine which is firmer than seems to be the case at first sight, even if it stands in need of articulation and development'.[31]

The consequent articulation of the Anglican standpoint in chapter 3 consists in an examination of the revised 1975 Declaration of Assent at ordination and the 1976 Report *Christian Believing* which is spelt out in terms of the latter's attempt to formulate a common 'pattern', a framework within which Anglicans might co-operate; yet the Report:

> seems to have no conception of the fact that it is in itself nowhere near producing such a pattern and demonstrating how it operates, and no conception that the Anglican communion seems never to have produced a demonstration of this pattern properly applicable to its contemporary situation. The question, what binds Anglicans together, remains unanswered.[32]

Sykes' own resolution of the Anglican difficulty comes in the programmatic conclusion to the chapter:[33] breadth of toleration of internal doctrinal diversity (even to the point of contradiction) is recognised, but the focal point of what the Anglican Church stands for as an institution is moved firmly onto the level of liturgy and canon law, the content of which is to be subject to 'rigorous criticism'. Thus, by a subtle shift of emphasis, the repeated affirmation of certain doctrines, above all that of the Incarnation understood as 'the basis of dogma', is not to be understood primarily as a

[31] *Integrity*, p. 35.
[32] *Integrity*, p. 41.
[33] *Integrity*, pp. 51–2.

disputed item on the agenda of theological discussion but that on which the Church publicly stands. Thus the public liturgical transmission of the dogma provides as it were a functional justification: positive theology would in effect have to be the scrutiny of the 'function' of the dogma in the context of worship rather than through the conflictual discourse of the theologian. These aspects of Sykes' argument are combined in a contextual definition of the constructive theological task:

> Anyone can observe that the doctrine of the incarnation is basic to Anglican liturgical life as enforced by canon law. Almost anyone can, on the strength of a little theological education, write essays attacking or defending it. But it takes real theological skill to see how this doctrine both underlies and is interpreted by a worshipping body at once tolerant of theological criticism of it and yet aware of the responsibility as a matrix for the nurture of Christian character.[34]

Whether this definition is wholly true of the cohabitation of contradictory elements is open to doubt. It is questionable if any worshipping body has this level of consciousness and here we have, seen from a Hegelian standpoint, an 'optimistic' account of the reflection possible in the context of the dependent, passive *Knecht*-like status of the 'worshipping body'. Perhaps an even more apt analogy at this point would be Lukàcs' notion of 'imputed class consciousness': that is what the leadership chooses to attribute to the led. What this improbable set of assertions undoubtedly sanctions on Sykes' behalf is a pointed attack in chapter 4 upon an earlier document crucial to Anglican self-understanding, the *Report* on *Doctrine in the Church of England*, upon which William Temple set his stamp. The defence of the 'English mind' attributed to Temple and the

[34] *Integrity*, p. 52.

'poisonous arrogance' of the English dismissal of foreign influences are bad enough, but the betrayal goes further in that the complacent laziness of Anglican theologians leads Sykes to ask if it is not the case that 'their reluctance to formulate and defend Anglican theology is a serious disservice not only to their own communion, but also to the universal Church of Christ'[35] In chapter 5 Sykes reviews Anglican theological method beginning once more with a declaration by A. M. Ramsey. In 1945 the latter wrote that Anglican theology is 'neither a system nor a confession . . . but a method, a use and a direction' that resists definition but nevertheless it 'has been proved, and will be proved again, by its fruit and its works'.[36] Ramsey's setting of his re-assertion of the Anglican cultivation of scripture, tradition and reason over against the appropriation of either neo-Thomism or Barthianism in a transcendence of 'isms', Sykes treats with polite scepticism for, he maintains that:

> Anglicanism has a specific content, and that it ought to expose that content to examination and criticism; it ought also to encourage specific individuals to write systematic theologies or extended treatments of Christian doctrine.[37]

This call for intellectual action is made without any serious attention to the socio-structural factors which control the production, distribution and exchange of knowledge, save for a passing comment on the excessive burdens imposed upon tutors in theological colleges. What is, however, interesting and important is a commitment to an enhanced definition of the nature of systematic theology which

[35] *Integrity*, p. 61.
[36] 'What is Anglican Theology?', Theology XLVIII (1945). p. 2, cited *Integrity*, p. 63.
[37] *Integrity*, p. 68.

emerges from the critique of Temple, whose denial of the necessity and the desirability of a 'system of distinctively Anglican theology' is countered by Sykes' demand for reflection organised in the following terms:

> The *systematic* character of any systematic theology derives from a massive attempt at consistency in reasoning, an attempt whose seriousness can be gauged either by the sophistication of its philosophical equipment or by relation of each and every feature of the doctrinal structure to a fundamental understanding of divine revelation.[38]

Such reflection should, moreover, have an epistemology and an ontology and, in addition, express the attempt to create a uniform vocabulary. Sykes has set a high standard for those like himself who would venture out of the narrow English parochialism epitomised by Temple into the higher reaches of a putative Anglican systematic theology.

The concluding chapters 6 and 7 of the *Integrity* contain a modest and as it were experimental enactment of the reinvigoration of the theological tradition with regard to the doctrine of the Church and 'authority', respectively. The effective educational relegation of ecclesiology to 'non-fundamental' status because of its contentious nature did not impede, as Sykes rightly notes, the longstanding and highly questionable defence on both theological and historical grounds of the institution of the threefold ministry. Regarded in historical perspective Sykes' only comment upon these pretensions, that whereas 'it is true that Anglicans have consistently defended the retention of episcopacy for a variety of reasons, it is an innovation to suggest that Anglicans have regarded any particular theological interpretation of episcopacy as essential',[39] has

[38] *Integrity*, p. 57.
[39] *Integrity*, p. 84.

proved highly judicious, almost prescient in the light of intervening events. Sykes' exposure of the polemical use of the 'appeal to the historic Episcopate' as a 'direct challenge to the traditional theory of fundamentals' by Anglicans associated with the volume *Catholicity*[40] would appear to make it impossible to invest in the office of bishop anything remotely approaching an absolute validation of theological meaning or truth, given the emergent subordination of free theological reflection to the critical guardianship of the liturgy. This relatively low view of the episcopate would explain, in principle, Sykes' non-intervention in the bitter public controversy surrounding Dr David Jenkins' (the present Bishop of Durham) apparent dismissal of certain doctrines regarded as central to the tradition by significant groups in the Church. The truth-functional apparatus erected around the office of the bishop in minds of those whose religious security was rocked in the controversy could be seen as a mistaken conception when seen from Sykes' standpoint precisely because it did not touch upon the real 'power-base' of the Church in the liturgy and its management. Consistent with this concentration upon the dichotomy between theological reflection (and thus public controversy) as such and the pragmatics of ecclesiological power invested in the governance of the liturgy is an emphatic concentration upon the interpretation and magisterial theological rationalisation of existing structures and practice:

> The weakness of modern Anglican ecclesiology may be in part traced to the disrepute into which certain passionately held dogmas fell when exposed to historical criticism; but it must also be traced to the chronic reluctance of Anglicans to accept the fact that what they have inherited as institutions and practices in the

[40] (London, 1947).

179

Church unencumbered with sharply defined theoretical baggage has profound theological, especially ecclesiological significance *as such*. And it is only the theological exploration of the significance of such an inheritance which will begin to establish Anglicanism on lines significant for the future of the world-wide Church, not only on the bogus grounds of its status as a so-called 'bridge church', but on the grounds of its capacity to submit its inheritance to a searching theological appraisal.[41]

It is at this juncture that the local, internal difficulties within Anglicanism and the distinct gift that this tradition brings forth to the wider ecumenical community distinguish themselves. Thus, on the one hand, the Church has to devise new means of containing the conflict between the pursuit of theological reflection and the imperative demands of the 'norm of tradition' transmitted within the liturgy; and, on the other, Anglicanism by virtue of its wholehearted recognition of the inevitability of conflict within the Church offers this realisation to a wider ecclesial public. In the seventh and final chapter on authority in Anglicanism Sykes starts out with qualified approval from the 1948 Lambeth Conference Report on authority and paraphrases it as follows: 'authority is both singular, in that it derives from the mystery of the divine Trinity, and plural, in that it is distributed in numerous, organically related elements',[42] and he thereby places a distinct interpretation upon the notion of 'dispersed authority' that the statement contains. The realistic recognition within this text of the inevitability of conflict within the Church and the control placed upon potential tyranny through the 'mutually supporting, and mutually checking, life-process'[43] of dispersed authority contrasts, so Sykes

[41] *Integrity*, p. 85.
[42] *Integrity*, p. 87.
[43] *Integrity*, ibid.

argues, with the documents of the Second Vatican Council one of whose chief weaknesses is a conspicuous failure to expect conflict in the Church. It is, 'in such a situation that the whole Anglican history of the experience of conflict is ... of potentially great service.'[44] Sykes' second major book, *The Identity of Christianity* is effectively the translation of formal reflection upon the inevitability of conflict within the Church (evident from its New Testament origins) into a proposed resolution of the quest for the 'essence' or 'identity' of Christianity itself.

The major thesis adumbrated above is subordinated in Sykes' text to the immediate conclusion in which he clarifies the emerging juxtaposition of the theological reflection that manifests acute conflictual diversity on the one hand and, on the other, the contingent, managerial necessities of sustaining the continuity, direction and stability of the liturgical enactment of the tradition and its norms. The second cluster of issues is dealt with first in such a way as to implicate, however implausibly (along lines directly reminiscent of Newman), the laity:

> The point which I am concerned to sustain is that it is of the essence of the Anglican view of authority that it should be maintained in principle that the means of judging matters concerning the faith are in the hands of the whole people of God by reason of their access to the scriptures; and further, that it is distinctly Anglican that this means is given to them in the liturgy of the Church, backed by canon law.[45]

It is not our concern at this juncture to determine what precisely might be the socio-ecclesiological cash-value of the maintenance 'in principle' of the means of judging matters concerning the faith, except to observe that the role

[44] *Integrity*, p. 89.
[45] *Integrity*, p. 93.

of the 'whole people of God' is in effect identified with passive receptivity over against the agency of the donor. The reasons for conflict in matters of faith arise, so Sykes argues, not least from the inadequacy of language: 'those who preach the gospel are committed to making plain in words, and words are inherently and necessarily ambiguous'.[46] Whether this is a general remark about the imperfect character of all human verbal communication or a defect peculiar to theological reflection is not made clear. Much is made of the duty of careful discernment incumbent upon the Christian: both laity and clergy are as it were underpinned by the 'essentially conservative' character of liturgies and hymns which, Sykes asserts, puts them in a 'very powerful position when there break out, in the ordinary course of events, controversies as to Christian belief and practice'.[47] That such an assertion has, given the passive receptive role of those implicated in a conservative-tending liturgy, a misleadingly rhetorical tone is apparent to the author, who concedes that this is 'essentially a conservative position, unless steps are taken to ensure the theological education of the laity and their incorporation into the corporate decisions of the Church'.[48] This account of the role of the whole Church in relation to the liturgy is conceived almost exclusively in terms of the logic of conferral, marginally tinged with sympathy for the un-realisable and un-Anglican congregationalist ideal. Sykes characterises the place of the laity with succinct clarity: their role is essentially conservative as 'an element checking the power of Church leaders and theologians or, at the most, sharing (as in contemporary synodical government) in the process of decision-making on a carefully restricted

[46] *Integrity*, ibid.
[47] *Integrity*, p. 95.
[48] *Integrity*, ibid.

basis'.[49] In its fundamental structure this relationship is in the main one of agent and patient, of actor and reacted upon, of definer of theological reality and one upon whose behalf reality is defined; it is in short that of Lord and Bondsman. It is a polarity peripherally modified by the power to block excess, but it is never the power to act or innovate. A semantic collision takes place between the ever more strident rhetoric used to 'empower' the essentially static and conservative character of the liturgy itself and the actual decision-making processes affecting particular liturgies:

> Thus, for Anglicans, it still remains the case that the liturgy of the Church creates the power base for the Christian community as a whole. This was so in the early Church, and with the gift of the scriptures in the vernacular, it becomes still more the case in Anglicanism. And the conclusion for contemporary Anglicanism must be that what is enforced in the liturgies of the Church is the most powerful tool in the hands of ordinary clergy and the laity for resisting innovations which have no right to parity of esteem or equality of consideration when compared with the established traditions. Hence the decision-making process whereby liturgies are changed, as they must be with time, is the basic seat of authority in the Anglican Church, and the basic exercise of that authority is the power to enforce the liturgy.[50]

This somewhat heavy-handed exposition of the pragmatics of liturgical power which moves from the near rhetorical exaltation of the static conservative, resistive 'power' of the ordinary clergy and the laity by a series of steps to the statement of active *espicopal* power hidden in the final sentence, contrasts markedly with the depiction of the theologian, whose creative discrimination generates what may prove troublesome attempted innovation. The

[49] *Integrity*, p. 96.
[50] *Integrity*, ibid.

183

Christian, and here Sykes must surely have in mind the Christian with informed theological understanding:

> must exercise his judgement . . . But to put some flesh on the bones one might add that this judgement is like the judgement a novelist has to exercise when he or she brings a character to a particularly dramatic set of circumstances and must offer a plausible account of the character's response. It must be plausible in the sense that the character must act out of the resources which the novelist has created in earlier parts of the book and within the general limits of human psychology. In such a judgement there is both a predictable and a creative element, and the skill of a novelist lies in his ability to make the most of the fact that characters are interesting not because their actions can be predicted with certainty, but because the interaction of event and character creates genuine novelty.[51]

Whilst this analogy is readily adaptable to the pursuit of theology in the narrative mode, and the 'church has to act in character'[52] in relation to such resources, these latter are not in and of themselves authorities. Again resorting to the notion of 'process' introduced into the Anglican context in the Lambeth Conference Report of 1948, Sykes advances what can be construed as an eschatological dialectic of authority, a relationship with 'authority' which is subtly but significantly redefined in passing as 'norms of authority'. A behavioural and functional account of unending engagement with these 'norms' expands and arbitrarily displaces 'authority' itself onto the plane of the transcendental:

> While formally speaking, scripture, tradition and reason are norms of authority, the processes of decision-making in the Christian Church are never completed. Decision-making is not,

[51] *Integrity*, p. 97.
[52] *Integrity*, p. 98.

therefore, a matter of balancing one authority against another nor of holding authorities in tension, as Anglican writing has sometimes suggested. There is only one source of authority which is the freedom and love of the Triune God. In human life, in scripture, in the creeds, in the decisions of councils, in the liturgical order and canon law, in Church leadership, there is only the discovery of authority, not its embodiment.[53]

This amounts to a *reductio ad absurdum* of the idea of 'authority'; the concept is driven into a dialectical impasse as problematic in its own way as the extreme immediate pre-Reformation nominalist doctrine of justification. In this quasi-nominalist account of authority the 'norms of authority' identified with the dispersed elements of the Christian Church are understood as the diverse occasions of the 'discovery of authority'. One reading of this position would be to regard Sykes' argument as a quasi-Barthian investiture of the broken fragments of Anglicanism with an occasionalist authoritarianism. The 'dispersal' of the 'norms of authority' is effected with some thoroughness, notably as regards the episcopate which is strictly reduced, in a reworking of brokenness reminiscent of Ramsey, to 'oversight' (*episcope*) and to 'the interpretation of a partial and broken symbol of the continuity of faith'.[54] So perish episcopal pretensions inasmuch as they purport to depend upon authority in terms of a historical transmission or continuity of embodiment or possession of a peculiar donation of the Holy Spirit. Conversely, the ground is prepared for the rebirth of 'authority' as immediate, that is 'real' power.

So we may initially conclude that what Sykes has in effect executed is analogous to a dismissal of any realist theory of *transmitted* authority within Christianity. It is in

[53] *Integrity*, ibid.
[54] *Integrity*, ibid.

the context of a broken, incomplete collectivity at the centre of which is celebrated the ongoing liturgy of the Word that an authority-directed activity nevertheless takes place. There is, however, nothing which in and of itself *is* authority (it is merely a 'norm of authority'); but on occasions authority is 'discovered'. This latter discernment is not assimilated into a fully consistent 'Barthian' position, that is to the divine foreordination and construction of the subjective receptive capacity as well as its objective correlate in the Word. The 'discovery of authority' demands the capacity of discernment; that which is authoritative must be identified on the basis of its having an identity. The very dispersed nature of authority in Anglicanism universalises at a stroke its translation into 'norms of authority'; thus the alternative locations of authority taken up within other traditions are all equally open to this critique. Sykes, through his pursuit of the 'integrity' of Anglicanism, has confronted the wider Church and Christianity with the question as to its identity. The role of the theologian as the informed agent of discrimination emerges out of the romantic intuition of the analogy of novelist into the actuality of becoming the vehicle of life-giving insight into the identity of Christianity itself. This is an ambitious reformulation of the historic theological destiny of the Anglican Communion in relation to the world-wide Church. The dismissal of received authority as the basis of identity has now taken place and the conflict-laden quest for identity is to become the identity of Christianity itself. These proposals are of profound and far-reaching consequence, not least for the understanding of 'power' which is itself the leit-motif that displaces in turn the preoccupation with identity as such. How the judicious reader ought to interpret this progression is an issue yet to be addressed.

4. Identity: the assertion of essence

The *Identity of Christianity* is a substantial work consisting of three sections: the first is primarily theoretical; the second contains detailed studies of relevant aspects of the work of Schleiermacher, Newman, Harnack and Loisy, Troeltsch and lastly Barth; the third is largely a reworking and clarification of the earlier material. There is on all levels an increase in conceptual complexity in comparison with the *Integrity* in that the consideration of 'authority', transformed at the end of the earlier work, is now displaced into an explicit 'sub-plot'[55] involved in the analysis and prescriptive exposition of the concept of 'power'. Thus we learn in the introduction that although there is an apparently old-fashioned ring about the 'essence of Christianity' controversy, the author's specific purpose is to excavate from this discussion lessons applicable to the present. This is, as compared with the *Integrity*, theology in a new key, for the criteria employed are not merely historical but philosophical: in particular, recognition of the decline of the quest for the essence of Christianity into the 'essentialist fallacy', here interpreted as an error characteristic of those who place too high a premium upon modes of cognition, is axiomatic. Thus the 'essence' quest stands as an unresolved dilemma, that is as threatened by the hostile alternatives of historicism and by the descent into subjectivism. The necessarily conflictual character of this dilemma and its emergence (as illustrated by the historical examples) provides the main scenario in the *Identity*. As in the *Integrity* it was necessary to ask whether there was a distinctive Anglican theology or method, so on this more exalted level two basic and analogous questions emerge:

[55] It is this 'sub-plot' that is here interpreted as the 'structure' of Sykes' text, see note 2 above.

'What, then, *is* Christianity? Another way of putting the same question would be to ask directly, Do the differences between Christians matter:'[56] There is, however, a deeper intention, what Sykes calls a 'sub-plot' and this is an extended preoccupation with 'power' which consistently reflects the transitional interface between 'authority' in the *Integrity* and its corresponding transvaluation in the *Identity*:

> One of the themes of the book concerns the responsibility of the Christian theologian in his exercise of power in the Church, a power which resides in his or her articulacy, or power to communicate. I hold that a theologian must communicate to other than fellow theologians, and that clarification of meaning is one of the few justifications for occupying valuable time and money in the production and reading of works of scholarship.[57]

This characterisation of 'power' moves in some respects beyond the polarity that became visible in the *Integrity* between theology as free-ranging creative reflection upon the Christian character in the context of the narrative mode on the one hand, and on the other the strict control and interpretation of the 'norms of authority' dispersed within the Church but focused primarily in the liturgy and worship. Here the understanding of power bears some affinity with Habermas' conception of power as communicative action, exercised here in relation to semantic clarification undertaken on the part of a wider community. Such an explication does of course presuppose a complex set of social relations related to educational access and the distribution of resources; for the intellectual hegemony here articulated is apparently regarded as 'value-free' as regards its context in social stratification (and this is perhaps a little surprising on the part of a socialist writer).

[56] *Identity*, p. 4.
[57] *Identity*, ibid.

The effective formulation of a theory of power expressed in 'communicative action' and 'instrumental reason' (the 'power to communicate' and 'clarification of meaning', respectively) reflects a 'managerial', interpretative approach to social polarisation, not surprisingly alien to a more critical Marxist or Neo-Marxist analysis. Seen from the latter standpoint Sykes' conception of the theologian has a strongly ideological ring to it: the theologian orchestrates and refines the ideological superstructure of the Church, indeed hierarchy is conceptually translatable into intellectual hegemony.[58] It is, of course, precisely this latter danger, seen in the possibility of a 'tyrannous use of intellectual power'[59] to which Sykes is alert, but his explanation of the phenomenon takes the form of an incomprehensible allusion to the fragmentation of knowledge in the modern era understood as a cause of a theologian's over-estimation of his or her significance. There is here yet again no critical awareness of the hegemony embodied within the text itself: this is effectively suppressed by the diversion into pluralism. It is the intrinsic character of the interconnection of knowledge and power as *domination* that can provide a far more realistic account of the basis of this 'tyranny' than Sykes is prepared to concede. Thus it is that the essence/identity discussion overlies a sub-plot concerned with power and directed at the reconstruction of Christian praxis; it is the prescriptive, rather than the merely analytical and illustrative status of this proposal that encourages this reader to accord it ultimacy in the appraisal and construal of the strategy present in the *Identity* text:

[58] Antonio Gramsci's conception of 'hegemony' as a group or class creating a state of affairs in which their leadership and privileged position seem natural is relevant here.

[59] *Identity*, p. 7.

The purpose, therefore, of the sub-plot is to place the discipline of theology and the expertise of the theologian in an explicitly new relation to the total phenomenon of Christian identity, concerned as a body with unavoidable and restless internal conflicts.[60]

The exploration of the 'identity' issue is in effect the illustration and justification of the necessity of this relocation of the expertise of the theologian and thus of his power. The 'sub-text' of the *Identity* has thus a dual role: on the one hand it functions as a structure in relation to which the illustrative, clarificatory material concerned in the 'identity' is organised; on the other it provides the prescriptive conclusions, the translation of theory into practice. The 'structure' determines the direction of the argument which is reinforced and justified by oblique excursions into the 'identity' exemplifications in which the concept of 'conflict' is encapsulated as in a 'mediation', ostensibly an encounter with that which constitutes reality. Indeed, in apparent contradiction to Sykes' own definitions of the nature of *systematic* theology,[61] he resists global consistency: 'I do not claim here to have any general theory up my sleeve to explain why these features of Christian profession . . . should be of such importance'.[62] It will be suggested that this hesitancy *has* to be part of the strategy in the *Identity* if the author is to resist the discovery of the latencies within his text and to retain a grasp upon a position so radically equivocal in the light of the wider contextual critique formulated below. In other

[60] *Identity*, p. 8.

[61] 'The systematic character of any systematic theology derives from a massive attempt at consistency in reasoning, an attempt whose seriousness can be gauged either by sophistication of its philosophical equipment or by relation of each and every feature of the outward structure to a fundamental understanding of divine revelation', *Integrity*, p 57. Judged by his own criteria Sykes can be understood to have partly succeeded, provided 'divine revelation' is identified with 'power'.

[62] *Identity*, p. 8.

words undue recognition of the real 'structure' of the text would demand an interpretative act the consequences of which might well contravene the overt conclusion drawn by the author on the basis of a skilful, but ultimately misguided concatenation of proposals. As will become clear, the peremptory dismissal of contra-indicative evidence or conflicting standpoints becomes comprehensible when the restrictive, artificially contained character of the argument is analysed in the structural context of the hermeneutics of power, understood in terms of the universality of the Hegelian dialectic of aggrandisement. As against this, the virtual dismissal of the 'will of truth' – that is the textual subordination of the pursuit of truth to the manipulation of 'meaning' – and the marginally limited theory of the management of theological power constitute the least acceptable aspects of these proposals.

The first part of the *Identity* begins with an extended account of identity and conflict in early Christianity in which the author, using recent sociological studies of the New Testament, demonstrates that conflict is intrinsic within the tradition. Consequently:

> I shall argue that any realistic account of Christian phenomenon strongly suggests the inconceivability of there ever being complete agreement about the identity of Christianity. That is not to say that Christians may not be able to contain disagreement within reasonable boundaries. But contained diversity is, in fact, what unity amounts to.[63]

Sykes integrates into his study an analytical model of religion drawn from Ninian Smart and this serves him well. Smart's six-dimensional model is admirably suited to Sykes' approach because it expands the structure of a given

---

[63] *Identity*, p. 11.

religion and distinguishes categories and aspects without admitting excessively complex accounts as to how these aspects might interact. Thus the distinction, crucial to the argument, between the 'inner' and 'external' aspects of Christianity draws upon Smart's approach without the charges of mutual reduction or antagonism inevitable should a less 'value-free' and incommensurable set of analytical insights (drawn from Marx, Weber, Durkheim, Freud, Levi-Strauss *et al.*) have been built into the model. Thus whilst Sykes' method as applied to the 'generalisation' of New Testament material would, according to his own criteria, be indicative that he is writing 'systematic theology',[64] his use of the Smart schemata would indicate that he is not, at this stage at least, prepared to function in terms of a wider intellectual dialogue. The presentation of the New Testament materials is suggestive and illuminating, especially in the demonstration that stratified developments involve ambiguity. There is no primal unity in the tradition from which diversity is a deviation, even the teaching of Jesus 'has certain ambiguities which will give rise to different interpretations'.[65] The hermeneutical correlation between the New Testament era and Sykes' understanding of the present task of the theologian is remarkable (even if, perhaps, unintended):

> The view of Jesus' intentions ... is one which emphasises the possibility for the transformation of a religious tradition by a simultaneous retention of the core-meaning of a familiar term combined with novel treatment of its conventional associations, supported by particularly significant actions.[66]

---

[64] See *Identity*, p. 12–13.
[65] *Identity*, p. 23.
[66] *Identity*, p. 19.

Where Sykes is less satisfying is in his evaluation of
St. Paul's constant, seemingly obsessive concern with unity
in a Christian context which has, the reader is informed,
always and everywhere only been susceptible to unity
understood as contained diversity. The juxaposition of the
Pauline lust for unity and the conflictual diversity of the
empirical early communities can only be understood in
terms of the quasi-sociological explanation later educed on
the basis of Troeltsch's understanding of the transitional
steps in the development of the Church. There is no
eschatological 'discovery of unity' proposed here corresponding to the 'discovery of authority' posited at the end
of the *Integrity*. This hesitance is the more significant when
the extraordinarily important role of the Pauline language
and conceptuality of unity in eucharistic, liberation, and
ecumenical theology is taken into account. Moreover,
given the earlier isolation of the 'one source of authority
which is the freedom and love of the triune God'[67] in the
Integrity, the contrast between Pauline 'unity' and Sykes'
realistic and pragmatic 'contained diversity' is uneasy and
would merit further critical exploration. In addition,
consistent construal of Christianity as Schleiermacher
envisaged it, that is as through and through polemical,
carries with it obvious dangers of retrojection and retro-
spective over-determination.

So far Sykes has argued that the sources of conflict are
understood to stem from the inadequacy of words as a
medium of communication and from the ambiguities
inherent in a tradition transformed by the 'simultaneous
retention of the core meaning of a familiar term combined
with novel treatment of its conventional associations'.[68]

[67] *Identity*, p. 98.
[68] *Identity*, p. 19.

Whilst under certain circumstances *some* sources of conflict *might* so originate, it is fundamental to an informed sociological and critical perspective that the sources of conflict lie outside language and are *perceived* in the inadequacies of language. In concrete terms the sociological intepretation of the contemporary Church and its forerunner in the New Testament depends upon the analysis of class structure and hierarchy and their influence upon belief and adherence. It is difficult to understand Sykes' resistance to theory at this juncture given his definition of the nature of systematic theology.[69] An even more implausible source of conflict is postulated which again diverts attention away from the structure of power implicit within the *Identity* text. This purportedly more potent source of conflict is a dialectic intrinsic within Christianity which consists in the tension between the inner and external aspects of the phenomena of the Christian religion. For Sykes, the primary thrust of Christian polemicism is located in inwardness; for Christianity, 'its only chance of making clear what its own innermost nature is is by unmasking every false morality, or corrupt thinking, or impoverished religion'. So it is that the polemical character is not merely as it were external, but internal, for as Jesus himself (authentically) indicated, he brought a sword 'and by that he meant that the religion he founded would essentially be characterised by an unrelenting struggle for purity of intention'.[70] Out of these elements is constructed the core dialectic of Christianity which is to be understood as a struggle between inwardness and external manifestation spelt out in terms of the following schematic cycle. The first moment consists in the inevitable conflict; the second moment is the serious

[69] See note 61, above.
[70] *Identity*, p. 29.

struggle for purity of intention in response to diversity; the third moment is the enactment of the guidance necessary in cases of dispute, in short 'authority' is 'discovered'. Once more the 'conflict' here outlined is interpretable in Hegelian terms of a premature resolution of the dialectic in favour of the Lord's 'moment' in which reality is discovered and thus imposed without passage through the cycle of self-discovery postulated in the full theory of power.

In the second chapter of the *Identity* concerned with the tradition of inwardness, Sykes enlarges upon the factors that justify his isolation of 'inwardness' as the determinative core of the tradition. That virtual *autonomy* is accorded to inwardness (justified in relation to its origins in the teaching on the 'heart'in Old and New Testaments) is a step taken that demands some additional justification[71] without which the material that follows remains the illustration of a carefully unexplored position. The autonomous status of inwardness and the spirituality of conversion derived from the Psalms and Paul's conception of 'the inmost self' is qualified through an alternative scheme provided by H. Mol's study of identity and the sacred[72], a work of considerable importance to any theologian or Church official entrusted with the functional maintenance of a religion in a hostile, secularising context. Mol's analysis provides Sykes with some sense of a wider setting, but this is strictly subordinated to the formulation of an account of Christian reflection showing 'a characteristic oscillation between emphasis upon inward transformation,

[71] For a critical treatment of 'inwardness' see T. W. Adorno, *Kierkegaard Konstruktion des Ästhetischen, Gesammelte Schriften* (Frankfurt am Main, 1962) vol. 2, chs. 2 and 3.

[72] *Identity and the Sacred: A Sketch of a New Social-Scientific Theory of Religion* (Agincourt, 1976). The conservative orientation of this book admirably reinforces Sykes' position in a defence of religion as structural integration as opposed to alienation.

and an emphasis upon the importance of the cult, with a large number of possible ways of conceiving the relationship between the two'.[73] Despite the use of Mol's analysis, Sykes' argument is grounded upon a restricted categorial basis, scarcely expanded when he makes his first substantial references to Augustine and his understanding of the relation of heart and sacrifice in worship[74]. Sykes' narrow dual categorial plank projects over the the abyss of legitimate complexity such as that explored, for example, by John Bowker in *The Sense of God*,[75] a book which tends to expose the non-dialectical character of Smart's six-dimensional account of religion. The reader is bound at this juncture to inquire after the existence here of a developed epistemology and ontology, the necessary components of a true systematic theology in the terms indicated by Sykes himself. In earlier post-Enlightenment generations the assumption by a theologian of a narrow categorial base and the consequent 'reconstruction' of all the loci was a permitted strategy; it is a rank implausibility to attempt this procedure within the confines of a restricted and largely uncritical advocacy of Anglican piety rearticulated in terms of the assertion of the dimension of 'inwardness'. The absence of a theory of knowledge operable within the context of the human sciences and the purely assertive basis upon which theological claims are made places enormous weight upon the solution Sykes is to propose: the theory of theological power.

[73] *Identity*, p. 42.

[74] It is not clear how Sykes would reconcile his anthropological account of sacrifice made elsewhere with the principle of self-extinction proposed in the *Identity*, see 'Sacrifice in the New Testament and Christian Theology' in M. F. C. Bourdillon, M. Fortes *Sacrifice* (London, 1980), esp. pp. 80.ff.

[75] *The Sense of God: Sociological, Anthropological and Psychological Approaches to the Origin of the Sense of God* (Oxford, 1973). The major works of Eliade and van der Leeuw are also relevant.

5. Power: the transvaluation of authority

It is the third chapter of the *Identity* on power in the Church which contains the pivotal arguments; it is here that the fundamental hypothesis comprised in the sub-plot emerges most fully. Having established to his satisfaction that conflict was inevitable in a Christian movement containing inherent ambiguities from its inception, and that Christianity itself suffers from the pressure of constant revision of its externals on the basis of its inwardness, Sykes repeats the less than satisfactory inadequacy–of–words argument and concludes that 'diversity . . . is the norm for Christianity',[76] a state of affairs overlaid often enough by the rhetoric of unity. The main body of the chapter and its four-stage argument contains: first, a consideration of the problems of authority following the death of St. Paul; second, an account of Troeltsch's explanation of how the concentration of power took place in the early community; third, a general presentation of the theme of power in the New Testament; and fourth, the development of the implications of these factors for the contemporary management of power in the Christian Church. Before embarking on this, Sykes proposes a crucial *identification* of authority with power without which the whole general hypothesis would collapse. As noted earlier the dissolution of authority into 'norms of authority' took place at the end of the *Integrity* in conjunction with a move from essentialist definition to the designation of meaning through use. The functional definition of 'power' demonstrated in the control of the liturgical 'power-base' of the Church displaced any essentialist fictions contained in the notion of a historically-transmitted authority. It is therefore entirely consistent

[76] *Identity*, p. 52.

that the conceptual definition of 'authority' and 'power', drawing upon the wider discussion of the concepts in sociology and political philosophy, should comprise an effective *identity* between the terms and reveal, moreover, a shared intrinsic meaning which is compatible with and assimilable into the remaining steps in argument of the *Identity*. The earlier theological replacement of 'authority' by 'power' through the quasi-nominalistic reduction of the former and its displacement by the functionally-defined latter is therefore underpinned by a further, somewhat brief, conceptual survey[77] which merits close examination because it is the fulcrum around which the whole argument of the sub-plot, latent in the *Integrity* and explicit in the *Identity*, in fact turns.

In this brief transitional passage the author would appear to succeed in reinforcing his emancipation of Christianity from the trammels of its now disputed past by a reformulation of a 'discovery of authority' embodied in a new spirituality of real, managerial power exercised in the discriminating agency of the theologian and through the rejuvenated command structure of the Church itself, that is of the higher clergy. The embodiment of authority in its 'command-obedience connotation' in the authority of the clergy as 'quite frequently legitimate, that is based in the mutual acknowledgement of the divine sense of authority, and then the right to command and obligation to obey'[78] might perhaps be surprising to the less than percipient reader, but given the absolutely crucial *identification* of authority and power, it is entirely consistent and evidence of the integrity of the *systematic* drive and *structure* in the text itself. It is on this basis that a newly-found confidence in the power of God is won and a consequent celebration

[77] *Identity*, p. 54.
[78] *Identity*, ibid.

of power may take place. There is proposed a renewed fusion of charismatic power with Church office in a 'repetition' of the Christian gospel in principle adequate to our chaotic, pluralistic times. All of this would only seem possible, both in theory and in practice if we acknowledge, following Sykes, the identity of authority and power. Are we bound, however, to accept such a crucial identity? Are there not indeed certain dangers in such a redefinition of charismatic 'authority' as power in the Christian Church? How, indeed, might such a theology of the celebration of power develop as the latter clearly offers a category far more suggestive, complex and pervasive in human experience than a theology determined through mere inwardness might indicate?

Sykes' treatment of the distinction of power and authority is brief but decisive and consists in the reiteration of D. H. Wrong's definition of power and the listing of the sub-headings of the third chapter of the latter's recent book[79]. The sheer complexity of the history, contextual determination and analytical treatment of authority and power is, however, revealed in Lukes' survey[80] to which reference is also made in footnotes. The importance of contextual factors is particularly important in the religious understanding of the authority-power relation and the emergent conception in the *Identity* has affinities with a

[79] D. H. Wrong, *Power, Its Forms, Bases and Uses* (Oxford, 1979), see chapter 3.

[80] H. S. Lukes in 'Power and Authority' in T. Bottomore and R. Nisbett (eds), *A History of Sociological Analysis* (London, 1979) takes a contextual as opposed to Wrong's more discursive line of analysis. The many-sided, even eclectic character of Sykes' proposals about power is evident given the partial applicability of so many concepts of power to them. Future work will have to take account of Michael Mann's *The Sources of Social Power* (Cambridge, 1986) vol. 1, esp. ch. 10 which lays strong emphasis upon the role of Christianity as a means of ideological integration.

number of other examples, for example: Hobbes (the 'Great Definer'), Simmel (the stress on super- and subordination), Luhmann (a systems theory approach in which power can be conceptualised as a medium of communication), Weber (inequality and dependence as phenomena of the distribution of power within a community), Daniel Bell (authority based upon competence), and so on. The initial many-sidedness of Sykes' discussion of the authority-power relation up unto this point is then decisively simplified. The relatively weak definition of power (derived by Wrong from Bertrand Russell) and reiterated by Sykes, that power is simply 'the capacity of some persons to produce intended and foreseen effects on others' does not in fact correspond with the demands of the identity of authority and power promulgated in the *Identity*, which would in reality be far better served by the stronger Weberian definition. Weber maintain that power is 'the probability that one actor within a social relationship will be in a position to carry out his own will despite resistance, regardless of the basis upon which this probability rests'[81] and this would be congruent with the distinctive 'command-obedience connotation' attributed by Sykes to 'authority'. Thus the categorisation of types of authority and the structure and justification of its enactment have implications which verge upon the authoritarian. Sykes asserts that:

> Authority may be coercive, induced, legitimate, competent, or personal. In religion the authority of the clergy is quite frequently legitimate, that is based on the initial acknowledgement of the divine source of authority, and thus of the right to command and obligation to obey. It may also be personal, indeed charismatic in the precise sense; quite often personal and other forms of authority are combined in a single instance.[82]

[81] *Economy and Society* (vol. 1), p. 53, cited in Lukes, op. cit., p. 638.
[82] *Identity*, p. 54.

'Accordingly', Sykes concludes, 'so far as the use of terms in this chapter is concerned, Paul's authority is an exercise of power.'[83] The above extended statement is descriptive rather than analytical; but, beyond this, it certainly has prescriptive implications. In terms of the overall conception it is impossible to interpret this passage as anything other than a straightforward identification of authority and power. The basic point made is that there cannot be a *'mutual* acknowledgement of the divine source of authority' grounded in a historically and socially transmitted source (because this is ambiguous and conflictual) but only a quasi-charismatic assertion and reception, a discovery and an acknowledgement of divine power; this is the equivalent in the new context of the 'discovery of authority' proposed at the end of the *Integrity*. Sykes' formulation of the conception of authority and its transvaluation into a depiction of power bears a more than passing resemblance to his understanding of Jesus' own hermeneutical method, which, it may be recalled, 'emphasises the possibility for the transformation of a religious tradition by a simultaneous retention of the core-meaning of a familiar term combined with novel treatment of its conventional associations as supported by particularly significant actions'.[84] Sykes' sensitive remarks that, 'It is a common misunderstanding that in order to be powerful one has to be self-assertive' for 'On the contrary, great power can be exercised by those who locate the origin of their authority outside themselves, in God',[85] are fully commensurate with his sophisticated re-installation of the charismatically endowed, but institutional and legally-sanctioned office-bearer who will discern and define the

[83] *Identity*, ibid.
[84] *Identity*, p. 19.
[85] *Identity*, pp. 54–5.

identity of Christianity in his context and act (i.e. command) accordingly.

The following analysis of the highly complex and contentious area of the interpretation of the history of the organisation of the early Church consists of a critical review of Hans von Campenhausen's distinction between Paul and Clement's understanding of authority and the sacralisation of subordination, 'order here for him (i.e. Clement) became an abstract and autonomous principle of an abstract (sic) kind'.[86] According to Sykes, von Campenhausen removed Paul's theological position from its social setting and underestimated the chronic power vacuum left by the departure of the so-called 'apostles'.[87] The real difficulty in Clement's claims to authority (the setting of which is remarkably similar to Sykes' depiction of the present situation) is 'that *all* external norms, including authoritative persons, have to exercise their discrimination on matters concerning the inwardness of the Christian life'.[88] The sociological deficiences of von Campenhausen were to a considerable degree remedied by Troeltsch, whose three stage theory of early Church development earns whole-hearted approval. Troeltsch's scheme has three stages: first, Jesus' teaching focused in the idea of God; second, the rise out of this of a Christ-cult enjoining faith in Christ; and third, most crucially, a displacement of the Pneuma-Christ by the episcopate. This displacement is of considerable importance as it brings Sykes' own argument to the point at which it is possible to isolate and define the locus of the power that is itself the agent of definition. In Troeltsch's words:

[86] *Identity*, p. 57.
[87] *Identity*, p. 58.
[88] *Identity*, p. 59.

In a concrete way the episcopate was substituted for the earlier faith in the Exalted Christ and the Spirit: it is the succession of Christ and of the Apostle, the Bearer of the Spirit, the extension or externalising of the Incarnation, a visible and tangible proof of the Divine Truth and Power, the concrete presence of the sociological point of reference.[89]

It was precisely an analogous attempted repetition of such a displacement in the face, not of the departure of Jesus, the death of the Apostles and the consequent power vacuum, but of an ambiguous decline in the reality of a high Christology in the face of historicism, philosophical critique and secularising pressures, which has been, it was suggested at the outset of this paper, a fundamental feature of twentieth century English Anglican theology. Sykes' apparent reluctance to concede any particular theory of the episcopate in the face of the many earlier attempts at such a formulation was but a hesitation in the face of undue particularism. Being aware of the dangers implicit in the consequences of Troeltsch's acute analysis of displacement, Sykes asks (but significantly does not answer) the question as to whether it is true that 'the episcopate *replaces* faith in the exalted Christ?' Troeltsch's account is not disputed in principle, it is, he argues, inadequate to the complexity of the question of power in the primitive Church. In the third section of his consideration of power in the Church, Sykes' generalised presentation of the New Testament materials appears as a lightly modified schematic structure borrowed from Troeltsch: first, the power implication of the kingdom teaching of Jesus; second, the power conferred on Jesus' followers; third, power as understood in the Pauline and deutero-Pauline writings. The review of the New Testament materials is informed by the appropriation of

[89] O. Wyon (tr.), *The Social Teaching of the Christian Churches* (London, 1931) p. 32, cited *Identity*, p. 63.

C. K. Barrett's analysis of the distinction between *exousia*, understood as a potential energy or divine resource, and *dunamis*, its actualisation. The depiction of power in terms of high cosmic drama evinces the conclusion that, 'Seen, therefore, from the standpoint of the power involved, we may hold that Paul's aggressive understanding of the authority lying behind his preaching of the gospel involves no radical transformation',[90] that is to say of Jesus' own experience and conception of power, given the ample evidence in Paul's letters for the centrality of the conception of the 'power of God'. The process of exposing the centrality of power is seen as initiated in Paul's interpretation of Jesus: 'Perhaps with sharper insight into the essentially veiled nature of Jesus' own exercise of power, Paul perceives that the crucifixion itself, and the weakness of Christ, is a message of great power (1 Cor. 1. 18 and 24).'[91] The consistency of Sykes' interpretation emerges in that where Paul's power fails that of God takes over and sustains unbroken continuity:

> Here one must note particularly the dialectic of weakness and power in Paul. It is not that human weakness is identical with divine power; rather that human weakness constitutes a vacuum which the power of God can fill.[92]

There is here distinct evidence of an emergent systematic theology of power, a 'consistent potency' which becomes the category, the criteria of which are employed as hermeneutical principles in relation to Paul's experience. This in turn reflects the integration into three stages of the continuous unfolding and changes in the organisation and management of divine power in the New Testament as a

[90] *Identity*, p. 71.
[91] *Identity*, ibid.
[92] *Identity*, ibid.

whole. Thus, seen in its totality, the handling of the theme of power in the New Testament brings Sykes to conclude without reservation that 'the early Christian communities were highly power-conscious bodies'[93] and that 'to be a Christian is to be equipped with power, real power, as distinct from the outward form of piety'.[94] It would now appear that any traditional, static conception of the historical transmission of authority would be inadequate in the face of the 'real power' of Christianity:

> This power is the divine power, the power of the Spirit. It dwells in the gospel, and is evident at the points where it overcomes challenge, opposition and conflict. It is the power to convince, to bring about new life, to create loving harmony in the community, to withstand persecution, and to triumph over death; it is powerful, in other words over indifference and rejection, over law, over internal dissent, over external oppression, and over the last enemy itself.[95]

This triumphalist theological rhetoric is open to a variety of interpretations: it may be 'read' in different ways. As outlined here, 'power' is centralised, all-embracing, the onrush of enforced unity; it is, in a word, potentially totalitarian. We learn that inwardness, the focal point of 'real power' is localised in the 'powerful people' who lead ritual and liturgical action – indeed, 'Totally diffused power is indistinguishable from no power at all.' It is here that the inner integrity and the consistent character of the structure of Sykes' argument is apparent: the apparent declension of authority and its dispersal into the multifarious 'norms of authority' has been sublated by the 'discovery' of authority as *power*. Despite the recurrent difficulties of

[93] *Identity*, p. 72.
[94] *Identity*, ibid.
[95] *Identity*, ibid.

finding structures adequate for its embodiment (and here the New Testament itself is evidence enough), it is in the reality of power that is to be found the open secret of Christianity itself. Most disquieting of all is that no real analysis of this power is offered: it is, in effect, the power that itself defines; it is not definable, except, as we duly see, in terms of the rhetoric of conquest and the negation of anything that smacks of 'depotentiation'.

The centrality of power in Christianity allows Sykes to celebrate its presence and ability to sustain combat in the cosmic struggle with evil and to generate self-sacrifice. There is evidence, we are told, of a rather unhealthy, even craven evasion of the themes of power and authority, which is apparent when, for example, the spread of secondary education brings abuses of power perpetrated in the name of the Churches to the attention of a wider public. This oblique gesture in the direction of Donald MacKinnon's sensitivities to the long history of the corrupt abuse of power in the history of the Christian Church is not here accompanied by its familiar correlate. MacKinnon has repeatedly returned to the theme of *kenosis* (even calling, rightly in this writer's judgement, for a '*kenosis* of establishment')[96] whereas Sykes will have none of this. Although a longstanding concern with the humanity of Christ is evident in Sykes' thought (and this fits in with the schematic outline of English theology in the introduction of this paper), he nevertheless distances himself from *kenosis* and, as categorically stated in the *Identity*, from 'theological celebration of powerlessness'. In a passage remarkable for its intuitive rather than evidential insight the reader learns that:

[96] This paper is at least in part inspired by Donald MacKinnon's Gore Memorial Lecture: 'Kenosis and Establishment' in *The Stripping of the Altars* (London, 1964) pp. 13–40.

The theological celebration of powerlessness, based on what appears to be a misunderstanding of Paul's theology of the cross, has an altogether suspicious air of *post factum* justification for loss of political influence.[97]

The depotentiated theology of the cross (and here Sykes has the Tübingen theologian Jürgen Moltmann in mind) has its roots in 'the diminished political influence exercised by the Church in western societies', and although such correlations are 'notoriously difficult to verify',[98] Sykes attempts what amounts to a sociological reduction. There is, on the contrary, considerable evidence to suggest that Sykes' hypothesis is false. First, the West German experience of the Third Reich renders all uncritical celebration of power questionable and ambiguous in principle, and no-one is more aware of this than Moltmann. Second, in a further example, the history of the Roman Catholic Church following the loss of the Papal States and thus of political influence in the nineteenth century went hand in hand with the grosser forms of ecclesiological and Papal aggrandisement. In addition, it is plausible to interpret the Anglican theology of the Episcopate as the essential ministry in the face of secularisation along analogous triumphalist lines. Third, by extension, it would be equally plausible to apply our counter hypothesis (effectively verified in the other contexts) to Sykes' own position and regard the 'celebration of power' in glittering, adamantine Christian inwardness as an overcompensated spiritual triumphalism encapsulated in a highly distinctive interpretation of Paul's words in Ephesians 1.19: 'the immeasurable greatness of his power in us who believe.' Sykes' remark that, 'one is inclined to ask whether there are social reasons why modern theologians fail to make any such

[97] *Identity*, p. 75.
[98] *Identity*, ibid.

claim' (i.e. to power)[99] invites the converse response, that the reader ask why some theologians *do* make such claims. In all events the dismissal of 'depotentiated theology' and thus, by implication, of the kenotic motif, is entirely consistent with Sykes' position. A price has to be paid and it is the *exclusion* from this distinctive Anglican theological position and its correlative praxis of anything remotely associated with a 'theology of liberation' which might well bear traces of depotentiation, or, even more dangerously, make visible social stratification and the ecclesiological equivalent of class polarisation within the Church.[100] For Sykes, God's kingly power is that which unites and animates the Church with a single corporate will:

> If one of the functions of the mythological language of God's kingly rule is the mobilisation of the person to total commitment and to a sense of confident participation in an ultimate victory of the divine intention over contrary forces, then any response to that language which fails to elicit a corresponding confidence may be justly regarded as inadequate.[101]

This kind of language can be interpreted in a number of ways; evangelical zeal can under certain linguistic conditions have a less than salubrious resonance. As theological rhetoric directed at the admonishment and activation of the Christian community it succeeds; but if absorbed into the

[99] *Identity*, ibid.

[100] Those acquainted with Leonardo Boff's *Church, Charism and Power, Liberation Theology and the Institutional Church* (London, 1985) will recognise an affinity of intention with the contents of this paper. See chapter five 'The Power of the Institutional Church: can it be converted?', esp. Boff's question: 'Is it true that the Gospel needs power, prudence, concessions, the typical tricks of pagan power, all criticised by Jesus (Matthew 10:42), or does its strength lie precisely in weakness, renunciation of all security, prophetic courage, as practised in the Church of the first three centuries?', and his remark, pp. 55–6 on the relation of inwardness and institutional structure.

[101] *Identity*, p. 76.

structure of the 'sub-plot', the call to 'mobilisation', 'total commitment' and 'ultimate victory' could become the homiletic aura surrounding a theory of power with the authoritarian tendencies to which allusion has already been made, that is to a full-blown celebration of power.

It is at this juncture that evidence of pervasive problems within Anglican theology and indeed English cultural identity emerge. Neither Anglican theology nor English culture really knows where it is now 'placed' in historical or geographical terms. Even within the Church of England local identities are forged and micro-ideologies created on the basis of reconstructions arbitrarily inspired by episodes in the history of the Church, be it the primitive Palestinian community, a supposed Pauline hegemony, patristic orthodoxy, Reformation piety or the unfettered egoism of neo-Romantic catholic medievalism. In this setting Sykes' sophisticated, well-informed argument is, it is suggested, a hermeneutic of power ideally suited for the re-formation of the Anglican Church along lines which transcend the fragmentation of historically localised ideologies. The theme of emergent, later routinised and rationalised, charismatic and kingly power is deeply rooted in the biblical materials and in the subsequent history of the Church. This 'power' has been ambiguous, not just, as Sykes would have his readers believe, in terms of a dialectic of inwardness and externality, but in a far more complex set of relations between spiritual and temporal power, between classes within the Church stemming from at least the early distinction of *ordo* and *plebs Dei*, and between ideological superstructure and socio-economic base, and so on. Sykes' refusal of this 'complexity' (explicit with regard to Troeltsch – the 'complexifier with a conscience') and his development of what amounts to a monopolistic theory of divine power, albeit moulded and mediated through changing structures of Church government, is not an adequate substitute for this further, and to my mind indispensable, critical framework. The role of the theologian envisaged by Sykes not surprisingly conforms with the preceding argument and the hypothesis in the 'sub-plot', which contains, so far as ecclesial theory and praxis is concerned, the real substance of *The Identity of Christianity*. Here a new problem arises concerned with the nature of truth and the theologian's conflicting responsibilities. The theory of power that emerges in the sub-plot of the *Identity* confronts the theologian with the possibility of a dilemma latent in the following statements:

> It is . . . very rare to discover a theologian who has taken full stock of the power which he or she exercises. Theological responsibility is commonly defined solely in terms of obedience to the truth . . . But even if it be true that obedience to the truth is one of the aspects of the theologian's responsibility, it is demonstrated that other aspects entail the formidable use of power in the modern Church.[102]

In short, should the theologian's integrity be expressed in the pursuit of truth or in commitment to the management of power in the Church? This is no simple choice, it may in fact be a false dilemma if the argument is pressed too hard. But, given Sykes' absolutely uncompromising advocacy of the management and deployment of power, that is the power of God's kingly rule at the centre of Christianity, the theologian has, at the very least, to exercise some caution with regard to these proposals.

We have outlined the vertebral logic of the dominant sub-text of Sykes' argument. What follows in the middle section of the *Identity* is skilled historical appraisal of the essence of Christianity controversy and a demonstration of

[102] *Identity*, p. 77.

its on-going relevance. Sykes' answer to the difficulty exposed by the conflictual character of the Christian quest for identity is, however, already fully evident: it lies in the whole-hearted appreciation and appropriation of the role of power understood as practical management in theology and Church government. From the examples examined in the second part of the book are drawn qualifications of the power hypothesis; but by and large the 'sub-plot' is reinforced and unaltered. The presence of the historical material is justified in terms of the clarification of theological meaning: it does not directly pertain to power and managerial responsibility.

The *Identity* has a sandwich-like structure: outlying theoretical and analytical chapters enclose an extended central section which consists in a detailed scholarly appraisal of individual treatments of the essence/identity theme, subject, as Sykes himself concedes, to 'manipulation' in order to suit the thesis of his book. The latter concession does not appear out of place provided that it is always borne in mind that the exploration of the essence controversy is directed at the reinforcment of the hypothesis concerning power. In consequence, a series of illustrative beads are threaded onto the theoretical cord that binds together the three main sections of the *Identity*. There is first of all, in Schleiermacher, the concern to escape from the 'externality tradition' and to replace this with the determination of the essence of Christianity through the establishment of its 'inner structural coherence', that is its 'particular mode of faith' (*Glaubensweise*). The methodological decisions Schleiermacher made determined in turn the structure of his dogmatics and, indeed, informed his understanding of the permanent relationship of theology with the non-theological disciplines. In second place, Newman is shown to have proceeded along lines analogous to those of Schleiermacher and his approach is an example, *par excellence*, of the prominent exercise of theological responsibility. As a third example, the dispute between Harnack and Loisy provides contrasting accounts of the relation between the 'kernel and husk' of direct relevance to Sykes' own interpretation of the inward and external aspects of Christianity. Both tackle the theme of power and represent it in non-political terms: for Harnack it is the power of personality, a reality into which 'no research can carry us further',[103] whereas Loisy believed that 'ecclesiastical authority is not in true nature domineering, but educative'.[104] Each writer was above all else committed to the recovery of the original force of the gospel, an act itself the exercise of responsible theological power, whatever might be the inadequacies of the results achieved. Of particular importance for Sykes' supportive arguments is a juxtaposition of Troeltsch and Barth. Troeltsch set out precisely the relationship between historicism and epistemology in the form determinative of modern discussion and offered a strategy in direct opposition to that developed by Barth. Despite what is referred to as an unfortunate tendency to complexify issues, Troeltsch saw the necessity of Christianity's retaining of its naiveté[105] in the face of the qualitative discontinuity of pre- and post-Enlightenment thought. Troeltsch's understanding of the social-psychological character of Christianity as a communal reality contributed to an epistemology which complemented historical research into the reality of Jesus' life and teaching. The exercise of the former insight demands highly developed theological discrimination – hence the interrelation of the power and status of the theologian with

[103] *Identity*, p. 141.
[104] *Identity*, p. 142.
[105] *Identity*, p. 150.

epistemology. In sharp contrast Barth reinstated the power and primacy of the Word over against Troeltsch's combination of the socio-psychological and historical approaches. Barth's emphasis upon radical novelty and discontinuity in the renowned second edition of the *Römerbrief* and the expressing of this through the central ecclesial act of preaching is of particular importance to Sykes as he distances himself from a purely archaeological approach to Christianity. The demand for immediacy is singularly uncompromising, for, as the reader has learnt earlier:

> Hermeneutics must under no circumstances become a sophisticated way of clinging to the evacuated shell of a once living religion.[106]

This statement is one of the more memorable dicta in the *Identity* and the justification of this standpoint is largely in terms of a subtle and original exposition of Barth which is particularly illuminating with regard to the Christological treatment of power in volume IV/1 of the *Church Dogmatics*, which attains a level of 'confidence' sustainable only on the basis of a 'parallelism of language'.[107] This parallelism (what we might term the juxtaposition of rhetorical excess and the realism relatable to actual social and historical context) demands an interpretative strategy different from that of Sykes,[108] who notes Barth's consistent repudiation of the hierarchical concept of the ministry and yet his high view of the theologian. The assumption of Barth's dialectical 'parallelism' into his own

[106] *Identity*, p. 76.

[107] *Identity*, p. 203.

[108] See R. H. Roberts 'Theological Rhetoric and Moral Passion in the Life of MacKinnon's "Barth" ', in K. Surin (ed.) *Christ, Faith and Ethics: Pursuing the Thought of Donald MacKinnon* (Cambridge, 1989) for an account of such 'parallelism' in the English context.

position is problematic: Barth is 'so radical a representative of the inwardness tradition that nothing external can be said unequivocally to be an actual sign of the presence of divine power.'[109] It is at this juncture that Sykes distinguishes the realism of his own position and indeed that of Anglican theology from what he understands as Barth's 'unrealistic' dialecticism. The latter has in my view a fundamental, and from the English Anglican standpoint, an incomprehensible emphasis upon grace: the words are invested with the Word as an act of divine invasion, a justifying grace that for ever denies the proclaimer the possession of that Word or indeed, the manipulation of it in terms of human achievement. By contrast, Sykes reinvolves the Anglican principle of *via media* in a form of direct synthesis, more accurately a syncretic synergism:

> The language of sociology and the language of theology may be separate, but the reality of divine and human power is not. It is not parallel or merely co-ordinated, it is inevitably, and dangerously, mixed.[110]

Sykes' subsequent promulgation of 'the challenge of a more balanced and realistic interpretation of the identity of Christianity'[111] falls ironically into precisely that errant tendency he isolated and exposed in the *Integrity*, that is the taming and domestication of theological impulses within a manageable institution, which, when all is said and done, demands a theology able to serve within, rather than challenge its context.

In the third concluding section of the *Identity* the basic issues are reworked and clarified. The dialectic of inwardness and externality is regarded as fundamental and

[109] *Identity*, p. 207.
[110] *Identity*, ibid.
[111] *Identity*, p. 208.

presented in terms of three models: foundation-superstructure; spirit-body; and centre-circumference. Deep anxiety is expressed in Sykes' concern for the maintenance of a stable unity within Christianity sufficient to evince and sustain effective commitment on the part of believers.

The question of the relation of the pursuit of truth to the quest for identity is raised once more[112] and it passes yet again into a critique of 'depotentiated Christianity'.[113] Sykes' own position is expressed in terms of an elegant, pragmatic compromise:

> It is perfectly reasonable to enquire under what conditions Christianity is one thing. Such an enquiry performs a useful service in bringing into the open the natural assumptions about its diachronic and synchronic unity. The specification of these conditions would be a conscious construction or standpoint in Christian history, neither ruled out of court by historical relativism nor convicted of being a subtle deviation from the question of truth.[114]

Faced with chronic disagreement about the Christian tradition as a whole, there are, Sykes maintains, only three possible responses: the first is simply straightforward affirmation; the second the abandonment of the defence of even minimal continuity in the Christian tradition; the third, taken up and developed, is that of 'dialectical' management of the dispute through the incorporation and development of W. B. Gallie's notion of an 'essentially contested concept'.[115] This advocacy of the 'genuinely creative dispute' would, if taken on its own, appear to leave Christianity and indeed Anglicanism locked in a ceaseless

[112] *Identity*, p. 247–8.
[113] *Identity*, p. 249.
[114] *Identity*, p. 250.

dialectical altercation, treading the theological water in perpetuity. It is now surely apparent that this is *not* the intended conclusion: the rescue can be performed by the ordained theologian. Here the new 'prince of the Church', in whom 'a religious concern and a scholarly spirit are finely conjoined for the purposes of theoretical and practical activity alike'[116] must step forward and take up his authoritative relation to the community of worshippers. Thus the internal experience of new life can be interrelated with the external factors of story, myth and doctrine; it is, Sykes concludes,

> in the process of interaction between this inward element and the external form of Christianity that the identity of Christianity consists.[117]

The final definition of the identity of Christianity in terms of the relation of its inward and external aspects is incomprehensible to this reader. In the light of analysis of the structure of the dominant sub-text, the 'sub-plot' of which Sykes himself speaks, such a conclusion would appear to be a diversion and a foreshortening of perspective (possible as part of a negative strategy) imposed upon a concrete situation far more complex and problematic than is admitted in either the *Integrity* or the *Identity*. Sykes' overall argument is thus severely and unnaturally limited by a careful process of the inclusion and the exclusion of key issues. Most fundamental to Sykes' exclusion zone is

[115] *Identity*, p. 251.

[116] See *Identity*, p. 88. Schleiermacher's conception of the 'prince of the Church' appears to have had an unmistakeable influence upon Sykes' understanding of the role of the theologian: 'If one should imagine both a religious interest and a scientific spirit conjoined in the highest degree and with the finest balance for the purpose of theoretical and practical activity alike, that would be the idea of a "prince of the Church"', F. D. E. Schleiermacher, *Brief Outline of the Study of Theology*, T. N. Tice, (tr.), (Richmond, Virginia, 1966) par. 9, p. 21.

[117] *Identity*, p. 261.

that concern, central to liberation theology, and indeed present long before this in certain aspects of the English Reformation and Dissent, with the highly problematic relation of secular and spiritual power in the Constantinian and medieval, post-Reformation and the Established Church. Sykes' advocacy of the inevitability of power within theology is presented in terms of the 'dialectic' of inwardness and externality as though it bore no intrinsic relation to the *contextual* factors implicit in ideology, social structure and the distribution of wealth and educational resources and opportunities, and not least the concentration of patronage. Sykes' solution to the problem of the identity of Christianity is a shrewd and sophisticated recognition and reworking of the role of the theologian (and, it would be not unreasonable to assume, the theologically-informed ordained holder of senior Church office, that is ultimately the bishop) which is undertaken uncritically within the given structures of Establishment and the continuing crisis in British higher education. The un-challenged centralised hegemony implicit within Sykes' proposals falls all too well into a national, governmentally-led, strategic return to the contemporary analogate to the social structures that underlaid 'Victorian values'. Despite Sykes' gestures in the direction of a limited democracy in the Church (a vestigial lay veto on liturgical extremities) the threads of power lead back into the hands of a magisterial élite which, aware of its power, defines the reality in relation to which the believer is to sacrifice him or herself. It might well be that such measures are necessary if communities of endurance and a clerisy are to be sustained in the new Dark Age in England; if this is the case, then there is no point in disguising or unduly mollifying proposals which are in reality to do with the dominative, hegemonic management of power and the organisation of belief in a threatened Church and religious mental issues in the situation of contemporary Anglicanism and examined at some length one highly influential and representative response. Through an exposition of the historical context, an outline of method and a 'reading' of the integrity, identity and power hypotheses that are contained in the structure of Professor Sykes' 'sub-plot', in our terms the dominant sub-text of his work, we are now in a position to synthesise the methodological and substantial aspects of our argument.

If the revival of Christianity implies its recapitulation or 'repetition' at each new juncture in history, then the attempt to define the identity of Christianity we have subjected to critical analysis has involved the reworking of archaic, inherited structures which bear an undeniable analogous relationship with Hegel's representation of the Lordship and Bondage relation: the structure of power that involves domination and subjection. Despite the specific authorial disclaimer, a denial of a dominative understanding of power, we have shown that Sykes' re-endorsement of the legitimate power of the ordained ecclesiastic, the bearer of authority understood as the power to command and anticipate obedience, is wholly congruent with the structural sub-plot of his texts. In partly redundant intellectual mediation, Sykes has tried, unsuccessfully in our view, to divert attention away from the latent integrity of the structure of his own position through constant emphasis upon the conflictual character of Christianity as ostensibly generated through the difficulty of historical transmission and the intrinsic imprecision of language. Inasmuch, however, as the power-conscious theologian, a re-embodiment of Schleiermacher's 'prince of the Church', exercises his (or her) discrimination and defines Christian identity *for others,* then this 'princedom' manifests itself as Lordship, that is a *Herrschaft* in Hegel's sense. In fact, pursuing the analogy further, Sykes' argument takes the dialectic from the merely unconscious assumption of inherited essence, as in the case of a pre-critical embodiment of a transmitted *authority* in tradition, to its active post-modern assertion as *power*. In other words we move from the static, frozen authority of the ancestral juxtaposition of *ordo* and *plebs*, that is as a canonical authority conveying a deposit of faith (possibly modified through a hierarchy of truths) to a dynamic self-defining authority that self-consciously legislates reality for and on behalf of the *other*. When seen in the context of Hegel's presentation of the dialectic of power, this represents merely the first 'moment' related to the third 'moment' in the progression: we thus move from the static assertion of authority directly to the active exercise of pre-emptive power by the sublated Lord; but at the same time this is a misrepresentation: there is, in reality, no engagement with the middle 'moment', the 'other', that is with the Bondsman, the Slave, the plebs, in this case the spiritual proletariat, the laity. It has been our aim to articulate the position of the elided 'moment', the invisible Bondsman identical in terms of our analogy with a voiceless laity subsumed into a false mediation, a Christian foreshortening of the dialectic which prematurely assumes such conflict into a false 'reconciliation'. The dialectic is paralysed by 'containment' prior to the administration of the *coup de grâce* through the 'discovery of authority', that is, through the re-assertion of power on a new *'Real-theologie'* of spiritual *'Herrschaft'*.

If Christianity then persists in foisting a false reconciliation or 'containment' upon 'conflict' what, then, are the immediate consequences? Not least we may see that the Christian 'dialectic' can only subsist on a restricted plane assimilable into the post-Enlightenment pattern of 'reconstructionist' theologies; it can in effect only take up a position at an alienated distance from the real fabric of life. If it were to enter into the latter then the encounter (informed ideally by the full panoply of the human sciences) would expose the most painful discordance between these conditions and the residual, crucial 'rhetoric' of the Gospel. The suppression or elision of the rhetoric which posits (however unrealistically in Sykes' terms) an eschatological unity of humankind, that is, its construal as 'one in Christ', is evidence of a pervasive failure to recognise the conflict and relationship between different kinds of rhetorical discourse within theology, a problem which might be elucidated through the use of tools drawn from literary theory, not to mention the other relevant areas of discourse.

Sykes' downgrading of such Pauline conceptuality and his consistent avoidance of a sociological definition of the Church in terms of a quality of human relation, other than as super- and sub-ordination, is doubtless 'realistic', but do they do justice to the demands of the theological task? The displacement of original and final unity, the Alpha and Omega of the Christian rhetoric of salvation, has disastrous consequences: Christian identity is put entirely and exclusively at the mercy of the informed virtuoso, the writer of Christian character, the Prince-Lord of the Church legislating for the identity of Christianity. To 'mix' the parallel languages of Paul and of Karl Barth in a new theological 'realism' puts 'God' finally at the mercy of the constructive ambition of the theologian, male or female. This is a false mediation, a sophisticated diversion made possible only because of a manifest curtailment of the understanding of conflict and enabled by a theology that baulks at the prospect of a doctrine of 'total depravity', the universal fallibility of *all* human agency. To draw a veil over this is in reality not only to deny humanity its inheritance, and indeed, its need for an anticipated solution, however wrought, but it is also to incur the risk, indeed the inevitability, of the corrupt, obfuscatory manipulation of others through the management of power at the most fundamental and insidious level, that is in the construction of the self-consciousness of the other. It is this 'other' that dies in the Christian representation of the dialectic as embodied in the structure of *ordo* and *plebs*. This is not normally a violent public act but the quiet ecclesial practice of spiritual abortion, the unprotesting infantilisation of countless millions of embryonic believers upon whose behalf an essential ministry presumes to interpose. In the brutality of Hegel's dialectic there are to be found the means that may effect the raw exposure of wounded psychic flesh, the cry for existence embodied in the slave, the *Knecht*, the non-entity (*Unding*), deprived in the Christian context of the gift of Life itself. To disinter Hegel's terrifying dialectic at this juncture is, I believe, to unsheath once more what Hoskyns called the 'dagger of the Incarnation'. What is found here in Hegel's argument is a true and brutal reflection of that tension, even contradiction, traceable in Christianity to the Epistle to the Philippians, Chapter 2:5–7, rendered with uncompromising lucidity by Luther:

> Jesus Christus . . . welcher, ob er wohl in göttlicher Gestalt war, nahm er's nicht als einen Raub, Gott gleich zu sein, sondern entäusserte sich selbst und nahm Knechsgestalt an.

Such theology is neither genteel nor *'salonfähig';* it exists in a negative relation to the ambiguities of the positions we have subjected to critical examination in this paper.

In the final analysis our concern in this long paper has not merely been with the limitations and the questionable tendencies of two representative texts but with the larger situation in English and Anglican theology. We have in effect compared the arguments of texts which in different contexts struggle to come to terms with the relation of ancestral tradition and modernity. If, following Ernst Bloch, we test the texts in order to establish their progressive or regressive orientation, an interesting parallel is apparent. Hegel represents and subverts in narrative form the logic of epistemological dominance in the ontological parable of the Lord and Bondsman; Sykes likewise restates but ultimately re-endorses a theology of dominance despite all the cosmetic diversions which overlie the structure of his texts. Hegel was, at least in 1807, progressive; Sykes is, according to our analysis, *regressive,* despite valiant efforts at modernisation. What Hegel (and, following him, the critical theoreticians of a humane Enlightenment) have all understood is that the emancipation of humanity is to do with the realisation, through affirmation or through revolution, of the 'other'. The history of the disjoined, secularised relics inherited from the Christian consensus in socialism, even in its healthier forms, has doubtless been in many respects disastrous; the 'dialectic of Enlightenment' is itself a sombre intellectual episode in the history of the modern period. Nevertheless, if the Christian Gospel has to do with freedom, love or grace then it has to do with the affirmation of the other. Neither the traditional Anglican ecclesiology with which we began nor the sophisticated rethinking of authority and, as power, its unneurotic celebration in an Anglican Church of the future can, by any stretch of the intellectual imagination, be regarded as theologies of liberation. If the Christian Church in its Anglican form has not yet even discovered or recognised the form of the other, that is in the bondspersons or laity,

6

FAITH IN THE CITIES:
Corinth and the Modern City

by David F. Ford

Faith in the City, the report of the Archbishop of Canterbury's Commission on Urban Priority Areas,[1] begins its theological section by arguing that some of the teaching of Jesus is so simple and direct in its appeal and relevance that it requires no theology to drive it home. The call to have compassion on those in need is a prime example. Paul too assumes the validity of this teaching. He wanted his Churches to 'remember the poor' and only when they were slow to respond did he resort to arguments that would stimulate their generosity. The report supports this latter point with a reference to 2 Cor. 8–9. So a simple ethical maxim is the occasion for relating 1st century Corinth and its Church to modern British cities. Is there more to be gained for the theology and practice of the contemporary urban Church from Paul's Corinthian correspondence? That is the question this essay will try to answer.

Faith in the City is not much concerned to relate what it says explicitly to the Bible. The same is true of the other essays in this volume so far. That does not mean that either is 'unscriptural', as there are many ways of being in accord with the Bible other than doing direct interpretation of it. It is also easy to find examples of extremely dubious theology which supports itself by abundant exegesis. So it would be possible to argue that both *Faith in the City* and

[1] London 1985.

the previous essays are indebted to scripture for their basic conceptions, principles and horizons. Yet still the explicit link needs to be able to be made. A Christian report on cities and a series of essays on the Church need to be referred to scripture.

This is not just a matter of testing against the main touchstone of Christian identity. It is also a recognition of the fact that the Bible is today one of the few significant reference points for all the world's Christians, and so any policy or theology which wants to have a chance of wide acceptance is wise to make its case through scripture. But beyond any such Christian prudence is the experience of the fruitfulness of engaging as deeply as possible with specific scriptural texts. Theology or Church reports may be done by people steeped in the Bible and may presuppose it throughout, but even so they never grow out of the stories, poetry, prophecy, law, proverbs, letters and other genres that make up scripture. It is always tempting for theologians to think that discursive writing in doctrine, essays and similar genres is somehow superior to stories and the other biblical forms. It would be more appropriate to acknowledge that much of the Christian quality and wisdom of our theology depends on the depth of resonance with the Bible, and that the discursive form is often an abstraction which may be necessary (and we have been strongly affirming theoretical discourse of various kinds) but which is in the end dependent on that resonance ringing true. Above all, keeping the various genres in dialogue with each other prevents any premature closure and helps each to be fruitful in new ways.

So there is a case to be made for having the explicit scriptural essay at the end of this volume. It enables each essay, already conceived in dialogue with scripture, tradition and much else, to be brought into fresh relation with

the Bible. This can only be done fragmentarily, and I have
decided to do it through two letters, 1 and 2 Corinthians.
How does Paul perceive the Church? How does he build it
up? How does all this resonate with our essays on basic
conceptuality, God, various aspects of Christian tradition,
authority and Church reality? And one striking feature of
these letters is that they are addressed to a specific Church
and its problems in a Hellenistic Roman city. This urges a
similar particularity on us. If ecclesiology cannot help with
the issues facing modern Churches then its theory is in
vain. Some of the previous essays have already engaged in
this. The present essay will combine reflections on 1 and 2
Corinthians with some examination of *Faith in the City*,
and especially its conception of the Church in urban
England today. Presupposed behind the whole discussion
will be two long-term involvements: seven years spent
with my colleague Frances Young at work on *Meaning and
Truth in 2 Corinthians*[2] and eleven years in the congregation
of an urban parish in Birmingham. The aim is to see what
wisdom the letters can offer a situation such as this.

1. The Economy of God

First we will look at 2 Cor. 8–9 in more detail. They are
remarkable chapters which take that simple matter of the
collection for the poor Jerusalem Church and make of it
what might be called a sacrament of the Gospel and of
God's whole way with the world. Even the terms used for
the collection are loaded redescriptions. Paul never uses the
obvious *logeia*, but instead words which integrate it with
his Gospel and ministry: *charis* (grace), *koinonia* (fellowship, sharing), *diakonia* (service, ministry), *eulogia* (blessing, liberality), *perisseuma* (overflow, abundance) and

others[3]. Paul uses theological and empirical language simultaneously, and the theological is not 'just' metaphorical. What is at stake is the whole 'economy' in which we live and our fundamental ways of participating in life and dealing with material reality. The gospel itself is reconceived in economic terms ('for you know the grace of our Lord Jesus Christ, that though he was rich, yet for your sake he became poor, so that by his poverty you might become rich', 8.9) in order in turn to transform the understanding of ordinary finances.

Is this, as *Faith in the City* suggests, an argument brought in to back up an obvious duty to be generous to the poor, only needed because the Corinthians were being slow to respond? Partly that is so, and the chapters themselves bear this out by their appeal to ethical commonplaces with many Greek and Jewish parallels. There is presupposed what chapter one above called 'general sociality', symbolised by the aim of mutual care 'that there may be equality' (8.14). But the dominating image is not one of just redistribution, it is of the paradoxical grace of Jesus Christ and of the Churches of Macedonia, 'for in a severe test of affliction, their abundance of joy and their extreme poverty have overflowed in a wealth of liberality on their part' (8.2). Paul does appeal for equality, but his examples are of something which goes beyond it. He both affirms the best popular ethics of the day and says that actually something even better has been demonstrated. He backs this up with a conception of reality which radically challenges the popular views by portraying what might be called the economy of God. This is an economy centred on God, and is characterised by abundance and the possibility of extraordinary generosity;

[3] For a fuller treatment of this and of the whole conception of the 'economy of God' see Young and Ford, op.cit. Chap. 6.

its crucial, generative transaction is Jesus Christ's giving of himself; its basic units of 'currency' are selves ('first they gave themselves to the Lord and to us by the will of God', 8.5; 'I will most gladly spend and be spent for your souls' 12.15); the main imperative in it is the distribution of what is freely given (hence Paul's ministry); and the overarching perspective is eschatological, with the Holy Spirit given already as a downpayment of the future (1.22).

In 2 Cor. 8–9 the climax is a description of this economy which has all of what Werner Jeanrond in chapter three saw as the marks of the Church—proclamation, celebration and the sharing of the new life:

> And God is able to provide you with every blessing in abundance, so that you may always have enough of everything and may provide in abundance for every good work . . . You will be enriched in every way for great generosity, which through us will produce thanksgiving to God; for the rendering of this service not only supplies the wants of the saints but also overflows in many thanksgivings to God. Under the test of this service you will glorify God by your obedience in acknowledging the gospel of Christ, and by the generosity of your contribution for them and for all others; while they long for you and pray for you, because of the surpassing grace of God in you. Thanks be to God for his inexpressible gift! (9.8–15)

There is considerable contrast between these chapters and the approach of *Faith in the City*. The latter, partly no doubt because it wanted to speak to both nation and Church, attempts no vigorous redescription of reality beyond the best general English liberal ethics. This has its strengths, in line with the critique of exclusively Church- or redemption-centred conceptions in chapter one above. But it is liable, as we shall see later, to acute weaknesses when it comes to addressing the Church.

One question raised for contemporary ecclesiology by Paul's letters and their way of understanding all reality in terms of the 'economy of God' is how such a comprehensive, Gospel-centred reconception can be done today. Our essays try to think that through, and they can be enriched, illustrated, questioned and opened up to further discussion by bringing them into dialogue with Paul's letters to the Corinthians. A question raised for *Faith in the City* is about its failure to acknowledge that question. The report does help to enable an ethical and pragmatic consensus. But is this at the cost of not recognising how deep the need is for the sort of redescription of reality, with accompanying social expression, that would necessitate some explicit thinking about the Church? *Faith in the City* lacks an explicit ecclesiology, and its implicit one is inadequate by the standards both of the previous essays and of the critique and vision that Paul's letters embody.

2. Corinth and its Church

Paul had founded the Church in Corinth[4] around 50 AD and he probably wrote 1 Corinthians in 54 and 2 Corinthians in 56. So the letters were to a very young Church, with perhaps less than fifty members, coping with a major transformation of life and all the problems that being Christian brought: how to go on living in Corinth in the face of many pressures and with unprecedented decisions to be made, how to be the Church together, how to respond to the various types of Christianity that were introduced, and how to be part of the Christian network through the rest of the Roman Empire.

Most of the issues concerned their Christian identity. Their very origins through Paul's work were suspect to

[4] For more on this section see Young and Ford, op.cit. Chap. 7.

some Christians, Paul was the leading member of the mission to the Gentiles which originated in Antioch. It was very different from the original Jerusalem and Palestinian mission, not only in being directed towards Gentiles as well as Jews but also in its focus on key Hellenistic cities of the Empire. These cities were the product of a political, social and cultural revolution begun by Alexander the Great in the late fourth century BC. They had a cosmopolitan culture, shared the Greek language and had their own system of self-government and education. The Romans took them over, exercised political control and developed communications by road and sea, but had no alternative to the common Hellenistic culture. Paul and his co-workers adapted their mission to this situation. They founded churches on important trade routes, helped them to develop appropriate ways of being the Church in relation to the key urban institutions and patterns of life, maintained communications by visits and letters and found financial support both from Church congregations and earnings. The latter raised a problem symbolic of the challenge Paul posed for the Palestinian Christians and of the suspicion that extended to the Churches he founded, and it is worth further examination.

In Palestine there was a tradition of 'charismatic begging' which Jesus encouraged in his followers and which was a mark of the early Palestinian Church[5]. The authenticity of an itinerant preacher was reinforced by his dependence on local generosity as he went from village to village. But in Hellenistic cities there was no such tradition and beggars were more likely to be seen as lazy parasites. Besides, for Paul, there was the fact that he was an organiser and sustainer of new communities and because he often

[5] See Gerd Theissen, *The Social Setting of Pauline Christianity. Essays on Corinth* (Fortress Press, Philadelphia 1982).

antagonised the local Jewish community he had no natural source of support when he began his work. To have his own means of subsistence as a tentmaker[6] had advantages: it gave him financial independence from the Jewish community and also from the developing Christian community, which, in a society in which patron-client relationships were basic, was important for his freedom and authority; it also gave him contacts through his craft, both among fellow workers and suppliers and customers. Yet it had another side too: it would have taken a great deal of time and energy; and it was done side by side with slaves and meant 'being perceived by others and by himself as slavish and humiliated . . . suffering the artisan's lack of status and so being reviled and abused'[7]. Paul was open to criticism from the side of Palestinian tradition and the words of Jesus (earning his own living was probably seen as reliance on himself rather than on God, hence his defence in 1 Cor. 9, 2 Cor. 10–12) and also from the wealthier Corinthians who clearly would have liked to be his patrons and may have been embarrassed by their founder being so identified with slaves and artisans.

Paul defends himself on both fronts with various arguments, but fundamental to them is his appeal, past tradition and a legalistic obeying of the words of Jesus (which he interprets not as a command but as offering a right which he himself is forgoing, 1 Cor. 9.15 f.), to his conformity with the humiliation and death of Jesus (1 Cor. 9.19–23, 2 Cor. 11–12). In the death of Jesus he finds the relativising not only of the Jewish law but also of Christian tradition and of inherited ways of being an apostle and

[6] On the importance of his tentmaking for Paul see Ronald Hock, *The Social Context of Paul's Ministry. Tent-Making and Apostleship* (Fortress Press, Philadelphia 1980).

[7] Ibid. p. 56.

being the Church. It is a legitimation of discontinuity in Christianity which does not fit with modern 'liberal' or 'conservative' patterns. It is perhaps best described as a cross-centred radicalism which is freed to do what seems according to the Gospel in a particular context. It enabled his mission to found Churches which were not modelled on those in Palestine but were free (with all the attendant risks and problems, of which his letters are full) to be indigenous. Much of the rest of 1 Cor. is Paul's wrestling with the details of this process as they were being worked out. It could be argued that no later transformation of Christianity has been as traumatic and comprehensive as its simultaneous transition from a purely Jewish to a mixed Jewish–Gentile community and from Palestine to an urban Hellenistic environment. The Corinthian Church gives a glimpse of what resulted.

What picture emerges of the Corinthian Church? In recent years there has been a great deal of study in the area variously called the 'sociology', 'social history', 'social description', 'social setting', or 'social world' of early Christianity[8]. There is probably more known about the Corinthian Church and its city than about any other part of the New Testament Church.

The city was quite new. Old Corinth had been destroyed by the Romans in 146 BC for helping to lead a Greek revolt and Paul's Corinth had been founded as a Roman colony by Julius Caesar in 44 BC. The settlers were mainly freedmen (former slaves) from many parts of the Empire who were granted Roman citizenship. The recent origin and the variety and low status of the first settlers combined with its position at a vital junction for trade and travellers

[8] The most helpful on Paul's Churches are Wayne A. Meeks, *The First Urban Christians. The Social World of the Apostle Paul* (Yale UP, New Haven and London, 1983), and Theissen, op.cit.

to make it somewhat more open and less rigidly stratified than many other cities. It was also enjoying prosperity in Paul's time, fed by commerce, reliable banks, thriving exports of manufactures, the revival of the Isthmian Games, and its political and military importance as the governing centre of the province of Achaea.

How did the new Church fit into this? One way to approach an answer is to try to describe its group identity in relation to other groups and institutions[9]. The main relevant ones are the religious temples and cults, the mystery religions, the Jewish synagogue, the household, the philosophical schools and the voluntary associations with special interests in areas such as politics, a craft, a profession, philosophy or sport. The striking thing about the Church is that while it can be shown to have some affinities with most of these it emerges from the comparison as a new sort of group. It combined worship, holy meals, personal salvation with initiation ritual, great diversity in ethnic, social, economic and cultural composition, a network of communities spreading through the Empire, exclusivism in relation to other worship and cults, and a sense of being one family together with meetings centred on households. It was developing a new linguistic and cultural identity, with its own 'in' language, its gestures, ethical guidelines, decisions about boundaries, and ways of interpreting scripture. All of this was informed by the world of meaning and behaviour which was called above the 'economy of God'. This was centred on the Gospel and ritually enacted in baptism and eucharist. The resulting community made good sociological sense in

[9] See especially Meeks op.cit., Theissen op.cit., and Robert Banks, *Paul's Idea of Community. The Early House Churches in their Historical Setting* (Paternoster Press, Exeter 1980).

Corinth. It enabled a resilient, intimate fellowship in a pluralist setting.

A key factor in Hellenistic culture was that of status (reflected in the prominence of such terms as honour, glory, reputation, shame, reproach) and it was therefore very important how the new group handled this. The Church in Corinth had a minority with high status according to various criteria: '. . . not many of you were wise according to worldly standards, not many were powerful, not many were of noble birth' (1 Cor. 1.26). Meeks reckons that of the seventeen named Corinthian Christians about nine have high status suggested by offices held, services provided for the Church, and sufficient wealth for travel or owning houses. Yet even these often exhibit considerable 'status inconsistency' – their marks of high status are accompanied by other marks of low status (e.g. in ethnic origin, slave origin, occupation or sex). It seems that able people who had no clear social niche were initially attracted to the faith. Of the rest, some were slaves but the average Christian seems to have been an artisan or small trader. The diversity in status caused great tensions in Corinth, as perceptively analysed by Theissen. Discrimination according to wealth threatened the eucharist, the more educated and sophisticated felt freer than others to eat meat sacrificed to idols, and the divisions over gifts of the Spirit may have been linked to the attempts of those with less social power to play a fuller part. It is no accident that the theme of unity and community is prominent in Paul's letters and that issues of status, glory, boasting, authority and power are pervasive.

It is not unusual for groups of many types in all ages to have problems about money, legitimacy in relation to a tradition, boundaries, elites who tend to dominate in their own interest, freedom and order in meetings, authority within and outside the local group, relations between the sexes, and the whole area of rationale and *raison d'etre*. But how far is comparison possible? More specifically, of what relevance to modern ecclesiology is the study of the Corinthian Church?

3. The Relevance of Paul's Letters

Consider the following definition of hermeneutics:

> The art of enriching our language in conversation with others; also, reflection designed to raise this art to self-consciousness without reducing it to a set of rules.[10].

That is a way of seeing interpretation as the learning of a sort of wisdom. It is not intimidated by allegedly impassable 'hermeneutical gaps', nor does it seek for the one correct method. It recognises the importance of theory in the sense of raising the art to self-consciousness[11] but gives primacy to the sort of learning and enrichment that happens in good conversation. That is what I am attempting with Paul's two letters.

It would be easy to see the vast difference between the Church in 1st century Corinth and contemporary urban England as an insuperable barrier to relevance. A small, new Church in an alien culture and economic system, confronted with pagan cults, in close contact with its powerful and charismatic founder, shaped through a whole set of historical conditions and conceptions peculiar to its time: how can that relate to us now?

---

[10] Jeffrey Stout, 'A Lexicon of Postmodern Philosophy', *Religious Studies Review* 13.1 (January 1987) p. 21. For a fuller treatment of the hermeneutical issues with special reference to 2 Cor. see Young and Ford op.cit, Chaps. 4 and 5 *et passim*.

[11] For such an approach to some of the theory see ibid, Chap. 5.

A first answer is that we do not only learn from what is similar to ourselves. To enter the 'common sense' of another period is itself a learning process which helps to understand ourselves better. The value of appreciating otherness goes far beyond historical understanding and is relevant to the whole range of diversity and pluralism which are especially important in modern cities. It is a common experience that it is just by immersion in something very different in all its specificity that insights are given into other areas: a good novel can take us up into its world and then, in a way that is perhaps impossible to systematise or reduce to rules, can deeply affect our lives. With the Corinthian letters, as with other ancient texts, one of the roles of scholarship is to make sure that we recognise the differences and do not treat them as modern documents. It is in understanding their particularity back there then that we are more likely to have the insights into our own situation.

A second answer is more specific to the Corinthian letters. They became part of the New Testament and so gained an authority very different from what they had for the first readers and listeners. One of the consequences of this canonisation was to encourage forgetfulness of their original setting and instead to treat them as timeless truth to be applied directly in age after age. But the letters themselves subvert that way of using them. In relation to the Church they do not give blueprints. They are not a Koran offering timeless guidelines. Paul himself was innovating in his mission, Church-building and interpretation of scripture. He was breaking with tradition and giving Christian grounds for doing so — notably the cross and resurrection and the gift of the Spirit which realises God's future now. So any direct, legalistic relevance is ruled out, and the appropriate response should not be to try to restore or recover an imitation Pauline Church. Paul was fighting those who wanted him to have an imitation Palestinian Church. This can have negative relevance today by liberating Churches from identities which are largely backward-looking and determined by particular past periods. It is also of positive value to Churches in the throes of the modern urban revolution (which has now been going on for less time than that initiated by Alexander the Great had in Paul's day) to identify with a previous traumatic transformation of the social structure and context of the Church and to see that it is the events at the heart of the Gospel which Paul used to justify his daring response. This insight into the similarities is only reached by engagement with the differences and particularities. Part of the value of the New Testament canon is that it requires this engagement with these texts age after age.

Yet a third answer follows on from that: the sort of relevance cannot be determined in advance. We simply need to get on with the conversation now to the best of our ability, not too bothered if we cannot establish our conclusions as valid for all time according to universal criteria, but very concerned to do justice as far as possible both to the letters and to our contemporary urban situation. The possible pitfalls both in New Testament scholarship and hermeneutical procedure are endless, but having co-authored a book on those issues I now want to take the conversation further and do more specific and practical reflection.

4. How does Paul perceive and build up the Church?

It is a telling feature of Paul's perception of the Corinthian Church that it can give the material for the sort of social description exemplified above. Paul is strikingly concrete, full of details. It is all the more impressive because he is not trying to give this material; it comes in by the way. Colin Gunton's insistence on the contingency, particularity and fallibility of the Church, and Christoph Schwoebel's on the Church as a human field of action are well illustrated. There is no hint of a Church other than the visible group of Corinthians with all their failings.

Yet the failings can be overemphasised, because there also appears a remarkable quality of community or sociality. Again, this is almost more impressive when it is indicated indirectly. Paul's language constantly reveals an intimacy, mutuality and solidarity that are the presupposition for his agonies over the Church. The family and friendship terminology that was habitual in the community points to its self-understanding as bound together as strongly as possible, and it was not only a matter of language: suffering, giving money and hospitality, praying, obeying, forgiving, trying to overcome divisive quarrels and passions, and greetings 'with a holy kiss' (1 Cor. 16.20, 2 Cor. 13.12) were also involved. It had the sort of shared, coinherent identity that allowed Paul to write the remarkable first eleven verses of 2 Cor. We have also already seen it as a new sort of group in Corinth, both adapting and innovating in relation to other patterns of sociality. How is all this to be explained?

There is no doubt about Paul's main explanation: it is in line with the Reformation's understanding of it as 'the creature of the word'. Faced with the threat of division in 1 Cor., Paul goes back to the origins of the community in his preaching of the Gospel centred on 'the word of the cross' (1.18; cf. 1.17,23, 2.1–5). Faced with questioning of his own ministry in 2 Cor., he makes the same sort of appeal: 'For what we preach is not ourselves but Jesus Christ as Lord, with ourselves as your servants for Jesus' sake' (4.5). The Church's origin is in its calling (1 Cor.

1.1–2, 24,26), in God's choosing (1 Cor. 1.27–28) which takes historical form in the communication of the Gospel. The Corinthian Church is unthinkable without reference to 'the Gospel of God' (2 Cor. 11.7), and the most striking thing about Paul's perception of the Church is the way he gives primacy to this.

How does it work out? I have called it above a form of redescription in relation to the whole 'economy of God'. I will now reflect on examples of how Paul does this.

He meets the divisions in Corinth with the questions: 'Is Christ divided? Was Paul crucified for you? Or were you baptised in the name of Paul?' (1 Cor. 1.13). The social unity entailed by the Gospel was already underlined in the opening address 'to the Church of God which is at Corinth, to those sanctified in Christ Jesus, called to be saints together with all those who in every place call on the name of our Lord Jesus Christ, both their Lord and ours' (1.2). The key to it is clearly the death of Jesus, as summed up in what is perhaps Paul's best précis of the Gospel in either letter:

> For the love of Christ controls us, because we are convinced that one has died for all; therefore all have died. And he died for all, that those who live might no longer live for themselves but for him, who for their sake died and was raised.' (2 Cor. 5.15)

For this Gospel, a divided Church is a catastrophe, representing a divided Christ. It is of great importance whether and how this principle is appropriated by the contemporary Church too. How intrinsic to the Church is its visible unity? *Faith in the City* is a Church of England report encouraging maximum cooperation between Churches, which is clearly right and practical. But in the aftermath of the failure of unity with the Methodist Church and other discouraging developments, visible, structural unity (local and at the other levels) is not a very popular aim at present. The tendency has been to aim rather at fuller cooperation and perhaps intercommunion. A similar vision of unity which preserves denominational identities was the subject of much conflict in the World Council of Churches earlier this century. The 1961 New Delhi statement, affirming instead the goal of full visible unity, was (explicitly for some participants) a recovery of the insight into the Gospel in 1 Cor. 1. The issue continues to be urgent, and in our pluralist cities the good (of interdenominational cooperation which does not question and even strengthens the separate identities) can easily be enemy of the best (the sort of visibile unity of which the Church of South India is an example).

The relevance of the cross to unity is carried through practically by Paul into the sensitive area of status. Here the world's values are relativised by the 'foolishness' of God. An identity rooted in the crucified Son of God cannot appeal to education, wealth, power or birth to support a position in the Church. Nor may spiritual gifts be an instrument of domination rather than service. The climax of his argument in this area is about his own standing as an apostle (discussed separately below) which is also comprehensively redescribed in relation to the cross. Status in its many, often covert, forms continues to be a powerful factor in Church life, and one of the dimensions most difficult to face up to. The Corinthian correspondence can act as an aid to perception, reflection and repentance about this, with its sharpest critique directed to those in authority. This has consequences for every aspect of Church life including that of visible unity, the most obvious hindrance to which is the virtual unthinkability of those with denominational authority and standing deciding to give it up. A story such as that of the remarkable humility of some of the leaders of the Churches that became the Church of South India can give encouragement that Paul's application of the Gospel to such matters need not be wishful thinking.

In one area after another Paul relates Church issues to the Gospel. Some of the issues are obviously irrelevant today, on others Paul's verdicts will be controversial among Christians now as then. But throughout he shows in practice what Daniel Hardy described as a dynamic which is both affirmative and critical and also is capable of generating richer and more open-structured forms of social order. His theology of God's call and grace and of the dignity of the empirical Church allows what may seem like extravagant affirmation of the Corinthian Christians themselves (e.g. 'I give thanks to God always for you . . . You are not lacking in any spiritual gift', 1 Cor. 1.4.7; 'I have great confidence in you; I have great pride in you; I am filled with comfort. With all our affliction, I am overjoyed', 2 Cor. 7.4), while maintaining an inexorable critical thrust. And the form of social order aimed at is one which tries to respond to issues in all their complexity, recognising the sort of factors relevant to sociological analysis, and aims to enable a community of great diversity to realise a vision of the truth of sociality summed up best in 1 Cor. 12–14.

1 Cor. 13, perhaps the best known passage in Paul's letters, relates to what Daniel Hardy called above 'general sociality'. Its sayings have numerous Greek and Jewish parallels, and Conzelmann sees this pointing

in the first instance to the assumption of Greek motifs by Hellenistic Judaism and their transformation to the style of the Jewish Wisdom tradition . . . In Paul's sense this Wisdom teaching is *Christian* teaching, even if there is no explicit mention of Christology. For *agape*, 'love', is for him a given *Christian* concept (Rom. 5.3 ff; 8.35 ff), and indeed he links up emphatically with the values of the Christian Church. But at the same time he allows them to appear as universal values.[12]

So here precisely where he is describing a 'still more excellent way' than service through various gifts of the Spirit in the Church he resonates most deeply with the best in the general wisdom of his culture. Far from cutting the vision of 'common sociality' off from the specifically Christian, Paul sets a standard for the Church by it. The other side of this is his earlier affirmation of the intrinsic relation of all creation to Christ: 'one Lord Jesus Christ, through whom are all things and through whom we exist' (1 Cor. 8.6). This is a position in harmony with *Faith in the City's* general approach.

But there are still the two flanking chapters 12 and 14. These have perhaps had more influence and been more exhaustively commented upon in this century than in any other, due mainly to the rise of Pentecostalism and the Charismatic movement. Suspicion among many 'mainstream' Christians that they are dangerously subversive is well-founded. Their picture of worship is apparently non-liturgical and inviting broad participation. There is nothing like a clergy – laity distinction and no one ministry is given a special overall leadership role (the likelihood is that eucharists were presided over by the head of the household where they were held). The widespread recognition that 1 and 2 Timothy and Titus are post-Pauline removes even the argument that Paul later moved towards a more 'Catholic' pattern. None of this is a serious problem unless one insists on a certain sort of backward-looking legitimation for one's present form of worship and ministry, or

---

[12] Hans Conzelmann, *1 Corinthians. A Commentary on the First Epistle to the Corinthians* Transl. James W. Leitch, Ed. George W. MacRae, S. J. (Fortress Press, Philadelphia 1975) pp. 218, 221.

claims an exclusive validity for one line of development that refuses to recognise the diversity of the New Testament and Church history. But many present patterns have traditionally been justified in such fundamentalist, legalistic and historicist ways. The Corinthian correspondence and the other essays in this volume converge in undermining that sort of appeal. One result is that Church worship and ministry in our cities can be helped to a more thorough critique of its inheritance in relation to its situation.

What more positive wisdom can be learnt from 1 Cor. 12–14? One of the most striking features is the new characterisation of the Church as the body of Christ. Colin Gunton has already discussed some aspects of this (above p. 75). His point about its main meaning being that of interpersonal unity is well illustrated by a comparison with 2 Cor. There 'body' is not used but the same understanding of the Church is expressed in terms of mutuality, coinherence, communication, jointness and service. It is this which is most subversive yet also full of possibilities for both the Church and other sociality today. It is not just that Gunton's and Roberts' critiques of hierarchy are anticipated; there is also a vivid picture of social identity constituted by communication and service. There is portrayed a dynamic of communication from God, between the members and with outsiders which was clearly explosive and risky. Paul is very emphatic about encouraging the gifts of the Spirit to be exercised, with the stress on those with most capacity to build up the Church. There is a problem, especially with any legalistic modern application, over the role of women in 14.33–35. Yet however that disputed passage is interpreted,[13] in the light of the earlier

---

[13] Some see it as an interpolation, some as only ruling out conversation during the service about what is going on. See Young and Ford op.cit. pp. 205f.

instruction about women praying and prophesying (1 Cor. 11.2 ff.) it obviously does not mean their exclusion from the new freedom of communication in worship.

The positive feature of the Corinthian Church that is at stake here can be summed up as *parrhesia*, meaning freedom of speech, openness, confidence. Kittel sums up its meaning in the Pauline corpus as follows:

> Openness toward both God and men, and in the Gospel, is meant (Eph. 3.12; 2 Cor. 3.12; Eph. 6.19–20). The face that is open toward God is also open toward others (2 Cor. 3.7 ff.). This open face reflects the Lord's glory in increasing transformation by the Spirit. Openness implies a confident freedom of approach to God (Eph. 3.12). In its human dimension it has the nuance of affection in 2 Cor. 7.4 and authority in Phlm. 8.[14]

This *parrhesia* was a vital aspect of Pauline community and inseparable from the Spirit understood as the recurrent and fresh 'eventfulness of God', especially in communication and symbolic acts. The key principle is that of a Gospel-informed quality of communication through which a whole community is transformed and expands. *Faith in the City* rightly recognises this in some black Pentecostal Churches. One of the most powerful impressions of worship at its best in Pentecostal and Charismatic traditions is of the new life and dignity given to often damaged, oppressed or repressed people when they take part in a new culture of worship which enables and encourages *parrhesia*. *Faith in the City* also offers some hints towards a vision of worship that is distantly related to the quality of *parrhesia* suggested by Paul. But there is little encouragement of the idea that the whole Church community fulfils its calling of

[14] *Theological Dictionary of the New Testament* Ed. G. Kittel and G. Friedrich, abridged in one volume by Geoffrey W. Bromiley (Eerdmans, Grand Rapids and Paternoster, Exeter 1985) p. 795.

mission and witness most concentratedly and explicitly through the quality of its own worship and that there too the most devastating distortions of true communication happen. 'The corruption of the best is the worst', as Paul's affirmation and criticism of the Corinthians suggests, but the usual situation is of Churches not envisaging the best because of fear of the worst.

Does this mean that the lesson of 1 Cor. 12–14 is that mainstream Churches should all become 'Charismatic' in some form? Again that would be a legalistic generalisation. It will be true for some, though hopefully recognising the dangers that are widely instantiated. But Paul was taking the Corinthians from where they were, and offering a constructive critique of precisely their present form of worship. More important than whether the surface features of worship and community life are Pauline, Johannine or like one of the many other patterns so instructively being recovered by New Testament scholars, is the vision of a quality of communication made possible in faith, hope and love, and of salvation inseparable from a liberation of spirit that overflows in fresh speech and action. It is such transformative and attractive communication, with affirm-ation of God and of other people at its heart, that can be a sign, localised in a vast variety of ways, of the Kingdom of God. But even this at its most powerful is judged by the criterion of 1 Cor. 13.

Yet in that chapter, for all its universal values, lurks a problem for modern interpreters that elsewhere is even more apparent. 'For now we see in a mirror dimly, but then face to face' (v. 12). So far the eschatology of the letters has only come out in passing, but it is unavoidable and all-pervasive. It is especially noticeable in the ethical sections of 1 Cor., as summed up in 7.29–31:

I mean, brethren, the appointed time has grown very short; from now on, let those who have wives live as though they had none, and those who mourn as though they were not mourning, and those who rejoice as though they were not rejoicing, and those who buy as though they had no goods, and those who deal with the world as though they had no dealings with it. For the form of this world is passing away.

Paul obviously expected the imminent end of the world and was wrong. How deeply does this affect his whole message? The answers of interpreters vary greatly. Does he, as Bultmann says, have a largely existentialised eschatology which only needs to be disentangled from mythological elements, such as an imminent literal end, for it to be relevant today, with the passage just quoted being an excellent example of eschatological freedom in practice? Was the later Christian tradition right in its tendency to stress eschatology in relation to the individual after death and to ignore the interaction between eschatology and history now? Is some political theology correct in reversing the traditional emphasis in favour of the communal and historical in the present?

One course that does not seem right is to ignore eschatology completely. This is not only because it is so fundamental to the New Testament or because it has profoundly shaped the modern world (largely through its secular forms in beliefs in progress, the ultimate revolution, a nuclear apocalypse or a thousand-year Reich). It is also because it seems impossible to have a conception of the Church or any other historical community without some eschatology, even if implicit. What sort of story, if any, are we part of? How do we conceive the future? Is Paul any help in doing so?

In view of the large place of eschatology in modern

theology it is surprising that *Faith in the City* makes almost no mention of it. Its main statement is that the Church is called to be an anticipation of the Kingdom of God[15]. That is a good start, but it is worth pursuing further through Paul. His basic conception is that with the death and resurrection of Jesus Christ a new age, or new creation, has broken into the old, so that we are living in a time in which the ages overlap. The new is being realised now through the Holy Spirit, so the most urgent thing is to live according to the Spirit[16]. It certainly involves present eschatological freedom, hope beyond death and the significance of the Church in history (though inevitably qualified by his expectation of the end). But as regards contemporary ecclesiology there are two implications that seem most important. The first is that the determinisms of history are broken by the gift of the Spirit as the downpayment of what is to come. If God is free to open history from the future then the future need not mirror the past. In the Church this combines with the message of the cross to allow for discontinuities and innovations. The criterion for something is no longer whether that is how the Church has done it in the past or even whether Jesus said it (cf. Paul on his means of subsistence) but whether it embodies the new creation and its vision of love.

The second implication is indicated by the 'face to face' of 1 Cor. 13.12. For Paul the content of eschatology is christological and the final reality is face to face. The reason the timescale is not a major problem is that the focus is on

[15] *Faith in the City* op.cit. pp. 48, 52.

[16] The fundamental alternatives for Paul are living according to the Spirit, *kata pneuma*, or according to the flesh, *kata sarka*. These and their variants run through the Corinthian correspondence and provide perhaps the best theme in Paul to parallel Christoph Schwöbel's concept of divine and human agency. The latter are for Paul properly related in life *kata pneuma*. Cf. Young and Ford op.cit. pp. 48, 123, 136, 160, 181ff., 224f., 239f., 260.

'the light of the knowledge of the glory of God in the face of Christ' (2 Cor. 4.6). The fullest context for this is a doctrine of God such as that of Colin Gunton's,[17] with the face of Christ representing an *eschatos* who embodies the importance of the contingencies of history and the joys and sufferings of humanity. Whatever the consummation may be like it will validate the ultimate significance of being 'in Christ' a community of service, love and worship. That is what Werner Jeanrond describes as 'participating in God's future now' (above p. 105). And the next section shows that the 'face to face' is also the final reference point for the most controversial issue in the letters, that of power and authority.

5. Paul's Authority

The theme of Paul's own authority in relation to the Corinthians is present in 1 Cor. and reaches its greatest urgency in 2 Cor.[18]. Werner Jeanrond claims that there was in Christianity 'at least initially a radically reformed understanding of religious authority' (above p. 82). It is worth briefly summarising the evidence of the Corinthian letters about this, adding some detail to Jeanrond's broad strokes. He also stresses the need for a critical hermeneutic of suspicion, and Paul's exercise of authority is a frequent target for that[19]. So I will look at Paul's idea and practice of authority in the Corinthian letters and also some of the ambiguities involved.

[17] For my development of this in relation to 2 Cor. see Young and Ford op.cit. Chap. 9, where the matter of the doctrine of the Trinity is discussed in a way which reaches similar conclusions to Colin Gunton above.

[18] See Young and Ford op.cit. Chap. 8.

[19] The most devastating recent scholarly attack on Paul is perhaps Graham Shaw, *The Cost of Authority. Manipulation and Freedom in the New Testament* (SCM, London 1983). For a comparison of Shaw with John Howard Schutz, *Paul and the Anatomy of Apostolic Authority* (CUP, Cambridge 1975), which seems to me to be the best treatment of the subject, see Young and Ford op.cit. pp. 219f.

Paul's overt aim in vindicating his authority is clear: he sees himself as the servant of the Corinthians with the task of building them up as a Church. The main feature of his argument is also clear: he appeals to the Gospel and his service of it, especially his conformity to the message of the cross, and uses it to cut through or relativise other approaches to authority. For example, in 2 Cor. 3.1 ff. he mentions a common way of guaranteeing credibility in that patron-client society, the use of letters of recommendation. He appeals instead to the Corinthian Church, the result of his ministry, as his letter 'to be known and read by all' (v. 2). He goes on to sum up his Gospel-centred legitimation in 4.5: 'For what we preach is not ourselves, but Jesus Christ as Lord, with ourselves as your servants for Jesus' sake', and this is then supported by a description of the way his life reflects his message: '. . . always carrying in the body the death of Jesus, so that the life of Jesus may also be manifested in our bodies . . .' (4.10). Later when he defends himself most directly in Chaps. 10–13 his key argument is about his sufferings and weakness. These are contrasted with other forms of legitimation which are in terms of impressive personal presence, speaking skills, form of financial support, strictness in exercising discipline, Jewish credentials, visions, revelations and signs and wonders. Some of these Paul can claim too, but he walks a rhetorical tightrope by both ironically boasting of them while undercutting them all with the evidence of 'power made perfect in weakness' (12.9).

Paul's strategy can therefore be seen as one of testing authority by the Gospel, with a strong emphasis on conformity of life as well as witness. It is backed up by frequent appeal to God as the source of his authority, as in the openings of both letters: 'an apostle by the will of God'. But Paul is well aware of the ambiguity of the whole exercise, summed up in his simultaneous use and disclaimer of boasting, and it is easy to suspect him. Anyone can claim support from God. Paul's apostleship is a rather irregular one which by the criteria used by some of his fellow Christians is not true apostleship: he had not been one of Jesus' disciples or a witness to one of the original resurrection appearances. So naturally he wants to change the criteria. What he substitutes for them might seem to make a virtue of necessity, using weakness to gain power just as Nietzsche was later to accuse Christianity of doing. It could be seen as an ideological use of the Gospel, with his 'real' motive (even if subconscious) being a desire to maintain control, to manipulate the Corinthians into submission, and intolerantly to deny others any influence over 'his' Church. The great mood swings and the sometimes violent language are further objects of suspicion which could be developed into a psychological analysis of someone with grave problems. Yet all those suspicions could be plausibly argued against, and one is left with a decision which will largely rest on grounds which the text cannot adjudicate.

What value can this discussion have for modern ecclesiology? The ambiguities are instructive in themselves, pointing to the problems even with the canonised models of authority and sharpening the need for vigilance. It is not necessary to claim that Paul's exercise of authority was perfect in order to learn from it, and the vulnerability of it to suspicion could be a sign of his willingness to risk being a different sort of apostle and found a different type of Church. But it is possible to learn from his conception of authority and recognise that, whatever the 'other side' of it, it does represent a radical vision of authority purified by the Gospel, and it can act as a powerful challenge to contemporary forms and practices. It is worth summarising some of the principles that emerge from the two letters to the Corinthians.

The first is that Christian authority must *appeal to God and the Gospel*, but that the criterion for the authenticity of this includes both the fruitfulness of its exercise in founding and building up Churches and the life of the one given authority. An authority disconnected from conformity to the Gospel or from building up the Church is fundamentally suspect.

The second principle leads on from that: authority must be *embodied*, involved in all the ambiguities of group interest, personal loyalties, power relations in the local and wider Church, pressures of culture, sex, money, means of persuasion, example and shared experience. Paul faces all the messiness of actual life and conflict and refuses to take refuge in formal types of authority or position, and he takes the risk of giving specific guidance.

The third is that authority is essentially *persuasive and distributed*. Even in his harshest criticism Paul has respect for the fact that the Corinthians too are related to God and are 'in Christ'. The picture of God's way of having power and authority is of him distributing it through the Spirit. So if God does not act monarchically or individualistically neither should Paul. He sees apostleship as one of many gifts of the Spirit, which are all for service in communication with each other (1 Cor. 12). Apostleship is inconceivable apart from participation in this new sociality rooted in utterly joint participation in Christ. So the mode of exercising authority must be persuasive. Only an authority that wins hearts is adequate. Hence the many heart to heart appeals, arguments, warnings and agonised expressions of love and concern.

Those agonisings indicate the fourth principle: Christian authority is *vulnerable*. This is perhaps the most radical of all, directly related to the cross. Paul could have made his ministry less vulnerable in many ways, and in the quality of authority, as in other areas, he chose a risky way. By going for trust, confidence and obedience from the heart, combined with high expectations of the community, he laid himself open to constant disappointment and subversion. This fragility is built into it, vividly symbolised by Paul's personal subjection to dangers and contingencies and a humiliating trade, and is its most obvious and challenging mark. The question is raised for all exercise of authority: how far does it resist the many temptations to choose security based on domination, distrust, formal legitimation, or other forms of self-protection?

Finally there is the *eschatological* nature of Paul's authority. Its final vindication is at the consummation, so it is future-oriented. Perhaps on no other area are Churches so subject to legalisms, bondage to the past, entanglement with distorting interests and idolatries than in that of authority. Paul's clarity about his ministry as helping to realise God's future and his refusal to absolutise past or present is a principle of liberation with wide relevance. At its heart is the great symbol of authority, the glory of God, enabling freedom and confidence, inspiring a whole community in an energetic mutuality and glorifying of God, while recognising that the full transformation into that glory is to come (2 Cor. 3). And incarnating the glory of God is the face of Christ, the ultimate embodiment of a persuasive, vulnerable authority, freely distributed through his Spirit.

All this has far wider relevance than to contemporary urban Churches, but it does fill a gap in *Faith in the City*. The report gives a good deal of space to practical ways of having more effective ministry in our cities, but it does not challenge deep patterns in the Church of England's ways of distributing power and authority, nor does it offer a vision of what authority centred on the Gospel might be like. The Corinthian letters can help here too by giving principles and examples that can help to redescribe what is going on and what the priorities for the future are.

6. *Conclusion*

Interpretation of the Corinthian letters has led us, fairly unsystematically, to a variety of reflections on the Church and its contemporary urban reality. It has helped to suggest some constructive criticisms of *Faith in the City*. These include comments on its approach to Church unity, its need for more explicit ecclesiology and eschatology, its inadequacy in relation to the quality of sociality and communication, concentrated in worship, which is seen through the Corinthian letters, and its lack of penetrating criticism or Gospel-centred affirmation on the issue of authority in the Church. The result has been that a vivid example of the Church wrestling with its Gospel and situation in one place and time has offered a contemporary challenge, together with part of an agenda, some principles and, perhaps, wisdom.

Yet if justice is to be done to *Faith in the City* the severe limitations of such an exercise must be noted. The main aim of the report is to address the nation as well as the Church about a situation of economic decline, physical decay and social disintegration in parts of our cities. The letters to a small, young Church in Corinth, agonising over its identity and expecting the end of the world soon, were not at all concerned with comparable matters. Yet as *Faith in the City* argues well, it is very appropriate for the Church of England to be concerned with them today. It is a way of being as realistic and Gospel-informed as Paul was in relation to Corinth. The report's strengths are its courageous affirmation of this, its lucid and powerful description of the situation in one area after another and its practical suggestions for both Church and nation. Many of its recommendations do have the moral obviousness and force mentioned at the beginning of this chapter. Yet they too can be strengthened and deepened by learning from the Corinthian correspondence. Mutual responsibility with compassion and free, respectful communication can be rooted in a created and redeemed sociality which is not just seen as the right moral answer to city problems but as good news whose very recognition and celebration allows it to be realised further. The many strong points of *Faith in the City* can be grounded better with the help of these letters, perhaps most pointedly by a fuller understanding of 2 Cor. 8–9. Those chapters can sharpen perception of both the Gospel and of inequalities and injustices, at the same time as inspiring practical action about them and offering for imitation the risky generosity of the poverty-stricken Macedonians.

The discussion and application of *Faith in the City* has only begun, and the many possible criticisms are a tribute to the significance of the report. It is perhaps the most important Church of England statement this century, and even by now it must be the one that has not only been most widely read and debated but also most consistently followed through at all levels. In itself it has been the beginning of an education about urban England for many people and it is well written to give a cumulative effect of immersion in a situation which can be all the more vividly imagined because of the restraint of the presentation.

The main danger in all this is that it easily comes across as law rather than gospel. The devastating picture is met by recommendations which are sensible but may only weigh down with a bad conscience those who are aroused.

Typically, Chapter 3 on *Theological Priorities* begins: 'The teaching of Jesus makes many demands on us . . .' (p. 47). The failure in eschatology means that the dimension of Christian hope is muted. The weakness in ecclesiology leaves the impression of tinkering with the existing Church. The overall lack of a vision of 'the economy of God' and of a commensurable freedom to be as radical and socially creative as Paul, both in affirmation and criticism, leaves one with the fear that this Church could end up being relevant at the cost of its identity. That would be ironical because, as the report says, 'the main contribution of the Church to our cities is to be itself' (p. 135). Unless there are signs of hope, where what is being expressed is in the form of an alternative and creative form of community, it is hard to imagine the transformation in quality of urban life required by the report. Such a community was Paul's first priority and it is arguable that it is equally urgent today. It cannot imitate Paul's Church but it can be inspired to have as its vision a similar combination of cross-centred unity, *parrhesia* with God, between its members and with the rest of society, a practice of love which is committed to universal community, and an authority that is constantly vulnerable as it tries to enable the Church to be a sign of the Kingdom of God for love of the world.

SELECT BIBLIOGRAPHY

Althaus, Paul. *Die Theologie Martin Luthers.* 5th edition, Gütersloh, 1980.

Aulen, Gustaf. *Reformation and Catholicity.* Edinburgh and London, 1960.

Avis, P. D. L. *The Church in the Theology of the Reformers.* Marshall's Theological Library, London, 1981.

Bakke, Raymond. *The Urban Christian.* Bromley, 1987.

Banks, Robert. *Paul's Idea of Community. The Early House Churches in their Historical Setting.* Exeter, 1980.

Blank, Joseph. *Vom Urchristentum zur Kirche. Kirchenstructuren im Rückblick auf den biblischen Ursprung.* München, 1982.

Bonhoeffer, Dietrich. *Santorum Communio.* London, 1963.

Boff, Leonardo. *Church, Charisma and Power. Liberation Theology and the Institutional Church.* London, 1985.

Bornkamm, H. *Luther's World of Thought.* E.T. by Martin H. Bertram, Saint Louis, 1958.

Campenhausen, Hans Von. *Ecclesiastical Authority and Spiritual Power in the Church of the First Three Centuries.* E.T. by J. A. Baker, Stanford, 1963.

Church of England. *Faith in the City. The Report of the Archbishop of Canterbury's Commission on Urban Priority Areas.* London, 1985.

Congar, Yves. *Lay People in the Church. A Study for a Theology of the Laity.* London, 1957.

Dulles, Avery. *Models of the Church.* Dublin and London, 1974.

Farley, Edward. *Ecclesial Man. A Social Phenomenology of Faith and Reality.* Philadelphia, 1975.

Farley, Edward. *Ecclesial Reflection. An Anatomy of Theological Method.* Philadelphia, 1982.

Flannery, Austin. 'Lumen Gentium', *Dogmatic Constitution on the Church of Vatican II,* in *Vatican Council II. The Conciliar and Post Conciliar Documents.* London, 1975.

Forsyth, P. T. *The Church and the Sacraments.* London, 1917.

Forsyth, P. T. *The Church, the Gospel and Society.* London, 1962.

257

Hanson, A. T. and R.P.C. *The Identity of the Church. A Guide to Recognising the Contemporary Church*. London, 1987.

Hasenhüttl, Gotthold. *Herrschaftsfreie Kirche. Soziotheologische Grundlegung*. Düsseldorf, 1974.

Herms, Eilat. *Einheit der Christen in der Gemeinschaft der Kirchen. Die oekumenische Bewegung der römischen Kirche im Lichte der reformatorischen Theologie*. Kirche und Confession 24, Göttingen, 1984.

Jenkins, D. T. *The Nature of Catholicity*. 2nd edition, London, 1953.

Kühn, U. *Kirche. Handbuch der Systematischen Theologie 10*. (ed. H. Ratshow), Gütersloh, 1980.

Küng, Hans. *The Church*. London, 1968.

Lukes, S. 'Power and Authority', in *A History of Sociological Analysis*, ed. T. Bottomore and R. Nesbit, London, 1979, chapter 16.

Meeks, Wayne A. *The First Urban Christians. The Social World of the Apostle Paul*. New Haven and London, 1983.

Milner, B. C. *Calvin's Doctrine of the Church. Studies in the History of Christian Thought, 5*. Leiden, 1970.

Moltmann, Jürgen. *The Church in the Power of the Spirit. A Contribution to Messianic Ecclesiology*. E.T. by Margaret Kohl, London, 1985.

Owen, John. *The True Nature of a Gospel Church*. In *Works*, edited by W. H. Goold, Edinburgh, 1862, vol. XVI, pp. 1–208.

Ramsay, Michael. *The Gospel and the Catholic Church*. London, 1936.

Schillebeeckx, Edward. *The Church with a Human Face. A New and Expanded Theology of Ministry*. E.T. by John Bowden, London, 1985.

Schutz, John Howard. *Paul and the Anatomy of Apostolic Authority*. Cambridge, 1975.

Segundo, J. L. *The Liberation of Theology*. Dublin, 1977.

Sykes, S. W. *The Identity of Christianity*. London, 1984.

Sykes, S. W. *The Integrity of Anglicanism*. London, 1978.

Theissen, Gerd. *The Social Setting of Pauline Christianity. Essays on Corinth*. Philadelphia, 1982.

Tracy, David. *Plurality and Ambiguity. Hermeneutics, Religion, Hope*. San Francisco, 1987.

Young, Frances M. and Ford, David F. *Meaning and Truth in 2 Corinthians*. London, 1987.

Zizioulas, John D. *Being as Communion. Studies in Personhood and the Church*. London, 1985.

INDEX